Margrit Coates is the world's le
communicator, and the author of severe
books. She was a resident expert in the
Animal Roadshow, and has appeared on S.   ..ction, as
well as on numerous other television pro   ..cs. In addition
to her many media appearances and radio interviews, Margrit
has been the Pets' Corner columnist for the *Daily Mail* newspaper,
and her work has been featured in countless magazines and
publications worldwide. Highly sought-after internationally for
consultations, lectures and workshops, she has lectured at the
Open Center, New York and to post-graduate animal behaviour
students at the University of Southampton, England.

Margrit is also a gifted healer, which means that, besides
communicating directly with the animals that she is consulted
about, she always connects to them with healing energy too –
which gives her work its incomparable edge. A founding partner
in a clinic offering natural therapies for pets and horses, she is
passionate about helping people understand animal sentience,
how animals communicate with us, and the benefits of healing
energy for them. She lives in the New Forest National Park of
southern England, where her organic garden is visited by many
different bird and animal species.

For more information, please visit www.margritcoates.com

'In [*Communicating with Animals*], Margrit Coates
reveals many fascinating and compelling aspects of
this little understood "language".'

Virginia McKenna, OBE, Founder and Trustee
of the Born Free Foundation

'Margrit beautifully helps us see who the animals truly are ... not only our best friends but our best teachers, role models, protectors, and healers.'

Carol Gurney, author of *The Language of Animals: 7 Steps to Communicating with Animals*, and founder of the Gurney Institute of Animal Communication

'Margrit Coates creates a sound path for us back to what we have known in our hearts all along.'

Susan Chernak McElroy, author of *Animals as Teachers and Healers*

COMMUNICATING WITH ANIMALS

How to tune into them intuitively

Margrit Coates

LONDON · SYDNEY · AUCKLAND · JOHANNESBURG

5 7 9 10 8 6 4

First published in 2012 by Rider, an imprint of Ebury Publishing
Ebury Publishing is a Random House Group company

The Random House Group Limited Reg. No. 954009

Addresses for companies within the Random House Group can be found at
www.randomhouse.co.uk

A CIP catalogue record for this book is available from the British Library

The Random House Group Limited supports The Forest Stewardship
Council (FSC), the leading international forest certification organisation.
All our titles that are printed on Greenpeace approved FSC certified paper carry the FSC logo.
Our paper procurement policy can be found at
www.randomhouse.co.uk/environment

Author photo on back cover by Jon Banfield (www.jonbanfieldphotography.co.uk)
For picture credits, see page 252 as an extension of this copyright page.

ISBN 9781846043161

Copies are available at special rates for bulk orders. Contact the sales development team on
020 7840 8487 for more information.

To buy books by your favourite authors and register for offers, visit www.randomhouse.co.uk

Please note: Margrit Coates is not medically or veterinary qualified. The information given
in this book is intended as a self-help guide for you and your animals. It is not to be taken as a
replacement or a substitute for professional veterinary or medical advice. Before trying any of
the techniques in this book, or following the suggestions, a veterinary surgeon must always be
consulted about any concerns whatsoever with an animal or bird etc. Neither the author nor the
publisher can be held responsible for any loss or claim arising out of the use or misuse of the
suggestions made in this book, nor the failure to take professional veterinary or medical advice.

The Random House Group Limited supports The Forest Stewardship
Council® (FSC®), the leading international forest-certification organisation.
Our books carrying the FSC label are printed on FSC®-certified paper.
FSC is the only forest-certification scheme supported by the leading
environmental organisations, including Greenpeace. Our
paper procurement policy can be found at
www.randomhouse.co.uk/environment

MIX
Paper from
responsible sources
FSC® C016897

Printed and bound in Great Britain by Clays Ltd, St Ives plc

Contents

Introduction   7

1   Why Talk with Animals?   13
2   At a Deeper Level   37
3   Two-Way Conversations   55
4   What to Ask, How to and When   79
5   The Horse's Voice   107
6   Healing Thoughts   133
7   From a Distance   153
8   Beyond the Here and Now   173
9   Wild Talk   191
10 It's Natural   217
11 High Notes   243

Special Thanks   251
Index   253

Awakening to animals

I hear your voice
those silent whispers that nevertheless
are clear, loud and profound

I hear your love
which touches my heart with a soft kiss
whenever I am with you

I hear your soul
guide me as I walk through the maze
of ignorance and greed on planet Earth

I hear you as an equal
for I am nothing without the whole
and you are part of the miracle that is the Universe

I will hear you always
knowing how you hear me
in your mind, in your heart and in your soul

Margrit Coates

Introduction

I look around and pinch myself. I am at the Wetnose Awards ceremony in London, chatting with Brian May, the guitarist in Queen, who is a well-known animal rights campaigner. Later, Brian presents an award to Virginia McKenna, founder of the Born Free Foundation, and after that I have the opportunity to talk with Virginia about our mutual passion for making a difference on behalf of animals. I have finally met someone who has long been an inspiration to me, and to be able to tell her this in person certainly makes this a red-letter day.

Actors Martin Clunes, Lorraine Chase and Peter Egan were at the Awards too, as was the TV vet Marc Abraham, and it was wonderful to hear their animal stories. Ingrid Tarrant was recording interviews, and during a break we reminisced about a horse story that she had shared with me a few years earlier. There were, of course, some canine stars present as well, taking all the attention in their stride. Not having to wake up in the morning and fret about what to wear, it was no doubt less stressful for them to attend the ceremony than it was for many of the humans present. The dogs exuded that calm, laid-back air that only a dog used to attention can muster.

A year earlier, almost to the day, I had been at another event in London. On that occasion, I had found myself sitting in my very own Green Room at the BBC headquarters, waiting to be called into the studio to be interviewed for the TV series *Pet Nation*. Liza Tarbuck and Huey Morgan were the show hosts in a beautifully designed animal-themed set. During the time that I sat in the Green Room whilst the earlier part of the show was being recorded, I saw different types of animals arrive in the studio. The sight of them, with all their dignity and self-awareness, made me become very emotional. I grabbed a tissue and fanned my face. Raising my arms to the heavens, I sent out a silent *thank you* to all the animals who have been my teachers, guides and healers. And I sent the thoughts of appreciation to animals everywhere, for their perfect soul beauty.

I still find it amazing how much animals have brought into my life. But the most important part of my work as an animal communicator and healer is not the famous people I meet, nor the wonderful locations that I am sometimes invited to visit. No, it's about the animals themselves and all that they can teach us. I want to close the communication gap between humans and animals, and thereby bring awareness to the widest possible audience.

And that is one reason why I am writing this book: so that you too can connect with animals in the way that I have been so fortunate to do.

About this book

If you are interested in raising your consciousness through animal communication, rest assured that you are on the right path: this positive action will encourage the animals who share their lives with you to view you as a significant human that they will want to talk to. When you communicate with animals on their wavelength, you have the best possible chance of not only understanding them, but also appreciating the depth of their experience as sentient beings. Inspired to communicate with animals soul to soul, you will be filled with wonder when, through your intuition, you sense their response.

I encounter a wide variety of species and problems, and it is always rewarding and satisfying to be able to help wherever possible. The majority of people who contact me have a dog, cat or horse as a companion. However, all animals, no matter what the type, are unique, and the art of interspecies communication allows us to become aware of messages that each animal wants to get across. There are, of course, many challenges to overcome when communicating with animals, but it is great fun, because animals – when they are allowed to express themselves and be true to their nature – show us how to live life to the full.

All species have intuitive, sixth-sense abilities. Animals have honed these to perfection over millions of years, whilst humans have become somewhat lazy in this respect. However, everyone has the potential to connect with animals on a deep level and, thankfully, listening to what they say, and learning how to help and heal them is nowadays of huge interest to an ever-increasing number of people. More than ever before, people want to understand animals on the deepest possible level, and to enjoy the benefits of having soul-to-soul conversations. Animals are not only amazing teachers, but they are also our healers. My hope is that this book will help you to awaken your innate communication gifts, so that the bond between you and the animals in your life can be strengthened and any problems can be resolved. For those already practising intuitive communication with animals, this book contains unique tips and insights to help with your work.

Always room for learning

My own journey is one of continuous learning, and an apt lesson was taught to me by horse Radian during the photographic session for this book cover. Pura Raza Espanola (PRE) stallion Radian reminded me what communicating with animals is all about. On the day that I booked to have my photo taken with Radian, the weather was very changeable, one minute black sky and heavy showers, the next minute sunshine. The photographer set up his equipment under umbrellas and plastic sheets, whilst Radian inquisitively watched the proceedings.

The photographer seized on a dry break in the weather to take some photos, during which I sat on a tree stump whilst Radian stood close to me in all his breathtaking beauty. Apart from the looming rain clouds, there was a lot going on. Another stallion was grazing in a paddock behind me, and there were mares in adjacent paddocks. As a stallion, Radian is highly sensitive to his surroundings and other horses. Without realising it, I allowed my mind to become cluttered. Would the rain start again soon? Was I holding my head at the right angle; were my hands in the right position? Would Radian become more interested in the mares than me? Radian started to fidget and disconnect from me, then he moved away.

The photographer shouted out: 'Relax, you look tense.' I then realised that I had committed the cardinal sin of communicating confusing signals. It was my energy that was making Radian uncooperative because I was not following my own advice about paying attention to the conflicting images that our thoughts can convey. Taking a deep breath, I pushed the chattering thoughts out of my mind and focussed on harnessing a state of inner calm. The change in Radian was instant. He moved forward to stand before me, with a soft look in his eyes as I silently said to him, 'You are beautiful. I love you.' In return, I felt Radian's spirit radiate peace as we locked in a timeless zone of loving energy. The result was a string of stunning photos, one of which is on the cover of this book.

Secrets revealed

Animals have thoughts, feelings and opinions. They are also aware of our inner world, and how we are thinking and feeling. As we are physically connected to everything in the Universe, it makes sense to get to know other beings on the deepest possible level. We do this through developing our intuition.

Throughout this book, I explain the benefits of intuitive communicating with animals, as well as how to develop a strong skill in this. When we talk to animals and hear what they say back, not only can we better understand the animals in our life, but we will improve our understanding of ourselves too, and of the special communication and healing gifts that lie at the heart of our soul. Through my stories I hope to do the animals justice, so that their incredible communication power sparkles from these pages.

Animal Zen moments

Animals have impressed upon me just how amazingly aware they are. They have profound insights, demonstrating a philosophical understanding – of that I am sure, having experienced it many times. Often animals astound me with their pronouncements and subtle nuances, such as horse Boo who communicated: 'All good things come good.' The meaning stumped me, so I had to ask for clarification from this master of communication. Boo explained that the things we seek that are relevant to our spiritual path will come to fruition.

Throughout this book I have included messages that animals have communicated, which I call 'Animal Zen moments' or 'Horse Zen moments'. The word ' Zen' is Japanese for meditation as well as the philosophy surrounding it. An Animal Zen moment involves concentrating on the energy of the present instant in time. It entails a multi-layered experience of awareness. Have a dedicated notebook handy for writing down the Zen messages of inspiration that animals communicate to you as you practise the tips in this book.

Having worked as one of the trailblazers in the world of animal communication, I have taken a long, and often arduous, route to knowledge and wisdom, but I hope to share short cuts with you that will lead you to a similar place in a briefer time. As in my previous books, this is what *Communicating with Animals* aims to offer you. Endorsed by true stories*, I share insights into the ways in which we can develop our intuitive side and converse with animals, which enriches all our lives. My dream is that communicating with animals will one day become a normal everyday occurrence, practised by all people. The world will truly be a better place when all humans tune into other beings intuitively.

Talking life, listening life, intelligent life is all around you. Join in the conversations and enrich your own life.

MARGRIT COATES

Important note: *The techniques suggested in this book should not be attempted by persons under the influence of alcohol, drugs or mind-influencing medication.*

* All of the stories in this book are true, but in some cases names and other details have been changed to protect confidentiality.

1 Why Talk with Animals?

Communication is the best way to move from ignorance to wisdom.

The most difficult part of writing a book can be the opening paragraph, so I thought to myself: why not start with a true story to show how animals communicate with us through the realms of energy, and how we can tune in to hear what animals say through the same system, as well as send messages back to them? Whenever we do this, the result is a bountiful supply of mutual benefits.

When communicating with animals, experience has taught me that it is important to get a sense of what the animal is physically expressing, as well as what is being silently conveyed. My first impression was that Millie's gentle canine face revealed that she was sensitive and wary. A pointer-foxhound cross, four-and-a-half-year-old Millie had been discovered by Ruth at a dog shelter two years earlier, when she had been looking for a companion for her black Labrador, Murphy. At first, no dog had seemed entirely suitable, but as Ruth was about to leave she decided to check out the trail-hound section, where she noticed a dog cowering in the corner of a pen. As Ruth pondered over what to do, through her intuition she sensed a voice saying, *Take me with you.* It was coming from the crouching dog's direction, so without further ado, woman and dog went home together, with Ruth naming her new companion Millie.

Millie had a few problems. The shelter had assured Ruth that Millie was house-trained, but she was not, and in fact it quickly became apparent that the dog had never lived in a house before. Millie was also scared of men and of people looking at her; she hated anyone going near her neck and detested loud music of any sort.

However, within minutes of meeting Millie I was able to touch her all over, including her head and neck, with Ruth exclaiming that Millie had never been so relaxed about this with anyone else. The difference with me was that Millie knew that I could hear what she was saying, that I understood her messages and worked with healing energy.

Communicating with animals means picking up information in a variety of ways – as this book will explain in detail. Through tuning into Millie's memories, I got a glimpse of the damp, dingy, stone-floored room where she was born, one of a litter of shivering puppies huddling together in an attempt to keep warm. A sickly, malnourished mother dog and the death of a puppy were also remembered. Whenever a certain man entered that room, Millie would try to hide herself away and refuse to be coaxed forward, which infuriated the man, who would grab the pup by the neck, then shake her and throw her around. The man demanded obedience and there was no place in his world for a cringing dog. When she was old enough to be assessed for scent-hound racing, Millie showed little aptitude for this sport – hence the reason she had been deposited at the animal shelter.

The work of an animal communicator involves being a faithful translator of what the animal transmits mind-to-mind, as well as decoding the meaning behind various riddles, metaphors or symbols that can act as clues to what they are thinking. Sometimes these images are easy to interpret; at other times they have a tantalising complexity about them. On this occasion, a bunch of heather appeared in my mind's eye, seemingly associated with the name that Millie had been given as a puppy. When I asked Ruth, 'Was her name once Heather?' Ruth replied that it had been Lucky, but she had considered it inappropriate and, on asking the dog to help choose a new name for herself, the name Millie had popped into Ruth's mind. Wait a minute, I thought to myself, I needed to work on my interpretation skills a bit more! I was seeing 'lucky' heather, so the previous name *was* in the image I was shown, which I must admit was an ingenious clue. It was one of the most obscure pieces of information that I have ever been given by an animal.

Actually, now I come to think of it, there was once a little cat who threw something cryptic at me. He kept saying that I should tell his person to take care of her eyes, to which she would reply by insisting that there was nothing whatsoever wrong with her eyes. When she started to become irritable with me, I asked the cat for a further clue. I then saw a droplet of water, followed by another and another. The image of eyes reappeared and it dawned on me that I was seeing tears. 'Have you been doing a lot of crying recently?' I asked the woman, to which she admitted that she had. The cat was so pleased with himself, he got up to drape his tail around my legs. I was pretty relieved too. Anyway, I digress somewhat, so let's get back to Millie ...

Further communication from Millie was thankfully easier to deal with. She had known that a question mark hung over her future at the dog shelter, and had chosen Ruth as her saviour for a reason. When Ruth had stood in front of Millie that first time, Millie had experienced a frisson of energy and been astonished to see a being of light with a bright ball at the centre. Millie later came to know this nucleus of energy as Ruth's loving heart.

The final piece of information offered by Millie was that she had two guardian angels. One was the sibling who had died as a young puppy, and the other a rabbit who also passed away in its youth. 'Why a rabbit?' I asked Millie. She was a hunting dog and so I wondered whether she had been the cause of the bunny's demise. It turned out that in an adjacent room to the one where the puppies had been housed, rabbits were bred. Also highly sentient beings, rabbits have been shown in scientific studies to communicate telepathically across distances. One young rabbit had linked up with Millie and through the wall they had sensed each other's thoughts and feelings. Millie explained the connection as an instant transference of knowledge, in which flowing messages stacked one on top of the other in layers, without the time lapse that we get in human-to-human verbal dialogue.

Animal insight

There is something magical about a relationship with another species. When we approach such relationships soul to soul and see with the eyes of the heart, it is especially beautiful.

The session ended there and I thanked Millie profusely for her willingness to share a communication session with me. It's so simple to thank an animal: whenever we address them in an enthusiastic tone of voice, combined if possible with a stroke, they will feel honoured. Of course Millie read my heart too, to confirm that I meant what I said.

After a consultation, I am always intrigued as to what the outcome will be, because it's impossible to predict. Like us humans, each animal is uniquely different, and each case has many facets to it. I soon got an answer: 'I just wanted to let you know that already Millie is displaying more confident behaviour – the most amazing improvement is her increased boldness towards men,' emailed Ruth two days later. 'My parents both noticed that Millie was not so nervous of Dad but more interactive, even greeting him. I know it's early days and Millie still has some way to go, considering what she has been through, but already she appears to have let go of those horrible memories which have been troubling her.' A session of healing communication is often what is needed for an animal to feel better about him- or herself. A friend of Ruth's contacted me to say that on calling at Ruth's house, she had had to look twice to make sure that Millie was the same dog, because she was now so much more relaxed.

Five weeks later, I met up again with Ruth and Millie, who looked in better physical shape with more relaxed muscle tone. The mistrustful demeanour had gone and on this occasion I noticed that Millie did not chat about her past, but about things related to the present. On my asking Millie what she wanted to tell me that day, she transmitted a picture of herself shaking a blue toy, an activity clearly associated with great amusement for her. Ruth told me that the toy was Millie's favourite plaything and that it was in the shape of a film-character bunny. Laughing, I asked Millie if her favourite conversation theme was rabbits, but with that Millie's mood changed to a more serious one.

The brightness of the pictures that Mille had just shown me dissolved to a foggy grey, in the centre of which I sensed the form of a man, solid like an impervious block of stone. Millie's telepathic tone was now very different, her light and eager energy replaced by a dullness.

'There is an atrocious lack of empathy from him,' Millie telepathically conveyed in the manner of a conspirator. I was taken aback, because I sensed that the man she was referring to was a friend of Ruth's. Animals are always direct and to the point, and so sometimes I need to think about how best to broach a topic with an animal's guardians. 'Atrocious lack of empathy,' Millie repeated, emphasising the word 'atrocious' as you would something which has great meaning. Oh dear, this was tricky. What to do?

'OK, Millie,' I said aloud, letting her know I was about to divulge the message. With this prompt from me, Millie obviously felt encouraged to add a bit more:

' ... and he doesn't listen to another person's point of view.' It was a pretty outrageous statement to make, but Ruth understood. She had recently ended the relationship with her boyfriend and exclaimed that Millie was spot-on with her analysis. We marvelled at the fact that a dog would communicate with such notions to underline the severity of a character condemnation. Ruth mentioned to me that just before the final parting Millie had started growling at the man. 'Of course I did,' Millie communicated. 'Ruth was sending me subconscious signals that she didn't want the man near her, so I was warning him to stay away.'

The fog lifted and Millie had a final pensive message: 'Let's go forward into the summer, into the light of the sun.' This communication made perfect sense to Ruth, because she had purchased a camper van especially for going away with her two dogs at weekends and holiday times. There was much for the three of them to look forward to.

Animals in translation

My connection with Millie was a conscious one; however, it's a well-known fact that around 90 per cent of our communication takes place at a subconscious level. Just think how much information we transmit to animals through our chattering thoughts and imaginative minds. Not only do we emit messages that we are not even aware of, but we are surrounded by communications from animals, who are also communicating amongst themselves. However, these messages frequently get blotted out through the incessant distractions of our everyday lives. No wonder animals can become confused in our presence, with neither party really getting the gist of what is going on.

We humans can speak at will in order to convey our needs, wants, aims and desires, which can be understood by anyone who speaks our particular form of verbal language. When using verbal language, we can edit the information we present to the world at large, removing things here and there that we do not like or do not wish others to know. Sometimes we may even add bits to enhance our status or manipulate a reaction. Not only do we often contradict each other, we contradict ourselves as well in our attempts to master this sort of facade. Or we may say things which our actions belie. Whilst animals can make some allowances for our idiosyncrasies, because they are able to read our energy, in these situations they can become very uncertain about what the truth of the matter is.

Animal insight

It is limiting to believe that anything beyond the physical five senses does not exist. There is much to discover beyond the scope of physical perception. We are first and foremost a body of energy, and it is through this medium – energy – that we send and receive information.

There is often a culture clash between humans and other animals; nevertheless human intuition can come to the rescue as a means to connect with the 'language of animals'. Actually, the word 'language' is probably a misnomer in this instance, because when we use our intuition we are not learning how to speak an actual language as such – we are simply becoming fully aware. Awareness means being able to cut through confusion to have clear intuitive vision. When we manage to achieve this, we will awaken to animals on a deeper level than hitherto experienced.

It therefore does not matter what your own native tongue is; when connecting intuitively, you can communicate with animals anywhere in the world. Whilst animals understand verbal cues in the local vernacular, they do not need to distinguish between linguistic concepts or subtle nuances. Animals utilise a universal energy system to send and receive messages. Vibrations from your thoughts and emotions are automatically translated into this communal language. Even when you are speaking aloud, the animal will read the intention and meaning behind your words. In fact, the thoughts and images you project are more important than your spoken words. This is how animals detect insincere people, sensing whether their intentions are genuine or not.

A stumbling block for humans is created when our intuition is suppressed, thereby obstructing our awareness of what animals are attempting to communicate to us. In such situations, animals rightly regard humans as the dumb species, for it is when we are out of sync with what is being conveyed that problems between animals and the people who care for them are perpetuated or escalate out of all proportion. Taking steps to become more in tune with animals is beneficial all round, because if our relationships with our companion animals are happy ones, then this will reduce stress in all our lives, human and animal alike.

Animal species do not need to translate the communications that take place between them at an intuitive level, as on this plane knowledge is instantly absorbed. Animals share a natural ability to talk to one another through telepathic means, connecting with each other regardless of distance and time. It is not just a survival mechanism but their way of life. Animals convey truths and realities either about themselves, their experiences, or about us. This ever-changing and updating network of information is available to us all when we tune into their wavelength through developing our intuitive skills.

It's rewarding

There is nothing mysterious about intuitive communication. We all have the potential for it and, for those who take the steps to exercise it, picking up messages from animals and transmitting replies becomes a regular occurrence. Through becoming intuitively active you can:

- Ask what an animal needs, as well as find out how past experiences impact on current behaviours.
- Deepen the bond between you and animals.
- Gain insights into how an animal is feeling.
- Better understand the relationships that animals have with each other.
- Transmit and pick up messages in a clear way.
- Identify any discomfort or misalignment that an animal may be suffering from. Sense potential health issues before they become serious problems. Explain medical procedures or other treatments that may be necessary to an animal.
- Prepare your animal companion for changes, such as a house move, a new partner, animal addition, the arrival of a baby, people leaving home, or your going away for a period of time.
- Keep in touch with an animal from a distance, sending messages of support.
- Assist in finding a missing animal.
- Connect with animals in the afterlife.
- Improve your life so that it becomes more fulfilling and meaningful.
- Evolve your empathic connection to the Universe.

The main factor in effective communication is the ability to listen, which means becoming sensitive to incoming information.

No limitations

Space is not an empty vacuum, but is full of restless quantum energy – and the truth is that everything is connected. The energy pulsing through our being is the same energy that permeates all life forms, endlessly transmitting a wealth of information throughout the cosmos, the totality of what we call reality. As a matter of fact, the carbon atoms in our bodies, together with those in other creatures and plants, are made of the same stuff as the atoms in the planets and the stars. This means that we are all made of cosmic material, containing the spark of the eternal. In that respect, we are all equal and linked by a perpetual bond. Each of us, animals included, has a personal frequency which transmits thoughts, emotions and physical conditions. These things have an energetic resonance and tempo of their own. Later in this book, I explain how you can sense this through an animal's 'voice', which we can hear with our intuitive 'ears'.

In the same way that we constantly respond to whatever we are exposed to, the world relates back to us. Unfortunately, society and science today often encourage people to analyse what is actually visible or can be measured, as though this alone holds the answer to the meaning of life, which means that vital information may be missed. When judged from this perspective, paranormal events are often dismissed as illusory tricks of the mind, which to my way of thinking seems very much like an attempt to devalue the genuine experiences of ordinary folk the world over, and to coerce them into making conclusions based on analytical activity – thereby suppressing their inner guidance and independence. Moreover, this biased attitude diverts us away from exploring areas that lie beyond the known human sensory fields. One day it will dawn on researchers that they have overlooked a vital component in their studies – that we are first and foremost energy beings interacting with other energy forms in a vast interactive system. For the benefit of all life forms, scientists need to take the important first step of acknowledging that the minds of both humans and animals communicate in as yet unexplained ways.

As Albert Einstein so concisely put it: 'The intuitive mind is a sacred gift and the rational mind is a faithful servant. We have created a society that honours the servant and has forgotten the gift.' Let's all remember the gift that we have and, moreover, use it.

What is intuition?

Intuition may be described as extrasensory perception, which leads to unlimited sensory experiences. Our intuition provides quick insights independently of any reasoning processes. Animals possess an advanced level of intuitive ability, whilst in humans this faculty is often ignored because we tend to override our intuitive responses as they arise, as well as undervalue the benefits that intuition has to offer us. However, things are rapidly shifting in this respect, as more people today are awakening to the possibility of communicating with all forms of life.

How does intuition work and where does it come from?

Intuitive communication is filtered to our brain via our mind. Our minds are not confined to the inside of our brains, but extend beyond them through infinite energy fields. In a reciprocal process, we access information emitted by other people and animals, and we can develop our ability to 'read' this unseen communication.

Many ordinary people already possess an evolved intuitive sense. This is what enables them to know instinctively when a friend or relative is in need, and also what alerts them to danger. Many of us will have experienced 'vibes', a 'feeling' or hunch about a situation, person, animal, decision or place – but at the time we couldn't quite put our finger on what exactly the 'feeling' was trying to convey. We may therefore have ignored it and overlooked any guidance that it might have been offering us. This can be a great shame, because these instant and direct impressions are our intuition's way of trying to communicate what needs to be done in any given situation. In this respect, intuition acts similarly to our conscience, pointing the way to truths. Over the years I have come to the conclusion that intuition is one of the facets of the soul.

How do I know that I am accessing my intuition?

Something within us knows the best course of action to take; this is the power of our intuition. However, there are occasions when we get our

instincts mixed up with our emotions. During times when we are engulfed by strong emotions, fears and hopes can colour our moods so strongly that we cannot be sure whether we are responding to imagination or intuition. If there is a lot going on in our lives, it is advisable to give ourselves time so that things can become clear again. In this way, we can assess what is guidance from our higher reasoning and what to ignore.

Is intuition the same as the sixth sense?

The brain receives information from different sources and we can compare it to a radio receiver. A radio picks up different stations, some of which will be clearer than others. We pay more attention to well defined incoming signals, as opposed to scrambled, distorted, flickering or weak input. In the case of the brain, strong signals usually come to us through the five sensory inputs of sight, hearing, smell, taste and touch.

Information that comes to us through our five senses frequently muffles information that is transmitted to our conscious awareness via faint and elusive wavelengths, but which is nevertheless equally important. It is through a subtle frequency that our intuition operates, and this is our sixth sense. The sixth sense frequency is received by animals more clearly than by humans, owing to our dependence on gadgets and verbal language. Nevertheless, when we have the intention to do so, we can access it just as readily.

Animal Zen moment

Learning means absorbing understanding.

How can we develop our intuition?

Everyone has an intuitive side and some people may naturally tap into this way of being, but for others it can take a bit of effort and practice to build up strength in this area. We develop our intuition through usage, like exercising a muscle.

A good way to begin is by listening to, and acting on, our inner feelings. The more we align ourselves with our intuition, using and trusting it, the more potent our ability to tune into it becomes. It's important to set aside the ego and have an open mind, as well as to quieten the conscious, chattering mind of our thoughts. Here's an exercise to help you get started:

- Sit comfortably in a tranquil setting and, using your breathing, relax every part of your body. Next, examine your thoughts: is your mind buzzing with ideas or things that need attending to? Are worries clouding your thinking? Ask those thoughts to leave you and set the intention that you want a quiet mind. It is surprising how effective this simple step can be. Playing music especially produced for meditation purposes can help the relaxation process too.

- Once your mind is clear and you feel grounded, you are ready for the next step. Sit or stand by your animal. Don't actively think about anything, stay in the zone of the quiet-mind state. Something will pop into your mind about the animal – it may seem brief and meaningless, but no matter for now. The important thing is that you are tuning into the animal using your intuition, which can only operate cleanly through a quiet mind.

Can we lose our intuitive ability?

Intuition can atrophy through lack of use. One of the biggest obstacles to listening to our intuition is finding ourselves in an all-consuming state as a result of something going on in our lives. Thankfully our intuition cannot be erased and, no matter how long it lies dormant, it can always be awakened and developed. To keep your own intuition/sixth sense active, it is important to pay attention to how you feel during each decision-making process and when spending time with animals and people.

Is intuition the same as telepathy?

Telepathy can be defined as the direct communication between minds. Our state of being can be actively broadcasting and receiving telepathically without our actually realising it. Have you ever answered the phone and known who the caller was going to be? Or had a sinking feeling that something negative had happened, which turned out to be

true? Telepathy is part of the intuitive process; therefore, when you allow yourself to be guided by your intuition, you open yourself up to using your telepathic ability.

The telepathic traits which animals possess can be observed in cats and dogs who know when a person is on their way home, or who sense that someone is unhappy or unwell. Afghan hounds have a bit of a reputation for being dizzy blondes, but one day Sasha demonstrated an amazing telepathic ability in relation to June. When June was on her way home from work late one evening, her car broke down in the centre of London, so she called her husband Anthony for help and advice. The phone rang and rang, for it was past midnight and her hubby was already fast asleep in bed. Leaving the number ringing, June hoped that her husband would wake up eventually, and was relieved when after several minutes he did pick up the phone. Except it wasn't her husband, it was the dog.

At first, June did not realise that Sasha had taken the phone off the cradle with her mouth, dropped it onto the table and was listening while June anxiously talked. She got the shock of her life when Sasha started whimpering and howling, noises which she kept on making until Anthony was roused from his sleep.

Through her acute telepathic connection to June, Sasha had known that June was the telephone caller and that she was in trouble. This story also shows that animals can ingeniously plan a course of action, because Sasha knew she had to pick up the telephone receiver (something she had never done before) and then alert Anthony. When June finally walked in the door and was able to praise her clever hound for the exemplary assistance, Sasha howled again – this time, though, in delight.

From all around the world, people regularly send me similar anecdotes, demonstrating that animals tune into what is going on around them. When we are open and paying attention, the amazing intelligence of animals can reveal incredible things to us; each animal has something about which it can enlighten us.

Intuition is practical

When we initially start to tune into animals, we may wonder how we can differentiate between the workings of our intuition, our own wishful thinking, or whether we are tuning into something completely different. First and foremost when communicating with animals, our intention must be to help the animal – and not solely for our own benefit. A selfless desire to connect is what creates a clear communication channel. Intuition is not just about listening to our own feelings: while feelings can give us information, we must investigate what they mean in relation to the animal. Success comes when we balance logic

Animal insight

Communicating with animals means tuning into a particular frequency, which our intuition instinctively knows how to do. When we suffer from a lack of concentration or become distracted, the input may fade or become scrambled. Somewhere in the Universe there is a central hub that connects the entire network of frequencies one to the other.

with intuition. When it is used in this way, we will discover that intuition is a very practical tool. In fact, it is impractical *not* to use it.

The more often we take time to be still and quiet, and the more honest we are about our intention to help and learn, the clearer the information will be that we receive through the intuitive sixth sense.

Making a start

'If only they could talk' or 'if only they could tell us what is wrong' are statements that I hear regularly during the course of my work as an animal healer and communicator. On these occasions, the animals present may proffer a yawn or give me a knowing look, whereas some are so bored by this misconception that they simply walk away. OK, animals do not open their mouths and give speeches, but they possess extraordinary telepathic communication abilities. These also lie within humans, but we have forgotten about or neglected them into disuse. Communicating with animals is not just feasible but a reality and, once we recognise this and awaken our dormant telepathic abilities, animals have fascinating stories to tell.

There are those of us who experiment and try to connect intuitively to animals, only to feel frustrated. These are often the individuals who say to me: 'I tried it but nothing happened.' In today's quick-fix world, rather than achieve success through dedicated practice, many people want instant results – which is why they may become disillusioned if they do not quickly pick up on what an animal is saying, thinking or feeling. Our frustration, though, only leads to animals switching off from wanting to talk to us, in the same way that we would prefer to avoid chatting with an impatient person. That said, mind-to-mind communication with an animal can sometimes be successful the very first time that someone tries it.

After reading my book *Angel Pets*, Chris decided to make a conscious effort to connect telepathically with her black Labrador, Ebony. On their next walk, Chris took with her a pair of mittens, one of which she placed on the fallen tree where she sometimes sat while Ebony mooched around. Some minutes later, Chris and Ebony continued their walk, and after a short distance Chris attracted Ebony's attention by calling her name. When Ebony stood looking at Chris, she concentrated on sending Ebony a mental picture of the glove left behind on the tree trunk. Raising her ears Ebony turned around, went back to the tree, picked up the glove in her mouth and brought it to Chris, who – needless to say – was ecstatic.

Monica from Bresso, Italy contacted me after reading the Italian version of the same book. 'Yesterday,' she wrote, 'I decided to talk to my sleeping cat, Romeo, mind-to-mind. I sent the thought, "If you are OK living with us and feel well in this house, please lift your head and meow at me." Incredibly, Romeo turned his head towards me, opened his beautiful yellow eyes and meowed. I was so happy.'

And this is what happened when Ali, my secretarial assistant, tuned into her border collie Flynn: 'Every morning the routine at our house is generally the same. When I've showered and am drying my hair, Flynn takes the opportunity to bring his toy of choice, and a game of throw and fetch will ensue. One particular morning, I thought I would test Margrit's theory of communicating through telepathy. As I went past Flynn's bed after taking my shower, I sent the thought to him, "No toy today, Flynn, I'm running late." To my amazement, I dried my hair with no dog present. Ten minutes later with a smile in my heart I sent the thought to Flynn, "OK, I can play now!" Within milliseconds I could hear Flynn coming to make the most of my invitation. I now find myself tuning into the subtle complexities of what Flynn is trying to say. It's quite incredible how the bond between us has improved as a result.'

Don't be disheartened if a first-time communication attempt does not produce the desired effect, or if sessions are a bit hit-and-miss. Things often evolve over time and depend on circumstances, including of course whether the animal is interested in interacting at that particular time. There can also be a time delay between our sending a message to an animal and its responding. It can help, therefore, to keep, the image or word that we are transmitting in our mind for a short while.

Definitions

Throughout the book, I refer to some key concepts and terminologies, so I thought it might be helpful if I gave you some definitions now:

- **Consciousness** – to be conscious is to be fully aware of our own senses, perceptions, ideas, thoughts, feelings and surroundings. Humans mostly adopt a fragmented approach to life, seeing themselves as separate from the whole, but this is a delusion of consciousness. We can liberate ourselves from the confinement of an insular perspective by embracing all creatures and nature. Then we will discover that we have some catching up to do, because in many ways animals are more conscious than we are – especially through their use of intuitive and instinctive knowledge, which transcends mortality, being passed on from one generation to another.

- **Sentient** – this means being self-aware. It is about having knowledge and a perception of our own existence and the plight of others. Animals as well as humans have this quality.

- **Altruism** – this is the quality of an individual who shows selfless concern for others. An altruistic action may even benefit another or a group at the individual's own expense. For a long time it was believed that animals and birds did not possess altruistic qualities, but thankfully this notion is now consigned to history. The world over, increasing levels of data, as well as people's own experiences, show just how altruistic animals can be.

- **Spiritual** – spirituality is about tuning into our non-physical dimensions. As they are so sympathetically attuned to the natural world, animals tune into non-physical aspects all the time. Acting as interspecies communicators is one way that we too can tune into non-physical aspects with relative ease, which in turn will help to develop our spiritual nature.

- **Communication** – receiving information through touch, taste, sound, sight, smell, insight, the sixth sense, telepathy and intuition. Interspecies communication is about developing an effective, authentic and harmonious skill in terms of our being aware of information on a variety of levels, and from different sources.

- **Heart** – whilst in physical terms the heart is an organ essential for pumping blood around the body, it also contains the largest electrical field in a body. Heart vibrations come out of our hands, giving animals information about our emotional state when we touch them. In this way, whether you are aware of it or not, you are continually sharing what is in your heart. In spiritual terms, the heart is a place as vast as the Universe. Information from all that exists is contained within the heart's energy field, ranging from each leaf to each life, past, present and future.

- **Soul** – the life force or vital essence of an individual being. Rather than think in terms of having a soul, realise that you are a soul within a physical body. Most importantly, we need to always remember that animals are soul beings too.

- **Soul conversation** – this takes place when we connect to an animal intuitively through good intention. Soul to soul, we silently communicate with, and listen to, the animal.

- **Animal** – a member of a nation of species. Our teachers, healers, spiritual guides and soul mates. For the purposes of this book, animals are distinguished from humans, although humans are animals too.

- **Human** – a member of the human race and, as such, a potential animal guardian, caregiver, spiritual partner, healer and soul mate. Throughout this book, I have deliberately avoided using the term 'owner', which suggests an unequal relationship between animal and human.

- **The Universe** – a limitless place, extending far beyond the boundaries of what we already know.

- **Animal nations** – for many years I have used the term nation when referring to animal species and groups such as, for example, dog nation, cat nation, horse nation, bird nation and so on. There are several definitions to the term 'nation', but I mean it in the context of a society, community, tribe and population, and believe that these designations can be applied to all beings.

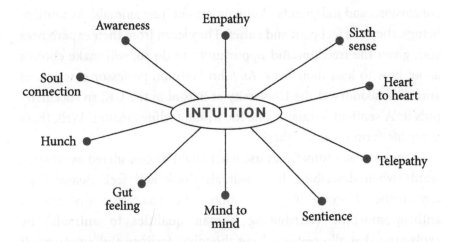

Awareness

Empathy

Sixth
sense

Soul
connection

Heart
to heart

INTUITION

Hunch

Telepathy

Gut
feeling

Mind to
mind

Sentience

Some key links to our intuition.

Why is it important to hear what animals say?

In this millennium, we are lucky that many societies in the world enjoy ample opportunity for freedom of expression, although there are some that still have a long way to go. Alongside this, a parallel movement is evolving whereby people are beginning to recognise that animals also deserve this right. However, as animals cannot verbalise or write things down, people need to become the animals' voices to ensure that they are heard. Deeper and more meaningful relationships with animals are being sought by many of us and, in order for this to become a reality, we need to be aware of what animals are really thinking and feeling. This will also help us to better understand ourselves.

Who do emotions belong to?

History has not been kind to animals in terms of acknowledging their aspects of consciousness. Reasoning had it that, being lower down the species ladder than humans, animals could not possibly feel the same way as we do – a conjecture that I have never understood. Thankfully, it has now been conceded that animals act in ways that demonstrate they possess emotional and mental powers concerned with forming conclusions and judgments. Animals are not 'just animals'. As sentient beings, they can feel pain and suffer. They learn from their experiences and, given the freedom and opportunity to do so, will make choices about how to lead their lives. As John Webster, professor emeritus of animal husbandry at the University of Bristol in the UK, so succinctly puts it: 'A sentient animal is one for whom feelings matter.' Well, that's every life form on earth, then.

In my stories, I sometimes use what could be considered as emotive words when describing how animals think and feel. Before I go any further I would like to counter the accusation that this is anthropomorphic (attributing human qualities to animals) by explaining that all creatures have thoughts, feelings and emotions. If they did not, they would not be able to survive. Our planet is populated by billions of sentient beings, the great majority of which are non-human. In terms of populating planet Earth, humans are the new kids on the block, with the oldest human remains dating to around 400,000 years old. Yet animal remains go back many millions of years. Indeed, the relics of a five-foot penguin that waddled the Earth around thirty-six million years ago have been discovered in Peru.

Because they have been on this planet long before us, animals were therefore the first beings to experience emotions. When their offspring were raised, older members became sick, territories were established, food hunted, objects utilised or their safety threatened, animals experienced feelings. Actions in group situations involved complex personal interactions, and still do. There are no emotions exclusive to mankind. Sadness, happiness, fear, anger, jealousy, ecstasy, confidence, shyness, care, depression, annoyance, anticipation, nurture, empathy, rage, pride, affection, grief, despair, excitement, elation, ardour and, of course, love – animals experience all these and more.

Somewhere along the path of human evolution, animals were deemed to exist in a jumble of indifference, and the concept of emotional intelligence was hijacked as belonging solely to people. The reason is that animals do not utilise verbal expressions to describe how they think and feel, and, labelled as 'dumb', they began to be used and abused. If animals had spoken language skills, then just think how vastly different our world would be today. Animals would most likely be living alongside us in their own harmonious states, not under human domination and control. Had evolution unfolded differently, we may even have become mere curiosities to non-human animals.

We have to be careful, though, that we do not project our feelings or our interpretation of emotions onto them. Every being experiences subtle variations in what they feel and how they feel things, so our human way is not the benchmark for normality. Emotional surrogacy should be guarded against. Dressing animals in replica people outfits, painting their nails or hooves with glitzy colours, colouring their fur and talking to them like babies are activities that cross over into the domain of treating animals like humans, which they clearly are not.

Paws of kindness

With the advent of CCTV, phone cameras and the internet, people en masse are able to record examples of animal sentience, and publicise the message that love, hope and helping are not attributes that belong solely to humans. In countless YouTube films, paws of kindness have touched the hearts of many people. One example is the dog on a highway in Chile who dragged an injured dog to safety across several lanes, dodging the murderous traffic. The dog didn't run from danger, but instead went into rescue mode. Another YouTube video shows a feisty squirrel scaring off several crows as he protects the dead body of his little mate. A few years ago, film footage appeared on TV stations showing a crow which had adopted a stray sickly kitten. Over some months, the crow was filmed in a couple's back yard, feeding the kitten

PAWS UP

Verbally communicating about anything and everything – in effect indulging in small talk – helps an animal to feel secure. Small talk also helps us to engage with the animal and, before we know it, we stop using words and find that the conversation is silent but just as powerful. Small talk can become our intuitive talk.

worms and other food and, as he grew healthy, kitten and crow played together like siblings would. In their companionship, species conflict was obliterated.

My morning newspaper intrigued me with the headline 'Zoo keepers stunned as moose rescues marmot from watery death'. Keepers at an Idaho zoo had been concerned when they noticed Shooter, a four-year-old elk, acting strangely at his water trough. Baffled, they watched as the elk tried to dip his hooves into the drinking trough, before dunking his whole head under the water. When ten-foot-tall Shooter lifted his head from the trough, he was clutching a tiny marmot between his jaws. The gentle giant placed the forlorn rodent down onto the ground, nudging it with his hoof as if checking it for signs of life, before watching it scamper off into the bushes.

10 good reasons why we need to develop our intuition and communicate with animals

1. We share this planet with other species and need to co-exist with them.

2. Animals have thoughts and feelings.

3. Animals want us to be happy. The least we can do is to return the favour.

4. Tuning into animals prevents our disrespect of other species.

5. Communicating with animals helps us to understand them better.

6. Communication leads to a more empathic approach all round.

7. Because each animal is unique our potential for learning from them is limitless.

8. Animal communication will help us to become more self-aware, and therefore develop our potential.

9. Love needs to be unconditional in order for us to be contented. Animals teach us how to love in this way.

10. It matters to the animals.

There is much to be learned from the eons of collective animal wisdom. When we first tune into animals, it may seem that something extraordinary and supernatural exists which is generally hidden from us. I believe that this is not so for animals, for whom there are no cosmic or celestial mysteries – only common knowledge. By tapping into this knowledge for ourselves, we can expand our own appreciation of existence.

It takes a lot to move a human away from the two-dimensional state that we so favour to the multidimensional level that animals inhabit, and which they invite us to experience with them. Increasingly, people are seeking to bridge the divide that remains within our verbal and written communications by conversing intuitively. By considering things from another species' viewpoint, we reach an improved level of observation and, ultimately, of understanding. This brings an additional dimension to our animal relationships, enabling us to gain a deep insight whenever it is needed. The next chapter offers insights into topics such as species behaviour and body language, and is aimed at avoiding communication breakdown.

2 At a Deeper Level

Animals appreciate being understood not just for what they are, but for *who* they are. Every living being is unique, even within species, and whilst there may be some character similarities, we need to look for the differences as well as the resemblances between individuals.

The foundation work of communicating with animals is actually rather mundane. As much as we might like to think it's all about hearing their voices and receiving astonishing bowl-you-over messages, or getting close to them spiritually in a meditative state, the truth is that understanding species behaviour also plays a very important role in animal communication, including the range of traits associated with each species – and of course making allowances for individual nuances. Such themes should form an important element in our studies as animal communicators. There are behaviour differences between species, and even between groups and family members. Animals can either follow their genetic heritage or set their own style of movement and actions. If we lack a basic awareness of animal behaviour, we may be drawn to incorrect conclusions based on our own random thoughts or opinions. Animals communicate plenty, but often feel helpless when a person judges them subjectively.

Each being is an individual intelligent soul, and whilst humans may be more complex and varied in their approach when it comes to expressing intelligence, the diversity of all creatures is amazing. The more that we respect this, the more interactively an animal will respond to us. It is helpful therefore to:

- Learn as much as possible about what makes animals tick.
- Remain objective.
- Make allowances for an animal's individual ways.

In order for our sixth sense and our reasoning to be in sync, it's essential to gain as much prior knowledge as possible about the type of animal that we are communicating with in order to avoid making fundamental interpretation errors.

Matching physical actions to unseen language

When we tune into animals, the telepathic communication that filters into us from them will be backed up by their body language, i.e. their physical actions. We may get the gist of their obvious body movements, but there are subtleties of outward expression that we can miss if not giving them our full attention. Animals direct a combination of body language and unseen language to each other as well as to humans. Dogs in particular are adept at signage. At an agility show, I got chatting to a woman whose Australian shepherd dog was obsessively focussed on her. At the point where I said, '... dogs read images from our minds but lots of people don't realise it,' the dog flicked his head round at me to communicate, 'Too right they do!' before resuming his attentive gaze. Wide-eyed, the woman commented that her dog had read my mind, whereupon I couldn't help but mimic the dog's phrase by saying, 'Too right he did!'

Becoming intuitively aware enables us to better understand the world of a particular animal. After all, we appreciate it when we feel understood by others, and it is the same for our animal friends. A symbiotic communicator is one who pays close attention to the combination of an animal's outward and inner expression, which helps overcome any potential misunderstandings about the animal's behaviour.

A woman contacted me in a panic because her male budgie was regurgitating to a favourite toy. Male budgies in breeding condition display affection to a mate by regurgitating, and I was able to reassure the woman that if no such bird is present, it is normal to display to a toy instead. Female rabbits, cats and dogs in season may begin to make nests and can become more difficult to handle. Horses can act skittishly, as their acute hearing can pick up sounds that we are unable to register. A golden rule is to always check unusual behaviours with a vet, as well as a species expert, in case they are signs of something for which the animal needs particular help.

Animal antics

Animals often back up a message with a physical movement. Horse Johnny had given me a variety of information to pass on to to his person Kathy, before telling me that he was puzzled as to why, when she rode him, Kathy spent so much time looking at her watch. 'What was this all about?' Johnny wondered. Kathy didn't have a clue what Johnny meant and, when she said this, the horse's attitude changed. From standing quietly by my side, Johnny strode across the stable and, thrusting his nose at Kathy's watch, promptly bit it. Pay attention – *this watch!*

'Oh yes, I get it now,' Kathy murmured. 'I keep checking my timings as I practise riding my tests.'

In biting Kathy's watch, Johnny had made it plain as can be that he was listening to both of us, and with his body language had added an extra dimension to the conversation.

Springer spaniel Alfie was another strong character – and hilarious. He greeted me with tail wags and a great sense of drama, before lying down with his head resting on his front legs. I detected sadness emanating from Alfie and when I mentioned this to his guardian, Jo, Alfie immediately raised both paws and covered his eyes with them, making me laugh loudly. But feeling sad is not a laughing matter, so I

Animal insight

Animals know everything about us – in many ways they know us better than we know ourselves. When we realise this, we can more ably understand animals.

quickly got back to the business in hand, which was to help Alfie tell his story. On passing on to Jo the reasons that Alfie revealed were the cause of his sorrow, we were startled to see him jump up, run over to me and bury his head in my lap.

'Gosh,' said Jo, 'Alfie knew what you were saying.' Indeed he did, reinforcing the fact through physical actions. If Alfie had been a human and acted in movies, he would have been nominated for an Oscar.

Educating a kitten

I have witnessed animals doing things with body language that show educational foresight. Some years ago, I took in a stray cat called Mitzi and her three-week-old kitten Floyd. Mitzi was a survivor of street abuse and from the off her mission was to teach her kitten essential life skills. The first time that I let Floyd out of the house at around twelve weeks old, Mitzi hovered by his side. The outside world was astonishing for Floyd to behold and he slowly moved along the garden investigating the smells and textures, before coming to the edge of a grassy bank which dropped down to a lane. As Floyd looked about him a rumble signalled the approach of a motorbike. With her paw, Mitzi struck Floyd sharply on the head three times, sending him reeling, then fleeing back to the house as the motorbike passed. For the next few weeks, Mitzi deployed this tactic whenever traffic came down the road, teaching that engine noise and cats were not a safe mix. Consequently, Floyd developed a sensible lifelong fear of roads, staying well clear of them.

What it's like to be an animal

We can get a sense from the above anecdotes how complex animals' actions and thought processes can be. When we first start communicating, it can be hard to connect, and even if we are quite accomplished there are times when we get a bit stuck. Visualising swapping roles with the animal is a good exercise as it helps establish empathy:

● Whilst sitting in a quiet place with the animal, imagine what it would be like to be him or her. Feel fur, hair or feathers cover your body. Take a moment to ask yourself what that feels like. Now allow your mind to take in the sensation of your having absorbed other body parts of the animal that you are with, as if they are your own features. What is it like to have four legs, wings, claws, webbed feet, hooves, a long neck or a tail, for instance? As you think about each aspect, realise what it is like to live in such a body and how you would see the world as a result. In this way you can get a sense of what makes an animal tick.

Developing our potential

In my experience of treating animals, I have found that there is often a correlation between an animal's state and the person who shares the house (or in the case of horses, a proximity) with him or her, so we need to be willing to consider how to change ourselves in order to help the animals in our lives. As we have seen, the world responds to us just as we react to it. We can realise our potential by becoming self-aware, and the first step towards this is to recognise what sort of energy we are sending out. As beings formed of energy, we each emit a personal frequency that transmits our thoughts, emotions and details of our physical condition, giving out information that can attract or repel others.

Becoming self-aware and claiming our power isn't about becoming a controlling person, but about mastering how we would like to respond to events. We can begin by separating our core identity from our thoughts: start to think in terms of saying 'I feel' instead of 'I am'; for example, 'I feel upset' rather than 'I am upset'. This type of energy is more attractive for others to connect with. Once we start becoming a 'feeling' person, our thought patterns begin to break free from stuck tendencies. Then decoding animal communication becomes more logical to us, and we are increasingly able to help them. This has a two-way effect – we don't waste our innate skills, and the gifts offered by the animals in our life are not wasted either. It becomes a win-win situation.

Becoming aware exercises

Being aware means tuning into a heart-centred place and a still state of mind, so that our intellect does not override our incoming impressions. This can be difficult to achieve, as society expects us to value our intellect above all else. Yet if we want to tune into animals, it is important that we place a high regard on our intuition, and this can actually stimulate our intellectual processes in turn.

Animal Zen moment

There are many places where souls exist. Earth is one such place; significant but small.

Breathing exercise

Being filled with tension is a real block to becoming intuitively aware. If we wish to become centred and clear unwanted energy, transformational breathing is a powerful technique:

- In a quiet place, focus on your breath for a few moments. Breathe deeply and evenly to reconnect with your natural breathing pattern. Over time, our breathing can become shallow in reaction to stress, and this becomes habitual for many of us. Stress can also cause too-rapid breathing. On the inhale, take in love and allow this to spread through your whole body. On the exhale, send out unwanted thoughts, opening your mouth and softly blowing as you do so. You can do several breaths like this. The practice of using the breath to calm your body, thereby allowing the heart rate to settle into a more coherent form, will help clear your mind.

- Listen to your core, the place in the centre of your body between your heart and solar plexus. Hold your hands over this place and imagine it expanding until your hands are pushed away. You will now get a sense of your whole field of energy. This is what you are.

Awareness meditation

With your eyes closed, visualise yourself in your favourite place – perhaps on a beach, walking through a garden, or sitting by a stream. Allow yourself to be infused with the magical healing of that place, bathing in the sense of calm that surrounds you. Encircle yourself in a ball of blue light and ask for an inspirational message to be given to you from the collective animal consciousness. Make a note of the communiqué. Repeating the meditation at another time may result in the same message or a different one.

Regular meditation is known to reduce stress levels, and this will help our relationship with animals. As well as improving our overall health, working on clearing our mind helps our intuitive status. To manifest peace in other beings, we must first be peaceful.

In the moment

We may struggle to make sense of our lives; we may be tortured by reason and find ourselves easily distracted as we strive towards whatever seems bigger and better, thereby missing the gems in each passing second. This can result in our sleepwalking through life, snatching away the potential of our present through past recriminations and disillusioned by a future not yet upon us. Animals have memories like we do and they too can be weighed down by their past or fearful of the future, occasionally even both at the same time.

By their very nature, when given freedom to do so, animals will choose not just to tolerate a moment, but rather to cherish it. Animals generally seek to embrace each moment, paying attention to what each second teaches, buoyantly extracting from it as much as possible. People, on the other hand, often impatiently focus on the negative aspects of their lives. Being with animals help us to appreciate each moment, for the future can be shaped by our enjoyment of the now.

Animals act in the moment whilst living in the whole of time, and as such teach us how to be 'present'. Being present involves the full engagement in each moment with all of our senses, including the sixth sense, and means being reconciled to the here and the now. It is a place where we are neither dreaming of the future nor reminiscing about the past. This is also described as 'being in the moment', through which we are able to acknowledge exactly what it is that we are experiencing.

React to each moment with animal friends as if it were your last second on earth. This will also help you to avoid any feelings of guilt when these animals pass away, as otherwise you might be left wondering about all the things that you could have done differently.

A sense of self

Certain skills are considered key signs of a high mental ability. These include possessing a good memory, a grasp of grammar and symbols, self-awareness, the ability to imitate others, understanding another's motives, being creative, problem-solving and having a sense of the 'I' of our individuality. Bit by bit, researchers have documented these talents in species other than humans, gradually chipping away at what we thought made us distinctive and superior.

Animals have a sense of self-awareness. Just after I had discussed this fact with a friend, right on cue, her large shaggy dog, Fly, gave me a demonstration. Fly strolled up to a floor-length mirror in the hallway and, with a soft, inquisitive look in her eye, proceeded to look at herself, slightly turning this way and that, all the while studying her reflection. Actually, I sensed that Fly was doing more than that; rather than making a superficial assessment, she was connecting to the energy of her whole self. It was obvious from the expression in Fly's smiling eyes that she had done this before, and it was utterly fascinating to watch.

Being who we are

'To dream of the person you would like to be is to waste the person that you are.' Reading this on the information board of a hotel, I understood how these words related not just to people, but also to animals. The gifts and opportunities that animals have to offer are often wasted, because either the sort of lifestyle that is imposed on them is not in their best interest, or humans are not listening to what the animal is saying. This means that the animal wishes for change, in effect dreaming of the 'person' that he or she would like to be.

It was when horse Arthur said about his rider, 'Ask her: *why can't you love me for who I am, not what you want me to be?*' that a breakthrough came in the consultation. In stunned silence, the rider learnt how Arthur sensed her resentment that, owing to his conformation, he was not winning shows. From that moment on the rider began to love Arthur for who he was, which meant amending the things they did together.

I remember another 'problem' client: Maisie was considered a 'boring' dog and generally acted in an insecure manner. Although her people had been trying to help her, what had being missed was the fact that Maisie fantasised about doggy games and sharing a bed with a pal, and then went on to dream of doing it all again the next day. After I passed Maisie's wishes on to her people, the family introduced madcap Zola to the scene and everyone was delighted at Maisie's new-found confidence and how fast she could run whilst yapping her head off. With her new canine companion, Maisie had become the happy dog that she had wanted to be.

'I'm not pitiful,' said the dog

An animal's sense of self can be at odds with how we view them. When Miki and her mother Michiko, from Osaka in Japan, went to buy toys at a pet store on Christmas Day, they saw an eight-month-old Cavalier King Charles spaniel in a cramped cage. After some deliberation, the two women took the wretched dog home to join Betty, another recently acquired puppy. It became apparent that the pet-store pup, who was given

the name Machan, could not stand or walk properly and the vet diagnosed hip dysplasia with surgery as an option. Whilst the vet was talking, Miki heard Machan communicate, 'I want go home, don't leave me here.'

So surgery was shelved and Machan grew into a strong dog. Now six years old, she runs, climbs stairs and jumps. The women believe that what helped Machan become healthy is their love and positive thinking, based on a lesson that the dog taught them about attitude. In the early days, when talking to her friends, Michiko would refer to Machan as *that poor dog*, because of her physical problems and earlier neglect. On one such occasion, Michiko heard Machan protest in an angry voice: 'Don't say I'm a pitiful dog!' The women then understood that Machan did not care what had happened in her past, nor about the state of her legs. Machan was focussing on the present, never wondering *why am I like this?* Each moment that Machan is with Miki, Michiko and doggy pal Betty makes her very happy. Such examples remind me to strive to look on the bright side of life.

Meant to be

Here is an example of another animal with self-awareness, which the animal used to contribute to a future outcome. Petra told me how a cat gave her her first lesson in animal communication. One Saturday afternoon, Petra had gone to visit a local cat shelter at which she occasionally volunteers, but she had barely entered the place when a young tabby started crawling all over her, yearning to be petted. Finally the cat fell asleep under Petra's caressing hands and she sensed that this little fellow was someone very special. At home Petra already had seven cats, two of them terminally ill. Common sense argued it wouldn't be a good idea to take in yet another feline. Petra picks up the story:

> Stupid me, I should have listened to my intuition. I didn't ask the tabby's name, only learning that he was four months old and the last remaining of a litter of six. When I drove home, I just couldn't get him out of my mind; now I know that he must have been sending me telepathic messages.

The next day, whilst gardening – which has a meditative effect on me – I saw the tabby's face in my mind's eye together with a brief glimmer of a name, barely enough to let me realise that it started with an L and ended with an S. I was sure that I hadn't imagined this and, contacting the shelter, I felt a shiver go down my spine on being told that the cat's name was Louis. I was also informed that a family was taking the tabby as a new friend for their cat, who had recently lost his brother. Although I felt miserable at not seeing Louis again I reasoned to myself that it was for the best.

A week later, the shelter manager called to let me know that the people who had taken Louis were going to return him, as their resident cat had been horribly upset to find his brother replaced by an interloper, had gone astray and been found dead a couple of days later. The family declared that they never wanted a cat again, and at that moment I finally realised that Louis was destined to live with me and no one else.

Louis has been my teacher and my guide – in topics such as unconditional love, opening my heart and my mind to the inspirations coming to me, animal communication, patience and positive thinking. I've got a deep and powerful relationship with all of my cats, but Louis stands out amongst them. I feel that he's a very old and wise soul that's been sent to help me follow my spiritual path and give me guidance along the way.

Positive outcomes

Machan was able to quickly move on from her past neglect and Louis was not unduly upset about his time in the shelter or brief unsuitable rehoming, but all animals are different in their response to difficulties or abuse. There are animals that I come across who are so traumatised by past experiences that they remain locked into a state of shock, only allowing themselves to trust one or two people. By tuning in to hear what animals say and sending positive messages back to them, we offer them the best possible chance of feeling at ease so that they can start to come out of their shell.

Unconditional and generous

A comment that is often made is that animals love us unconditionally. However, we should not confuse an animal's instinct to survive and their being dependent for food and water, with appearing to love a human who abuses them. Ironic as it may seem, unconditional love from an animal is actually offered to us with a condition: that we respect and honour the animal, if we seek to be regarded in the same way. It is vanity to expect to receive something more from animals than we ourselves are prepared to give to them. It also allows a person to act badly, thinking that an animal will always forgive them no matter what. Animals ask us to earn their love through giving our own love unselfishly, graciously and generously. To an animal we are all potential friends – it is up to us to prove our worth. When we love unconditionally, we are ready for a spiritual experience, as happened to my friend Roly.

The secret garden

When he was driving home one November night in the pouring rain, Roly's intuition told him that an animal needed him, so he stopped his car and had a look around. Lying on a verge was a young buck roe deer which, whilst injured by a blow to the head, was alive. As it was so late, none of the local animal societies were available to contact, so Roly lifted the deer, which he estimated to be around five months old, into his car and took him home to see what could be done to help the animal.

The deer seemed to have a strong will to survive. He lapped water and nibbled at some food, but was obviously groggy and unwilling to stand. Near midnight, Roly called me to ask if I had something suitable that could be read to the deer to help create a healing atmosphere. Immediately I thought of the 'Awakening' poem which I had written for the dedication page of this book, and emailed it off to Roly. A few minutes later, whilst offering love to the deer, Roly started to speak the first line of my poem: *I hear your voice, those silent whispers that nevertheless are clear, loud and profound* ... and the deer became calm and sleepy. Looking down at the dozing animal, Roly couldn't help but feel privileged to be so close to a wild creature that he normally only saw from a distance – but if only the circumstances were not so grim.

The dawn did not bring an improvement in the deer's condition, and telephoned advice from a wildlife specialist was to take the buck to an animal welfare centre to be euthanised. As the authorised person there stepped forward with a captive bolt gun, Roly asked her to give him a few minutes to say his goodbyes to the deer, which rather took the woman aback ... say goodbye to a deer? Whatever next!

I can understand how Roly was feeling at that time: the responsibility of taking a life was weighing heavy on his shoulders, combined with a sense of a wild animal's vulnerability. Kneeling down by the deer, Roly opened his heart and started to communicate telepathically. What he said is this: 'I am sorry that I haven't been able to do more for you. Please forgive me. Wherever you are going, I wish you a good life and eternal peace.'

Roly went to stroke the deer's head, and at that precise moment the deer raised himself to lick Roly's palm, not once but twice. During the hand licks, Roly described to me how he felt engulfed by a huge surge of energy within his body, followed by stillness. It was like he had been removed to a completely different and unfamiliar realm, a dream-state glimpse into another dimension that we are not normally privy to. Roly summed it up with: 'It was the unexpectedness that shook me. I could not help judging myself for being inadequate, but from the deer there was no judgement – instead with generosity of spirit he departed, giving me a priceless personal gift. The deer showed me an inkling of what is possible to sense.'

When you love unconditionally the connection to the being, of whatever species, adds stardust to your soul. The first time we are gifted with a spiritual experience like this with an animal, it is like taking a peek into a secret garden, suddenly finding that we are going beyond our everyday reality, which now seems drab compared to the vibrant interior of the secret garden. If this sort of thing has not already happened to you, be assured that it can at any time. These experiences come out of the blue, so don't set any expectations; unconditional love will transport you there.

The big picture

Make an effort each day to observe what is going on around you. People tend to rush around, only taking in bits and pieces of information. Animals observe everything using their complete sensory range; they take in the big picture and the minute details all at the same time.

Looking through the lens

For a few minutes stand still and look about you. Think about what you see, the shapes and colours of the world before you.

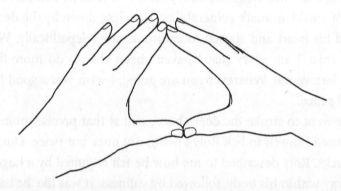

Next, place your fingers and thumbs together to create a lens shape and study an area within this outline. What can you see in this small space? Are the colours and textures different from the bigger picture and, if so, in what way? Do the details reflect the general scene or do they differ? There is a world of dynamic information going on in this relatively small area, even compared with the large view you just looked at.

Compare the information from the two worlds – the big picture with the smaller selection: the macrocosm with the microcosm. One cannot exist without the other.

Doing this exercise regularly helps us develop a stronger focus for interpreting messages from animals. When communicating with them, we juggle information – minute details come along, coupled with large pieces of data. It is like peering through a lens whilst looking at a globe. This may sound difficult, but isn't once we get used to expanding our mind and fully engaging with the world.

Duffy

A communication session can produce a roller coaster of messages, showing many aspects of an animal's nature. This is exactly what happened when John and Sarah brought along four-year-old Border collie Duffy, together with his doggy pal, Miss Milly, to see me.

A couple of years earlier, Duffy had been found wandering the streets in a poor condition and ended up in an animal shelter. An error of judgement was made in allowing Duffy to go to a busy family with boisterous children. Too active for the family to cope with, the dog was sent to a trainer who used discredited techniques, which resulted in Duffy becoming resentful and fretful. It culminated in the family's youngest son offering Duffy a pie, then taunting him by snatching it away. Duffy lunged at the pie and the boy's fingers got bitten in the process. Taken back to the shelter, Duffy was labelled an anti-social canine until Sarah and John came along and recognised the dog's good nature.

When I tuned into Duffy, he took me back to the time when he was thrown from a truck, landing on his head and right shoulder. For a few minutes the dog lay helpless and confused, pounding rain drenching his body. After a while, bruised and sodden, and wondering why he had been abandoned, Duffy had hobbled along trying to follow the direction of the truck, but the scent had been washed away.

PAWS UP

Consider every situation from the individual animal's viewpoint. This will prevent you from projecting your experiences onto whatever that particular animal's problem seems to be.

To prevent the prejudices of your own perspectives from taking over, consciously employ your intuition. Ask yourself, if you were that animal right now, how would you be feeling about your life? Based on this knowledge, are there any improvements that you could make to help the animal become more content and fulfilled?

Keep your senses on alert in a positive way – this means having your energy antennae switched on, so that you can pick up the information that animals wish to pass on to you.

For a several weeks, Duffy lived by his wits, drinking from puddles and eating what he could scavenge, before someone took pity on the stray and transported him to the shelter. Memories of mistreatment by the unkind boy and the intimidating trainer were also blurted out to me. It was important for Duffy to express his troubles as a component of his healing. From time to time, Miss Milly, who lay with her eyes closed, would open them and glance over in my direction, keeping a check on whether I was on the ball with my interpreting. I seemed to be doing OK.

Then the mood changed and Duffy became more upbeat. 'Tell him to give me more chips' – and with that comment came an image of big fat juicy fries. Oh dear, this was not normal dog food, but when I conveyed what Duffy had said, John roared with laughter. Once a week, John treated himself to chips with his evening meal, and he would save two, one each for Duffy and Miss Milly. As John described this to me, Duffy was salivating.

'Anything to say about Sarah?' I asked Duffy, changing the subject. To which he replied, 'She has changed her perfume recently and I don't like it as much as the previous one.' Sarah was now laughing too, commenting that she would set aside the expensive scent and revert to the cheap brand.

But Duffy was not done yet. He confided that there had been a recent situation concerning someone near their home. Detecting 'a being of sadness' passing backwards and forwards behind the garden fence, Duffy had sent this person doggy healing. Until that communication, John and Sarah had no idea that Duffy had been aware of their elderly neighbour's plight: the neighbour had passed away a few weeks earlier after anxiously waiting for an operation.

A day later, I received this message from Sarah: '... the thing for which we are most grateful is the "release" which you evidently gave to Duffy. He is so much more relaxed and this shows in his beautiful eyes.' Burdens can weigh heavily on an animal's shoulders and we can all do something to lighten the load.

A deep level of feeling exists within all beings. Who are we to judge that one species feels less than another, or less than us? It is all relative, and using our intuitive side gives us insights into the magnificence of other worlds, as well as into the life of other beings.

Special moments

Appreciating animals for their uniqueness encourages them to be expressive. During one of my teaching trips to New York, a woman brought her cute Papillon dog, Dino, along to the class. During the first meditation, as I asked the class to tune in to receiving a message from animals, Dino came towards me, whereupon I picked him up to hold in my arms. As I spoke the meditation, I noticed Dino looking at the engrossed faces of the people in the room, and when the meditation ended and eyes were opened, the teacher that greeted the class was Dino.

My heart is full of special moments like this, all of which add to my understanding of the insightful nature of animals. Send out loving thoughts to all the animals that you meet, without regard for their species or physical appearance. This is attractive to animals, who will be drawn to your compassion, so that you engage in a two-way conversation – the topic of our next chapter.

3 Two-Way Conversations

Animals are magnificent. They help us to decode the complexities of communication. More than that, they instruct and inform us.

Every interaction that we have with an animal is a two-way conversation. All life forms are energy transmitters and receivers, and the fact that each being is different makes life very interesting. We constantly send and receive information without effort, even if effort is required to make sense of what we do pick up on. The concept of energy exchanges flying around, crisscrossing the Universe, can be hard to take on board, but I do believe that there is a structure to this process. 'Connection to all there is' means different things to different people. Depending on our individual beliefs, we may link to God, Allah, Buddha, the Force, the Goddess, Angels, Spirit Guides, the Divine, the Flow, Saints, the One Mind, the All, the Source and even the Sun, the Moon, or the stars.

Personally, I like to use the term 'The Oneness' out of respect for all the different individual perceptions that we have of this force. I believe that The Oneness holds frequencies, rhythms and resonances matching those of the individual signals of the billions of Earth's creatures. All thoughts and messages flow through this location from every species, making it the all-knowing centre of an infinite Universe. It is a weightless state that we effortlessly connect to even without motivation, because it is everywhere, within and around every being. Therefore, as well as a link to other creatures through common atoms in our bodies, we are also united with each other through being part of The Oneness. The emerging information is continually assessed by the planet's creatures, which does not make them any more or less spiritual than we humans are – rather just more tuned into the universal communication focal point.

Every time I am with animals, I am reminded of the simplicity of their raison d'être, doing things just because they can. It is this ability to accept existence unquestioningly that makes animals appear more spiritual. They view us as inclusive of all that there is, rather than adopting a fragmentary approach towards the world like humans tend to do.

Hanging out with an animal without asking questions or seeking answers brings us into their spiritual zone, where supernatural experience is always possible. This togetherness doesn't require activity such as touching or grooming; it is just a question of our being close to them. Sharing energy without wanting anything in return is itself a form of communication and is often what an animal has been waiting for us to do. It is a solid platform to grow from in terms of intuitive awareness.

Helping out

As I've tried to suggest in the stories that I've shared so far, communicating with animals is essential for many deeper reasons than merely for our own interest or amusement. Animals don't perceive themselves to be spiritually separate from us and so they can offer us insightful revelations to help guide us on our pathway through life, exercising their guardian-angel qualities. When I have important decisions to make, I like to run my fingers through the fur of chatty cats, wise horses or expressive dogs and ask them to inspire my decision-making. Sometimes they help guide me to actions that I would not normally take, but which nevertheless turn out to be the most fruitful.

Animal insight

Through allowing yourself to connect soul to soul, you become whole. Instead of being a fragment, you harmonise into a vast Oneness, where your true value emerges. You find yourself communicating with other species.

Going through a tough time some years back, I sought the company of a favourite confidant, a dog called Sam. Talking to Sam about two possible decisions, I described them as options A and B. With the first option, Sam quizzically cocked his head from side to side; when I ran through option B, he turned his head away. Of course the decision had to be mine, based on many complicated factors, but intuitively I felt that Sam was guiding me, so I chose option A. It is one of the best decisions I ever made and ultimately led to me changing careers to where I am today.

Cats are particularly adept at displaying psychic qualities. When I picked up the message 'Stop the car' from Abyssinian cat Rufus, I thought that it was because he hated going to the vet, and associated the car with his being transported there. The mystery was solved the next day when the car in question broke down and was found to have a mechanical problem, which could have caused an accident at any moment. Somehow Rufus knew that danger was imminent and had wanted to prevent his people from being hurt.

The soul-voice

No other person in the world is like you, and your voice pattern is as unique as your fingerprint, which is why we can recognise people by hearing them speak. Animals too have a unique voice pattern. Vocalisation is the sound produced by humans and other vertebrates using the lungs and the vocal folds in the larynx. However, a voice is not always produced as speech, and animals may bark, meow, growl, screech, squeal, moo, grunt, moan, chirp, whistle, twitter, roar or whinny. Toothed whales produce sound through their blowholes, whilst baleen whales use the larynx to communicate – as they are without vocal cords, the exact method of sound production is uncertain. Humpback whales have been found to use their own syntax to build phrases that can be combined to form songs lasting for hours.

There is also the voice of the soul, which we can sense or mentally hear when an animal communicates through the unseen energy system. This voice is the expression of the individual being that is housed inside its physical body. We humans also possess such a voice, which we utilise whenever we tune into animals through telepathy. This works in tandem with our intuition, which listens to guidance from our soul-voice. Wherever I go, I am aware of the informative beauty of animals talking, which creates a subliminal chorus in the background, the ripple effect of voices enhanced or receding as appropriate. There is no such thing as complete silence, only an ongoing symphony of soul-voices.

The voice, whether an oral sound or a silent expression, helps us to define character, mood and health. Animals too have their own distinctive soul-voices that match their individual personalities, idiosyncrasies and attitudes. These soul-voices come in an array of tone, quality, rhythm, resonance, pitch and volume. When you are tuning into an animal, don't get bogged down trying to work out what the timbre of a voice means – it is what it is. As you communicate over several sessions, the soul-voice sound may or may not change. However, if you are communicating with a group of animals, you will find that you can begin to distinguish between each individual through their soul-voice signature.

These words define various soul-voice qualities in animals that I have come across:

Soft	Melodious
Gentle	Breathy
Loud	Whispering
Throaty	Staccato
High-pitched	Flowing
Sad	Intense
Strong	Subtle
Lilting	Wavering
Monotonous	Weak
Excited	Deep
Quick	Powerful
Slow	Undulating
Ponderous	Resonant

Hearing an animal's soul-voice is a wonderful experience. When you have proven that you have made a genuine connection by getting the details right, then you truly know you have made contact at the deepest, most authentic level.

Mix and match

'Who' an animal is will influence his or her mode of communication. Be prepared to be surprised when you connect with an animal, because that animal's soul-voice may not always match his or her outward appearance, personality or actions. I have met small docile cats with booming expressions, bouncy dogs with high-pitched utterings and big heavy horses with dulcet tones. My Chihuahua dog friend, Faun, has a high-pitched bark, but possesses a deep, bass-tone soul-voice, whereas a vocally active Burmilla cat I know called Ethel has a weak, almost inaudible soul-voice. Anne the four-ton elephant, who I write about on page 209, has a soft breathy way of communicating. I have worked with many thousands of animals, but never come across identical voices, and I am sure that animals think the same about humans.

I decided it would be interesting to ask a dog what my own soul-voice sounds like, so I put the question to fourteen-year-old Shetland sheepdog Lillie, because in the pack of five dogs who share her home she is the observer. I was apprehensive in case I was told that I sounded like a foghorn, but was relieved to be informed that my soul-voice was lilting, linear and with occasional swirls. At the same time that I heard the description from Lillie, she showed me a picture depicting my voice pattern, which I subsequently recorded in a drawing. Lillie communicated her approval when I showed her the sketch.

Ask an animal that you have a close relationship with to describe your own soul-voice. Through your mind's eye see what pattern your soul-voice makes.

Conversations come and go

Nothing is constant in the way in which we communicate, or how animals choose to behave conversationally. In the reciprocal process, conversations can come and go like the ebb and flow of a tide. It is not possible, practical or reasonable to expect to be tuning in constantly to an animal's thoughts. We live in a human dimension and other species are in their own sphere. We can dip in and out of an animal's world as required and, if we have an open consciousness, this means that any time an animal wishes to send us a message we will hear it. This transmission may be about an animal's health or wellbeing, a necessary course of action, or a helpful warning. A spiritual message of enlightenment may also be offered.

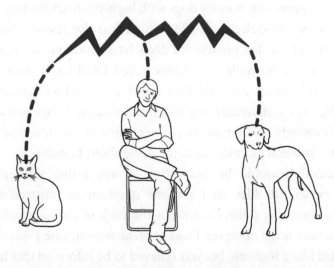

Energetic information is continually being transmitted and received by all beings.

All in good time

Because they hear each other, animals do not realise that humans often neglect to sense the discourse. There are some animals, therefore, who are so used to not being heard by people that they stop attempting to communicate with them. This is why it is essential when we are communicating with animals to let them know that we are prepared to be patient, because they deserve to be allowed to express themselves in their own way, in their own time, and to have a choice about whether to respond to us. This brings me to the subject of free will, which we humans generally seem to take as the exclusive right of our species. Animals have a will of their own and as communicators we must adopt moral integrity by recognising this, and listen to what the animal is saying about what they would like to happen.

Let's not forget either about personality interactions. An animal is not duty-bound to resonate with us as a person, in the same way that we do not get on with every other human being on the planet. We need to make allowances for this and not always assume that the animal is at fault when communication channels do not open or break down. A genuine love of all animals, no matter what they look like, is a very important foundation to work from. When trying animal communication techniques, people may find that they have difficulty connecting with a particular animal. Well, it might be helpful to think of it like this: if we walk into a room full of people, there will be some who will want to talk with us, others who will be reticent, and a few who simply aren't interested.

When I first met him, Beethoven, a long-haired Jack Russell, ignored me to the point of acting as though I was invisible. He is the resident dog at a place where I was teaching in Holland. During the coffee breaks, he would hang around, indulging in dog pursuits such as sniffing about, sunbathing and rolling on the grass. However, as I got out of the car on the second day, a fluffy ball of dog hurled himself at me, greeting me as a dear friend. It was Beethoven, talking nineteen to the dozen and wanting to engage me in conversation, an attitude vastly different to his aloofness of the previous day. Beethoven had needed time to come out of his shell and he turned out to be funny and cheeky, even posing nicely when I asked him if I could take his photo.

Frostie, an English cocker spaniel, was also very wary of me to begin with – and understandably so, having recently been subjected to internal veterinary examinations which had been an affront to her dignity. In fact, so much so that when she first met me Frostie growled, warning me to behave respectfully towards her. Throughout the whole of our first meeting, Frostie eyed me with suspicion, and so I channelled healing energy to her by holding my hand away from her body. Apart from verbal warnings, Frostie did not communicate with me on that occasion.

This was to be the pattern of our next four meetings, although after the second Frostie was content to be touched by me. When Frostie arrived for the fifth session, loudly communicating 'Hello', I realised that something had shifted. She went on to express her appreciation that I had not pressurised her into connecting with me by asking questions or getting physically close to her until invited, because, Frostie explained, she was quite shy. Thereafter Frostie would lead her person to my clinic whenever she was booked in, eager to convey her messages.

Lily, one of my cats, lacks confidence when meeting new people, and often even with folk who she knows quite well. The situation is not helped by her gregarious brother pushing her out of the way to grab as much attention as possible. Therefore I ask people to spend a bit of time quietly talking to Lily, and this allows her self-assurance to improve. Interestingly, when encouraged, Lily has more sage wisdom to impart than her more vocally chatty brother.

Many horses suffer from people's impatience and their individual ways are ignored or they are punished/admonished for expressing their free will. It is a very sorry state of affairs, which is why I have written three books about horses with the aim of helping improve this situation.

Sorting out a meaning

Sometimes the conversation that I am having with an animal does not make much sense at the time to the humans involved, so they have to go away and think about it. Usually the penny drops quite quickly after their subconscious has given them a nudge, often followed by a call to me saying: 'I was on my way home when I realised what the message meant ...'

This was the case with Gillie and Tanya. Gillie brought her German shepherd dog, Tanya, to my practice and during the consultation Tanya communicated that she had received a traumatising bang to the head when she was a young dog. Gillie confessed to being bewildered, but soon got back in touch with me, having remembered a car accident five years earlier. The car had left the road and rolled down a hill, resulting in the driver being hospitalised. Tanya and a couple of other dogs in the car had escaped, and when rounded up seemed fine. Now we knew that

Tanya had suffered a blow and as a result had been bruised and become sore and headachy. Ensuing problems from head injuries can include long-term neck, limb and back dysfunction. Tanya's story shows how tuning into disclosures from our furry or hairy companions can assist us in helping them after an incident, as well as in keeping a general check on what is going on with them health-wise.

Lessons from species

In our dealings with animals, we need to remember that we are animals too. Humans can suffer from human-centric thinking and bias towards the interests of their own group, whilst overlooking the importance of global integration and balance. This is something that the animal kingdom encourages us to learn about, for there is a vast diversity of life on Earth, with over one million known species of animals and an estimated total of over eight million different species of life forms, including plants, protozoa and chromista, such as algae. Three hundred thousand plant species exist and six hundred thousand fungi.

Animal Zen moment

Communication is not about asking – it is about listening.

So we can see that we humans are only one species amongst a total of many millions. There are some who may say that all this is irrelevant, because humans are the most advanced species. However, a sobering thought is that if animals and insects disappeared off the planet, it is estimated that humans would only have a few years of survival. Yet if humans left, other species would carry on regardless.

Humans are part of nature and to progress we must do far more than ignore, or half-heartedly attempt to communicate with, other species. We are joined with all creatures through the intricate web of life. When we use our intuition to enter a conversation with them as equals, the true meaning of these relationships can be revealed.

Insights from species

I have long pondered over the meaning of species – why life is divided into different groupings in the way it is, as well as the essential qualities of various species, how they relate to us, and what we can learn from them. In doing so, I have come to the conclusion that the attributes of other beings are pointers to the life lessons that we can learn from them. The insights that come to us when observing other creatures are filtered through our intuitive self. These are some of my conclusions related to various creatures I have encountered:

Butterfly

The butterfly is a delicate creature that evolves through impressive stages of transition. The egg becomes a larva, then a chrysalis and finally emerges as a butterfly. Chinese animal symbolism views butterfly wings as an undying bond between lovers.

Life lessons relevant to us: the caterpillar considers his life is ending, but the butterfly knows life is beginning. We can responsibly embrace changes in our environment and body as we progress through our own stages of evolution. As we go through transitions in life, we should keep faith, accepting each metamorphosis until we emerge in soul-beauty. This could be thought of as unfurling our spiritual glory.

Deer

Deer have a swift, graceful and tender beauty, for which reason the Celts linked them to the arts, poetry and music. Native Americans observed deer to be skilled at finding healing herbs. As I know from personal experience, deer are able to play a role as messengers from the angelic realms.

Life lessons relevant to us: deer invite us to explore our creative nature. They represent a spiritual approach to the environment, and teach us to be graceful in whatever we undertake. As the deer has an uncanny sense of where to find the goodness that the Earth provides, so we can seek our inner treasures. If you find yourself out walking in an area where deer live, send out a thought asking them to lead you deeper into spiritual consciousness as you go through life.

Dog

Dogs use a complex language system of vocal noises, body movements and telepathic messaging. In this way, they gain from each other vital information about the status of their surroundings. The ancient Egyptians, Romans, Greeks and Celts regarded dogs as sacred guardians of other worlds and ephemeral domains. Native American wisdom deemed dogs to represent assistance, fidelity, friendship, protection and communication.

Life lessons relevant to us: canine energy invites us to explore generously all aspects of communication and sensory perception. Dogs teach us to gain vital information about our inner state, other beings and our surroundings. Listening to lessons from the dog can guide us towards realising our limitless potential.

Cat

Possessing an independent, mysterious air, cats act as guardians of the unseen world. They are keepers of secrets and gaze with guile on people who do not understand the depth of cat knowledge. In ancient Egypt, cats were sacred and depicted on the head of the lunar goddess Bastet, whilst in ancient Rome the cat was sacred to Diana, the moon goddess.

Life lessons relevant to us: the cat can be aloof and therefore offers a message that we should distance ourselves from unwelcome situations or people that we do not resonate with. As cats are synonymous with psychic power, they represent the ability to harness our telepathic abilities as an asset. Cats also teach us to have an overview of the world at large.

Horse

The horse is the greatest contributor to the enhancement of human civilisation. The horse's attributes are power, strength, beauty, endurance, nobility and wisdom. The spirit of the horse is symbolic of the Universal life force. Native American culture viewed the horse as representing freedom, which could be harnessed to benefit the tribe. In Chinese culture, the horse is associated with devotion and stability. Buddha is said to have left the Earth plane riding a white horse, and the acclaimed psychoanalyst Carl Jung claimed that the horse represented the intuitive aspect of human nature.

Life lessons relevant to us: the horse shows us the darkness that can prevail from deprivation of freedom, resulting in limitation and domination. Thus the horse reflects the light and shadow natures of humans. The horse asks that we see through the intuitive portals of the heart and soul, and in doing so become truthful ambassadors for the rights of all beings. Because the horse has a natural grasp of spatial awareness, he encourages us to know the infinite parameters of energy. A powerful message the horse offers is that, like the herd, we are all interconnected whilst remaining separate entities.

Bear

The bear, despite looking ferocious, has an amicable, easy-going nature and is acutely driven by the seasons. The mother bear has a fiercely protective commitment to her offspring. Hibernating through the winter, the bear emerges to gorge on nectar-rich food in the spring and summer, before finishing with a berry fest in the autumn.

Life lessons relevant to us: the bear invites us to accept the cycle of waxing and waning of experience, including being prepared to hibernate with an idea until the right time presents itself for developing that thought. Inklings of an idea can be brought to fruition by tapping into bear determination. The standing bear reminds us that we too can become larger than life by rising up to fulfil our inherent potential.

Eagle

The eagle sees finite detail and its streamlined wings represent the balance between male and female energy, the Chinese concepts of the yin and yang. Effortlessly surfing thermal currents, the eagle represents our being synchronised with the movement of healing energy as it radiates throughout the cosmos.

Life lessons relevant to us: we learn from the sharp eagle eye that we can intuitively pinpoint detail through developing the accuracy of our psychic vision. We are invited to expand our vision to encompass our sixth sense and, in doing so, utilise our ability in a laser-like fashion, focussing on the reality of a situation. We can discover how to connect with energy in order to revitalise our lives.

Coyote

The coyote is super-sharp and highly sensory-activated. Native American cultures view the coyote as a trickster and shape-shifter. The Navajo never kill these animals, believing that they accompanied the first man and woman into the physical world. In Shoshoni tribe culture, the coyote indicates an ending, which paradoxically is a new beginning.

Life lessons relevant to us: coyote energy encourages us to develop a sense of humour. We need to be mindful of our actions no matter what mood or state of affairs we find ourselves in. Shape-shifting means flexibility and allowing ourselves to see the flip side of situations, so that we are always dealing with the whole story.

Hummingbird

Hummingbirds are amazing migrators, known to wing their way two thousand miles to reach a destination. Hummingbirds actively seek the sweetest nectar, and their fluttering wings move in the pattern of the infinity symbol. Thus these birds represent eternity and continuity.

Life lessons relevant to us: be persistent in the pursuit of your dreams by adopting the tenacity of the hummingbird. Seek out the good things in life and the beauty in each day. Realise the source of your joy and how it feeds your soul, whose life is eternal.

Dragonfly

The dragonfly's iridescent wings are incredibly sensitive to the slightest breeze, and on catching the light they reflect beautiful colours to brighten the day. Dragonflies are also attracted to water, where they hover, skitter and dance over the surface. The lifespan of the dragonfly is short, so it knows it must live to its fullest potential. These creatures are symbolic of change.

Life lessons relevant to us: look deeper than scratching the surface. Pay attention to emerging thoughts and be mindful of what you wish to achieve. Be prepared to be flexible and go with the flow. Live, as if each moment were your last.

Elephant

A behemoth of incredible power, the elephant has an acute sense of family responsibility, taking great care of its offspring and elders. The elephant displays determination, loyalty and social connection, standing up for others and defending members of the group. Elephants sometimes travel to a specific place to die, and the social group performs intense grieving rituals. In Roman philosophy, the elephant was legendary for its longevity, so the animal became symbolic of immortality and of living in harmony with divinity. Ancient Hindu texts depict an elephant as a stabilising influence holding up the world. The elephant is a symbol of physical and mental strength, as well as responsibility.

Life lessons relevant to us: when we believe in something wholeheartedly, we have the power to forge ahead. We have a responsibility to be protectors and defenders of the weak, the helpless and the voiceless. Whilst we cannot take all the burdens of the world onto our shoulders, in our sphere we can be a dependable and loyal friend to all creatures. Spiritual strength becomes a key mantra in our lives and, through our intuition, we link to the harmonies of the Universe.

Squirrel

Squirrels are sociable animals, often seen in pairs or groups. They are vocal creatures, utilising an extensive range of sounds, particularly when playing or if feeling threatened. Being practical, squirrels store nuts for digging up in the winter, although only around 10 per cent of these are ever recovered. The rest do not go to waste but act as seeds, growing into trees, thus perpetuating life.

Life lessons relevant to us: squirrel antics make people laugh, so when we see them it is often a message to take ourselves less seriously and have more fun. The squirrel asks us to be mindful to ensure that the metaphorical seeds we sow will come to fruition. When planning for the future we should always include some benefit for nature, so that we help replenish the planet.

Bee

Bees operate through intricate modes of communication and beehives are examples of impressive architecture, combining perfect storage with efficient living space. Pollination by bees is vital for crops and fruits to be able to continue their life cycle, and for this reason bees sustain life on earth. The honey produced by bees has valuable health benefits for other creatures. Bees are symbolic of structure and order, as well as the virtues of adhering to a perfect plan.

Life lessons relevant to us: bees ask us if we are communicating effectively. Are ideas you are formulating based on productive thinking or are you wallowing in areas of negativity? The by-products of industrious efforts at communication include valuable knowledge as well as more meaningful relationships. When passing a beehive or seeing a bee, a message may be for us to establish greater levels of organisation within our home, workplace or thinking.

Dolphin

Communicating with sonar 'clicks', each dolphin has a signature whistle – its own unique identity. Dolphins are known to have extraordinary intellects and emotional IQs greater than those of humans. Using sonar, they can look into each other's bodies and detect certain temperature changes that indicate changing emotions. The dolphin symbolises emotional depth.

Life lessons relevant to us: use your sixth sense to navigate through the murky waters of life towards enlightenment. Don't retreat from responsibilities and be comfortable with your unique self, rather than trying to emulate others. Explore the depths of your feelings and emotions so that, rather than remaining deeply buried in the fathoms of your consciousness, they can surface to be dealt with in whatever way is appropriate. This creates a clearer channel for intuition to flow through.

Animal insight

Communicating with animals is about being with them, not doing things to them.

Grasshopper

Grasshoppers use their hind legs as a catapult and can both jump and fly. They do not have a territory, but roam to find food and escape predators by hiding in long grass.

Life lessons relevant to us: aim high with ideas and plans and you can get there. Leaps of faith can result in consistent forward momentum. The grasshopper advocates that we listen to our soul stirrings, which are indicators of our inner beauty and creativity.

While I was writing down the notes for the last paragraph, a grasshopper literally jumped onto the page! A movement caught my eye – on the wall above my desk, a green grasshopper was rubbing his legs and wings together. I read aloud what I had written about grasshoppers and in response the little fellow became still, before he took off to land on my notebook. How marvellous that the Earth's creatures, large and small, sense what we are about and, when possible, will come forward to say, 'You are on the right track.' Gently cupping the grasshopper in my hands, I freed him into the sunshine of the garden with my very best wishes.

Keep a journal to make notes in, and share the information with friends and family, encouraging them to do something similar. As you go out and about, what insights come to you from the animals, insects, birds, sea dwellers and wild creatures that you meet? There is a wealth of knowledge waiting for you.

Blessed by a butterfly

Any creature can come to us as a messenger; we just need to look about us to notice where they are, rather than rushing through life oblivious to the significance of events.

During a coffee break at a conference where I was teaching, a delegate called Ines came to stand beside me as I looked out of the window. It was an early spring day, the sun was shining and daffodils were beginning to unfurl their glorious yellow trumpets. Those first warm days after the gloom of winter are particularly welcome.

'I am so happy to be here,' Ines said to me, beaming from ear to ear.

'I am also very happy,' I replied.

With that, two butterflies landed on the windowsill in front of us, right by the glass. As Ines and I stood shoulder to shoulder, the butterflies mirrored us, touching each other with their tortoiseshell-coloured wings. We became mesmerised by the radiant beauty of these creatures, joyous in their ballet after the prolonged cold months.

The butterflies could have flown anywhere to bask in the welcome sunshine, but they had come to the exact spot where my new friend and I stood expressing delight in each other's company. Through radiating healing energy, we had communicated an acceptance of animal messengers – thus attracting the nearest ambassadors: these butterflies.

A very long day

Entering a dialogue with an animal comes with great responsibility and we can never predict where it will lead to. This was one of those occasions.

Flops was in despair. His canine body was tense, his breathing included bursts of panting, and his vacant eyes flicked from side to side. If he had been a human, I would have concluded that Flops had been crying. A large, black crossbreed, Flops had been at the Humane Society in Manhattan, New York for several weeks. As a puppy, Flops had been taken on by a man from the same place, and for over eleven years the dog had enjoyed a good life until circumstances changed and, in a distraught state, the man had driven Flops back to the Manhattan premises and given him up.

Kneeling down by Flops, I sensed that owing to his predicament he didn't want to talk very much, which was understandable. It was like there was a wall between us built from pieces of broken heart, so I let Flops know that I was there to help him as best as I could. Great sadness engulfed me from Flops's direction and I felt the raw emotion so acutely that my chest actually ached. The overwhelming sense that came to me was that, minute by minute, Flops was waiting for the man to return.

It was such a delicate situation to deal with. Communicating with Flops about his tragic situation, I outlined as best I could the things that cause humans to make certain decisions. Being a dog, Flops did not judge, because he did not really understand human reactions to cause and effect. All the same, my talking to Flops was obviously therapeutic for him. His panting eased and he became more interested in his surroundings, as if seeing them for the first time. Now I heard Flops's soul-voice, surprisingly strong and rapid in its transmission: 'It's been a very long day.'

It was such a profound statement that I was, very unusually for me, struck speechless, for it wasn't just the actual expression that hit me. In those six words, Flops had provided an erudite synopsis full of significant meaning, far beyond what I could ever have come up with if asked to sketch his plight. In this dog's company, I was left feeling poorly served by language.

Weeks had gone by since he had been returned to the centre, yet Flops had aptly summed up the situation, because for him time had lost its linear isolation and rolled events into a single moment: *It's been a very long day.* When I finally found my voice to pass on to the facility workers what this master communicator had said, I struggled not to sob. Not out of pity, because Flops did not invite that, but because I felt helpless to make his situation better. Gazing solemnly down at Flops, a

PAWS UP

- As an analytical process, thinking can block intuition, which is a sensory mechanism. Allow your mind to freewheel when you wish to connect to an animal soul to soul, as this allows your senses to feed you information from the animal's perspective.
- Sensing through intuition is like following a connective mesh that binds us one to the other. One of the biggest obstacles to our understanding what animals are experiencing is when we become consumed by thinking. This switches off our telepathy and sixth sense, leading to confusion about what is going on with our animals if they start to act up.

teacher in a dog's body, I wished that I could offer him a home, but I lived thousands of miles away on another continent. The least I could do to make Flops's circumstances more bearable was to communicate that I would pray for his contentment and peace. 'Yeah, let's go for that' was Flops's parting comment, as he dropped a weary grey muzzle across old paws.

Talking to an animal about their difficulties is very important to them, heavy though their burdens may be. Just knowing that someone is aware of what they are going through can be healing for them, allowing the animal to feel that they are important enough for their voice to be heard. In this respect, all of us can do something to help an animal's 'long day' become more bearable.

Animals never fail to amaze me with their often philosophical or poetical expressions. Each occasion changes me irrevocably and I am grateful that this is so. Whenever I think that I have reached a plateau, an animal like Flops comes along, showing me that I am but a sapling with a long way to go before I become a wise, old oak tree.

The love conversation

Cat Ginger was another charming animal, who I met at the same venue and who stole a special corner of my heart. If Ginger were able to hold a pen, perhaps this is what he would have written about our meeting:

> I talked to a human today who heard my voice. As we looked into each other's eyes, in unison we said, 'Let's hug.'
>
> Although I was only held in the woman's arms for a short while, the love shared was limitless. We became the energy of love, the sense of love and the feeling of love. I was beloved to this woman, and she to me. We became love itself. We pressed our faces together with a mutual knowing smile and it sealed our love.
>
> There was more to the love in which we blended than an emotional attachment, because healing flowed between us. As the woman's hands embraced my body, I got a sense of what it would be like to be

loved like this for the rest of my life. When the woman put me down, we had both changed, because when you love, no matter how briefly, your heart and soul respond.

On my return back to the UK, I telepathically kept in touch with Ginger, sending out positive vibes for him to be chosen by someone looking for a cat companion. I was over the moon when that eventually happened. Ginger is now called Jack, and utterly adored in a home of his very own.

Blending with animal energies

- When you wish to tune into an animal, visualise a silver thread extending from your heart area, which attaches to the animal in a similar place.

- Now ask for information to travel along this connection. Mental, emotional and physical sensations relating to the animal can be detected in this way. An energetic bubble will form, enveloping both of you. In essence, you become as one and in this state intuitive communication flows easily between you.

- You can connect to any species of animal or bird in this way. Actual contact is not necessary; you can be some distance away from the subject.

When you have practised blending with animal energies, you are ready to move on to the next level of communication, and the following chapter includes tips on what to ask and when.

I'd like to end this chapter with a poem, which I hope will inspire you on your way to becoming a compassionate animal communicator. The words of my poem 'Message from the Animals' were given to me in a meditation whilst I was with horses, dogs and cats – and birds were landing all around us. I had asked the animals the question, 'What is it that we need to know?' in readiness for the next chapter, and they were only too eager to passionately infuse me with the following words ...

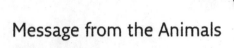

Message from the Animals

Be a voice of the voiceless,
and allow those who are mute to speak through you
so wrongdoings can cease.
We are unable to fight for our rights
but we have you to speak on our behalf .
This is our greatest hope for a better world.

We link soul to soul, now and for eternity
and what you do matters for it cannot be undone.
Open your heart more than ever before;
hold out your hands to embrace healing energy,
and be a student of your intuition
so that you know who you are.

Come to us without ego,
your worst enemy and of no interest to us.
We read the consciousness of the Universe,
moments of truth our pleasure.
Join each one of us in the dance of love,
for when you know who *we* are
communication flows between us …

4 What to Ask, How to and When

When rigid thinking releases its hold, we are able to shift to an intuitive state of being.

Our collective intuition is saying, 'Listen to me, because in doing so you will hear the animal's voice.' This appeal is in response to an escalating desire in people to bond with animals on a level deeper than has hitherto been considered usual. It's contagious too, with the clamour reverberating globally. In this chapter, I have put together as much information as I can about what questions to ask when you are communicating with animals; about how to go about doing so; when to pose particular questions and how information can come to you. Make yourself comfortable and enjoy the tutorial – I hope to offer you the equivalent of a workshop contained in just a few pages.

First and foremost, be yourself. Animals say: 'Come in truth and you and I can have a meaningful conversation.' During my workshops, I tell people: 'Be who you are, maybe for the first time in your adult life.' When people let themselves go in this way, they describe a feeling of lightness, as the strain of trying to keep up with others' expectations falls away. Time spent with animals, therefore, helps us resolve the age-old question of 'Who am I?'.

Individual expression

When it comes to communicating with animals, there is no such thing as a fixed personality type, and you are not one either. It is restrictive to use labels, and interspecies communication cannot have a tick-box method. Personalities in all creatures, including humans, are mutable states. As our animal communication skills develop, a reciprocal evolving of personas always takes place.

Sally regularly brings three dogs to me, two German shepherd dogs, Tess and Babe, and cavalier spaniel Ella. Their individual responses to my healing communication work are fascinating to behold. Tess becomes so sedated, her eyes open but glazed over, that the first time I tuned into her I had to check that she was still breathing and alive. Babe sits calmly but decides for herself when she has had enough, then bounces around inquisitively, as if the place were new to her. Ella was a very nervous dog when she first came to see me, but has generally made great strides in the confidence stakes and now strolls in wagging her tail. Each time I meet these dogs, things evolve and I learn something new about how to be.

Levels of communication

We can't help but make connections with other beings, yet whether we are aware of this is a different matter. There is sometimes a misconception about what communicating with animals actually means. There was the time when I was teaching an animal-healing class during which a student expressed her disappointment that I had not touched on the communication side of things. During the practical session, the woman had described a sensation of unusual heat in her hands and had seen a glow around the animal's back. I explained that these things were *all* aspects of communication.

PAWS UP

Try doing these things simultaneously to help develop your communication skills.

Energy – send out empathic feelings. This triggers a resonant connection.

Images – project your intention of helping the animal, which triggers telepathic connection.

Words – speak your question or message aloud. The animal will pick up the meaning behind the words.

Combine mental telepathy with visualising an open window in your heart area, through which love leaves and enters.

Our bodies respond to energy from animals, and various sensations, including temperature changes, tingling, butterflies in the tummy or goose bumps, can result from this. As humans, we may have pre-set assumptions or expect too much from the time that we spend with an animal. To help combat this tendency, allow your senses to give you information rather than rely on the prejudiced and conditioned rational brain.

Précis of important points for communicating with animals

- Have patience and send out love whilst communicating.

- With love shining from your eyes, ask the animal, 'Who are you?' By posing this question, you begin to resonate with the unique personality of the animal.

- Feel a genuine like for the animal, and don't compare its looks with others you have met.

- A great deal of information can come from an animal just through your being intuitively aware, and without asking a single question.

- Don't expect communication to follow a format. Setting an agenda prevents you from listening to what the animal wants to say.

- Avoid being subconsciously distracted by something else that you need to be doing. Make quality time for the session.

- Your mood or state of mind will influence how animals react to you. Negative thoughts can have an adverse effect on organisms, and animals will try to block any negativity. Angry, bitter, vindictive or depressing thoughts create a barrier to communication because animals will want to avoid such negative energies if we carry them. When you want to communicate about a specific issue, tune in when you are not focussing on yourself or any problems of your own.

- Have an open mind, so that information can come through without it being blocked by your thoughts.

- If you do not get a response right away, wait. Check your energy state in case you are transmitting anxiety or an overwhelming desire to succeed. Remain in your neutral zone and avoid critical analyses.

- If the animal moves away, do not become irritated or annoyed. Animals know when they disappoint or irritate us and, if this is the case, it will not provide a platform for harmonious interaction. Too often animals feel under pressure to do what humans want them to do.

- When messages start to flow from the animal, be respectful of his or her feelings. Do not make the mistake of talking about an animal to other people present as though the animal cannot understand you, or does not have an opinion on what you are saying.

- Animals communicate in a variety of ways and at different speeds. Their messages may either tumble out or move slowly. Whole sentences may be offered or one word at a time.

- If an animal chooses not to communicate then another time may produce a different result. Forming a rapport with an animal can take several attempts.

- When you converse with an animal, it is part of a learning curve. There is no 'one size fits all' method, no right or wrong. We need to find what works best for us, and whether we have a preference for one mode of communication over another. Someone who is visual may get lots of pictures from animals and find it easier to communicate through sending images. Or a person who likes sharing ideas may sense an inner translation of sensory input taking place, resembling a dialogue. We may start out biased to one modus operandi, then with practice discover a variety of ways in which we can comfortably work.

- You can use a verbal phrase whilst sending a telepathic message. I frequently talk to animals verbally and non-verbally at the same time, and a multi-dimensional conversation ensues.

- Communicate often – you will get better with practice. Over a period of time you will notice more details about animals' responses.

- Once your intuition has become strongly active, you can operate in a state that resembles autopilot, a neutral state free from distracting thoughts, which I discuss in the next paragraph. In this mode, important information will come to you as and when required, such as sensing that an animal feels unwell before physical signs manifest.
- Thank the animal for being in your life.

The neutral state

When we communicate with animals, it's best to work from what I call a 'neutral state', which means having a core inner stillness. You can achieve this through doing a short meditation before going to talk to the animal, and keeping your breathing even and calm during the connection with them. When we are in a neutral state, we can readily move in any direction to follow what animals say to us, making sense of the way in which they say it. We can also think of the neutral state as like being on an observation deck, from where we can obtain an overall impression of what it is going on.

Remain in the neutral state whilst communicating. Being unbiased and self-aware are important both before and after tuning into an animal. This attitude also helps prevent you from absorbing the emotions or physical depletion of the animal, or from feeling drained at the end of a session.

Is it real?

When intuitive communication is first attempted, people are understandably concerned about how they can tell whether what is coming to them is for real. Are they making something up or is what they are sensing really a communication from the animal in question? The topic of communication authenticity and integrity came up during a conversation I had with Carol Gurney, author of *The Language of Animals*. This is what Carol had to say about assessing accuracy:

> The key to being sure you are really receiving messages from an animal and not making it up is getting information that can be verified by the animal's person. Always include questions that encourage specific detailed answers. For instance, say to a dog: 'Can you tell me about your favourite activities?' You may hear 'I like to chase balls', but as many dogs like doing this you cannot know if this is your own thought or his. This is a cue to dig deeper: ask what the ball looks like, where the dog chases his ball, and who is throwing it. When you hear that the ball is purple with yellow stripes and the dog chases it in a fenced-in field surrounded by trees, both you and the animal's person will know for sure you have connected with the right animal and are truly talking with him.
>
> When most of us start communicating with animals, we often get information that is not accurate – the dog never had a purple and yellow ball. Rather than feel discouraged, use this to your benefit. Remember what it was like talking to this dog. How did your body feel when you got things right? How about when you got things wrong? Perhaps you began to push yourself, to drift, or a bit of fear came up. With practice, you will realise the ways you disconnect from animals and go into your own thoughts, and what you need to do to stay connected and receive genuine information.

My own mantra is: 'Don't think. Feel.' Thinking and analysing during intuitive communication will cause us to digress from sensing. If you are not sure where a feeling, thought or image is coming from, pay attention to where your energy is centred. Is it in your head? Then the information is most likely interference from your thinking. Is your energy centred in your heart and from where you sense a transmission of love? Then most likely the message is coming from the animal. Confirmation can come in any shape or form, so be open to interesting surprises.

Note: *Taking in communication from another species is not the same as hearing 'voices in the head'. Persons with mental health conditions may sometimes say that they feel driven to do certain things by a voice inside them, urging them on. However, animals do not encourage us to harm another being, commit crimes, indulge in anti-social behaviour, act in a destructive way or become obsessive. Rather, animals teach us to be spiritual and loving. Their communications relate to things of benefit to themselves, other animals or people, and to us. They also guide us to take care of nature and our planet.*

Tuning in for a chat

A hectic lifestyle will hinder your ability to communicate with animals. Being bombarded by technology – the TV on, computers whirring and mobile phones bleeping – creates an energy mishmash and shortens our attention span, making it very difficult to detect the subtleties of an animal's soul-voice.

Whether in your own environment or someone else's, create the most conducive atmosphere possible for communicating with an animal by having all equipment switched off. Multi-tasking is confusing to animals; therefore we need to focus on one thing at a time, which in this case is tuning into them intuitively. Keep up a mindful presence at all times, by which I mean concentrate on being fully present in the moment. If, during a communication, you break off to do something else, such as take a phone call, your awareness will be shifted away from the animal, who will consequently lose interest in you as a competent communicator.

We can communicate with animals anywhere anytime, but when you are still gaining experience it's wise to select an opportunity when the animal is relaxed and not anticipating a meal, exercise or another part of the daily routine. If an animal is busy doing something, and wants to be interrupted by your communication, then he or she will make that choice.

Position yourself so that both you and the animal are comfortable. Some animals like close contact, even communicating whilst being caressed, whilst others prefer not to be handled. You do not have to be near an animal in order to pick up messages from him or her, and the animal does not need to be looking at you for a conversation to commence. The minute you start telepathically sending messages, the animal is attentive at soul level, which is where all conversations begin and end. For this reason, you can even send your love to a sleeping animal.

Asking questions

After you have prepared yourself, you are ready to ask specific questions. First set your intention and ask permission. This means letting the animal know what you are about to do and why. You can speak aloud or telepathically, saying the animal's name, followed by something such as: 'I'd like to chat – is that OK with you?' At this stage you may feel a sense of lightness within yourself, or hear a 'yes' as though someone just planted the word in your brain. If the animal senses that your intention is pure, he or she will usually feel safe about connecting. In general, the answers you receive will lead you to asking yet more questions. Animals are not into having convoluted discussions, and the communication window in which you work can be fairly short.

An animal's instinctive reactions will override its paying attention to you. If you are attempting to tune into a cat and a spot of light plays on the ceiling, or a dog and there is a squeaky noise within earshot, or a horse and another whinnies, you will not be the animal's immediate priority.

- **Keep to the point** Have a list of short questions prepared that you would like answers to and double-check that they are logical queries from an animal's perspective. Ask questions only when you have given the animal the choice of instigating a conversation and first saying whatever he or she wants to say. This communication may answer your pending questions anyway, or may divert you onto a completely different track. I consider it disrespectful to rush in and start bombarding an animal with questions without allowing him or her to engage first. The only time I would do this is in a crisis.

- **Clear and simple** Be clear with your questions, ensuring they do not become muddled up with unrelated images or thoughts in your mind. For example, it would be unhelpful to ask a cat or dog what their favourite toy is whilst you were also recalling what a child liked playing with last Christmas. Simple and direct questions are the best, rather than complex or verbose interrogations.

- **Be direct** A golden rule is not to ask loaded questions with a view to getting the answer we want to hear. Not only can that leave an animal feeling dispirited by our lack of empathy, but our interpretation will be biased and flawed.

- **Ask with care** Don't keep repeating a question if you do not pick anything up. Either you are not on the animal's wavelength, or the animal does not wish to answer the question. In any respect, being forceful rather than empathic is the quickest way to cut a communication cord.

- **No agenda** To start with, it may be easier to connect with someone else's animal, because we often set agendas subconsciously with our own, which are either based on the sorts of behaviour we wish to encourage in the animal or something that we seek to verify. For example, we may have bought an expensive dog bed and now hope Fido will say it was money well spent; we may want our horse to like a new saddle, or for Kitty to agree that not being allowed on the silk bedcover is a good idea.

- **Starter questions** If you have a question to pose to your own animal companion, go ahead and ask a simple question, then see what floats into your mind and how quickly that comes. With animals that are not part of your household, start by asking them about their favourite toys, games, places, things to eat and activities. In this way, you will familiarise yourself with who the animal is, as well as encourage him or her to be receptive to your more important questions. When responses to basic questions and their content are validated, you can progress to becoming more specific about any matters of concern.

Posing questions about wellbeing

These are some of the questions you can ask. You can say them aloud or direct them to the animal through your mind:

How are you feeling? This encourages input to come to you related to the animal's overall health – mental, emotional or physical.

Are all parts of your body energised or do you feel energetically depleted anywhere?

Does anywhere hurt and, if so, where? In response to this question an animal may use body language and either point with the nose to a certain place, lick an area, or scratch. Or you may sense where the animal has discomfort. If you pick up an area of pain, it is essential to inform the animal that you are going to advise seeking veterinary advice and, if communicating with your own animal, make the necessary appointment and communicate this fact. Animals need reassurance that you are a trustworthy communicator partner.

Is there a type of food that you need? Animals often display an inner wisdom about things lacking in their diet, but do discuss your ideas with a vet for safety.

In your day-to-day life would you like anything changed or improved? It's helpful to know about every animal's likes and dislikes.

Which animal or person do you particularly like being with? This question will give you a sense of the animal's relationships. Also ask for a description of the animal or person and a reason for the preference.

Is there is there an animal or a person that you do not get on with or want to avoid? Follow up the previous question with this one. If the animal says this is the case, seek to establish what the problem is.

How do you feel when meeting new animals or people? This will give you an insight into the animal's personality or whether there is something bothering the animal that affects his or her relationships.

Would you like to share with me anything from your past? This is a question I usually include in my communications. However, we should not probe like a voyeur but invite feedback with the utmost respect for an animal's feelings.

What can I do for you? What can your person do for you? Is there anything you want to either ask me, or for me to ask your person? These are all important questions to ask when you are communicating with an animal.

Somewhere in the communication, ask the animal if he or she has a message to pass on. I have found that the content of this can include virtually anything and may be transmitted as words, images or symbols.

Finally, when passing on messages to the animal, either your own or on behalf of someone else, check that they are coherent and rational.

Sending pictures

Animals pick up information from the pictures that form in our mind's eye. You can send pictures intentionally by thinking of the action that you would like to take place (such as Chris's communication to Ebony in Chapter 1) or bringing into your mind a scene of a situation.

Always keep pictures positive. It is essential to keep thoughts of undesirable activities out of your mind – such as the dog getting up on the sofa, for example – because thoughts create subconscious mental imagery. Animals take their cues at face value and cannot differentiate between what you want and what you don't want in those types of communications. This leads to a lot of confusion in animals, who desire to please us, but the image in our mind conflicts with what we want to happen.

Being so independently minded, cats tend to pay scant attention to picture instructions, so the best way to communicate with them is via thought transference and through posing questions. Horses, however, are receptive to the mental images that we transmit to them.

Receiving messages

Here's where you let go of doubts and anxieties about what could be happening, or what should be happening. It is worth making notes because information comes in quickly. In my experience the first thing that comes to me after asking a question is the animal's reply, which frequently will be immediate. Any more than a few seconds delay, check your state of mind in case you have slipped into a thinking-and-analysing mode, which will block you from hearing what the animal is really saying.

How information appears Be receptive in the moment, rather than being tempted to plan your next move. Welcome any feelings, sensations, images, words or smells that come to you, in any combination, even if they seem nonsensical at the time. Messages transmit in a nanosecond, and when you receive a message the animal will literally have just sent it. When we are receiving information intuitively, it usually bounces in quickly, like when we get a flash of inspiration – a 'light-bulb moment' of insight. The most direct way that the information comes is when you feel that you 'just know' what the animal is thinking or feeling. This 'knowing' is a transmission of the total sum of what an animal wants to tell you.

Evidence of communication from an animal can include:

- The rhythm of your thinking changing as an animal's thoughts are superimposed in your mind.
- Ideas/thoughts popping into your head, unrelated to what you were previously thinking.
- An emotional or physical feeling appearing in your being, which wasn't there when you began the communication session.

- You get a sense of looking outside yourself, such as an awareness of what it is like to see the world as an animal.
- You receive a picture or words in your mind's eye, which according to mystical tradition is located inside your head just behind your forehead.
- You sense a word or words coming from the direction of an animal.
- The animal makes intense eye contact with you, even briefly. When communicating, keep the look in your own eyes soft and loving at all times.
- You sense or see a symbol; an example being the time I tuned into a donkey that had recently passed away and saw a packet of mints. It turned out that the last thing that my friend gave her donkey was a handful of garden mint. Messages may be conundrums, like one I received from the beagle who showed me an empty box before rolling onto his back. I then learned that the dog had undergone surgery to remove some tumours from his abdomen. When a cat showed me a carrot, I was nonplussed. Cats are not partial to raw vegetables, but when I figured out the message's meaning I discovered that the image related to an antioxidant supplement that had been prescribed by a vet.
- Voice and image. Be aware that information from an animal can come in what I call a 'twin transmission'. This means that the animal may make a vocal noise whilst simultaneously adeptly sending a telepathic message.

Just one - or a combination - of these things may occur in any one session. The overall communication can be fleeting or form a more lengthy dialogue. Whatever form it takes, allow the conversation to flow naturally, so that you get to know how this individual communicates.

Acceptance Don't judge what you get, or wonder if it is right; it is what it is - even if you do not immediately understand the overall significance. The more empathic we are and the less we are thinking about ourselves, the better chance we have of reading the animal correctly.

Interpretation We should not seek to interpret a message from our perspective alone, but remember that we are dealing with a non-human. Interjecting our thoughts into what we are receiving will distort our interpretation of the facts. And making assumptions based on our experiences is restricting and can lead to a false trail. It can take a bit of working out to interpret an animal's response, which is why we should always discuss our findings with the animal's carer. For example, a cat who describes fearing a man who shouts may be describing someone with hearing impairment, rather than an angry person. A dog who showed me an image of a kicking foot was actually depicting a woman with muscle spasms after a stroke. Another time, when I picked up an image from a horse of his rider waving a stick, it turned out to be information about her baton-twirling hobby, which she practised by the paddocks. Sometimes animals don't fully understand what is going on, so their communication may be confusing. This was typified by a dog telling me that father and son fought in the house, but in reality they were practising their judo. For the dog's sake, I suggested they stick to the gym!

If we receive a communication that we would not have thought of readily by ourselves or that suggests a state of awareness which differs from our usual experience, this is a sign that it has come from the animal. But even if you receive a seemingly obvious answer, such as the cat hates getting wet, a dog likes games, or a horse favouring grass, make a note because it may have a vivid association with a recent occurrence for that particular animal.

Always end the session by thanking animals for their insights and teaching. Take a note of how an animal responds to your appreciation, for that is another aspect of their communication.

Communicating confusion

As we have already seen, our thoughts and emotions broadcast strong instructions to the animals that we share our life with. Harry told me how his dog, Tom, would for 'no reason' start to bark when out on a walk. As Harry had a particularly stressful job, I suspected that it was probably worries spinning through his mind which made Tom apprehensive. I suggested that when out walking, Harry was to talk to Tom about happy things in his life. When he did, the barking eased.

I have a friend whose partner does not stay in the vet's office when their cat is being examined, because the man's fretting about the cat being unduly hurt emits danger signals, which used to encourage the cat to fight tooth and claw. When only my friend is in the room, maintaining calm thoughts, the cat acts more like the proverbial pussycat. And it's common knowledge in the horse world that a nervous or tense rider/handler will upset a horse.

In passing

Animals often communicate casually and spontaneously with what I call a 'passing hello'. Communicating with animals is frequently not about sitting down and focussing on set questions, but rather about allowing unforced simple messages to filter through, which nevertheless have value. Whilst teaching in an historic area of Belgium, I made friends with Charlie, one of the local barn cats. As the students were doing practical work, Charlie came towards us, greeting me telepathically with, 'Hello again.' Enthusiastically, I replied both verbally and silently, 'Hey, beautiful Charlie!' whereupon his tail quivered in delight. Animals appreciate it when we let them know that we are intuitively tuned into them, rather than superficially thinking, *Oh there's a cat/dog/rabbit/ horse.* We can't expect animals to consider us as interspecies communicators if we mostly go through life ignoring them.

A group chat

If there is more than one animal in the vicinity, we need to be aware that they may all be trying to chat to us at the same time and that their voices and messages can overlap. An individual may interact by joining in a conversation we are having with another animal. Whenever I visit a multi-animal household, each animal will usually want to interact and contribute to a conversation. There can be a cacophony of messages flying around. However, in some situations animals may ignore us in preference for a private dialogue amongst themselves. We are, after all, humans living in our own world, with all that entails; but if we can dip in and out of an animal's world when required, this will be to our mutual benefit, and will deepen the bond between us.

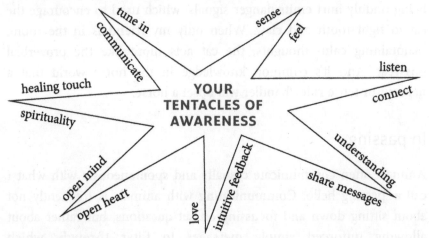

Spreading out tentacles of awareness enables you to create a sound communication platform.

Who said that?

Occasionally, an animal is flummoxed and unsure of how to react to my talking to them on their wavelength. I am obviously a human ... yet can communicate with them in the manner of a non-human. Bemused, the animal is not sure where the information is coming from, wondering *Who said that?* and *What is going on?*

When Tasha, a Canaan dog, realised that we were in rapport, she did not know what to make of it, so she circled the room whilst glancing over towards me. Stopping in her tracks, Tasha lowered her head and gave a low-pitched growl. However, it was not a warning grumble, but rather a noise that said: *This is a first for me and I do not know how to handle it.*

After explaining to Tasha what was going on, I had the sensation of energetically blending with her, and knew that she had stopped resisting the connection. Sure enough, Tasha progressed to offering insights into her life and times, after which she shook herself, yawned and quizzically stared into my eyes as she analysed the content of what had just occurred between us. 'You are a weird human,' Tasha concluded, then, tail wagging, she licked my nose in acknowledgement that I was now a special, if rather odd, friend.

One of the funniest things I have encountered was when I entered a room only for the cat in it to become wide-eyed and then flee the scene, tail fluffed out like a loo brush. I quickly worked out what was going on: I had just been chatting to some horses and goodness knows what remnants of that communication were still flying around in my aura. I made the decision to return another time, when thankfully the cat did not find me alarming.

As the little cat showed me, energy is something that animals are more sensitive to than humans. Never was this more evident than the time that I was with a horse called Bugsy, who was calmly eating hay when a friend who is something of a kindred spirit came up to say goodbye to me. We hugged and Bugsy leapt up in the air, snorting. The combined electrical energy of our healer-to-healer contact had zapped Bugsy. After I had stroked Bugsy and explained what had happened, he relaxed and went back to his hay.

> **Animal insight**
>
> Say to every animal you meet: *Talk to me if you need to, because I am listening.*

Careful approach

When communicating with animals, we need to be aware that things may not always work out as we hope and therefore care needs to be taken with our approach. I learnt this the hard way on a day that I had volunteered my services to an animal shelter. A scruffy, but delightful, terrier mix called Bobby was about to be viewed by a potential adopter. I communicated this fact to Bobby as the woman came into the room, whereupon Bobby ran over to her and placed a paw on her lap. I got rather carried away and sent Bobby a message to be on his best behaviour as this woman could soon be taking him home with her. Bobby couldn't have conveyed any more clearly that he wanted to be with the woman by the way that he clung to her side. The woman stated that she would be back a couple of days later to adopt Bobby, giving him a tickle under his chin as her promise.

Except that the woman changed her mind; the reason given was that Bobby was too much of a mutt and would stick out like a sore thumb amongst the glossy pedigrees residing in the woman's upmarket neighbourhood. That experience taught me to always take into account the vagaries of other people. In similar situations nowadays, I take care not to unduly raise an animal's hopes. Thankfully, a few weeks after my visit, a couple of guys fell for Bobby's charms and took him home with them, where he is very much doted on as the beautiful dog that he is.

The truth will out

On a few occasions when I've taken a booking, the session has been cancelled, with the client confessing that they were worried about what an animal might say to me. I find it intriguing to imagine what secrets those animals are carrying around with them.

Animals can sometimes reveal uncomfortable truths about what is happening in their and their people's lives. A small dog was being treated by a colleague physiotherapist for recurring leg injuries. When I got involved in the case, the dog showed me pictures of how he kept being tripped up by an elderly woman who hooked at his legs with her walking stick. The woman who had brought the dog to me later tackled her somewhat senile mother about this, who confessed. Thereafter, she was not left unsupervised with the dog.

An even more dramatic case involved Helen, who consulted me about her lurcher, Gemma. The dog had suddenly started to refuse to get into Helen's car and would now back away, shaking and panting. A couple of weeks after this, Gemma would no longer enter Helen's bedroom either, a place where Gemma normally slept in her own bed on the floor. The best way to find out what was going on was to ask the dog.

As soon as I tuned into Gemma and asked if she had anything to share with me about her newfound fears, I found myself experiencing an incident from her perspective: I had a choking sensation, sparks exploded into my head, there was ringing in my ears, my eyes felt as though they would burst and I started to black out. There was also intense pain throughout my whole body. Good grief, I had to get to the bottom of this.

'Show me what you see when this happens to you, Gemma,' I said to her. And, horribly, through the dog's eyes I saw a man pointing a small black device at me which made me scream uncontrollably. Whilst Gemma didn't understand what was happening, through my own awareness I knew exactly what was going on.

'Gemma has been subjected to electric shocks, and deliberately, by a man!' I blurted out.

For several minutes, Helen was too upset to say anything and tearfully bent down to pet Gemma, telling her how sorry she was. When Helen did speak, she explained that she had recently split up from her husband with some animosity. From what I had just described, it now dawned on Helen that both sets of Gemma's problems had begun after Gemma had been looked after for the day by the husband. He had always been jealous of the lurcher's attachment to Helen, and it seemed he had reaped a terrible revenge. Fitting an electric collar to Gemma, he had zapped her with the controller on high volume until the dog was traumatised into not being able to join Helen in the things that they usually enjoyed sharing together.

When Helen confronted the soon-to-be ex-husband, he admitted his guilt. Furious, Helen was so specific in her description of events that the man was convinced his actions had been witnessed. He demanded that Helen say who had revealed his mistreatment of the dog, but when he was told that Gemma had, he retracted his admission. The story, though, was included in the divorce petition to the court and animal cruelty cited as one of the reasons why the marriage had irretrievably broken down. Fortunately, once Helen changed her car and moved house, Gemma recovered from her ordeal.

It is immensely rewarding to be able to help solve problem cases through communicating with an animal. Thankfully most of the revelations are not so dramatic and some are amusing.

Jimmy

I once picked up a bizarre message from a green budgerigar called Jimmy, whose guardians had consulted me because their normally chirpy bird had suddenly stopped talking. A check-up from the vet found the budgie to be in excellent health, so everyone scratched their heads as to what the problem could be. When I tuned into Jimmy, he ventured, 'I'm not who they think I am,' whilst casting a beady eye in the direction of the middle-aged couple sitting on the sofa.

I asked the bird if he could help me out a bit and a hint materialised: 'Jimmy died.' Who was I to argue with that kind of certainty? Doing a bit of detective work, I learned that Jimmy's loss of speech had been noticed after the couple had returned from a cruise. As the budgie had been left in the care of a friend, it had initially been assumed that Jimmy was sulking. However, when asked, the friend reluctantly confirmed that the original Jimmy had indeed passed away in her care, having choked on a piece of cake. In shock and embarrassment, the woman had rushed to her nearest pet store with the little feathery body, whereupon she had managed to find a near identical, but of course younger, replacement bird.

No wonder the vet had found 'Jimmy' to be in such good health! It was good to help solve this mystery and eventually Charlie, as Jimmy was re-named, learnt a few words of his own. I still look back in wonderment that not only had Charlie known he wasn't the bird everyone thought he was, but he also understood the situation in its entirety.

Reading energy as a form of communication

We can gain information by reading the energy flow in an animal's body. At a livery yard, I noticed that a tabby cat had a crooked flow of energy running along his spine, which veered into a distorted loop around the left hip before making a zigzag journey down the right hind limb. A clue to what I was sensing came when the cat did the most peculiar stretch, sticking his hind legs out behind him and giving them a shake. On asking the cat what was causing the stiffness, fleeting images of an accident with a horse reached me. The yard owner confirmed that this cat had indeed been accidently trodden on by a horse when much younger, resulting in the cat requiring veterinary attention at the time. I could have simply dismissed the cat's behaviour as a quirky mannerism, but delving further revealed the reality of the situation.

On another occasion, whilst I was out dog-walking, a woman came along with a pooch who I noticed had blocked energy in one leg. Dogs get people talking to each other, so I took the opportunity to mention my observations, suggesting a visit to the vet. A muscle tear was diagnosed and the speedy intervention helped the dog recover before more damage was done.

Intuitive communication is a combination of observing an animal's energy field, watching body language, receiving messages and asking direct questions. In this way, we can glean the most comprehensive information.

Blocks to communication

In order for our intuition to be the most effective it can be, we need to take care of our physical, mental and emotional wellbeing.

Energy enhancers - raising awareness

Fresh wholesome food
Meditation
Being at a beautiful natural location
Adequate sleep
Massage, acupuncture,
    homeopathy, reflexology
    and osteopathy

Socialising with like-minded people
Laughter
Relaxing music
Creative activities
Gentle exercise, such as walking
Gardening
Loving thoughts

Energy depletors - lowering awareness

Alcohol
Smoking
Drugs
Pollution and electromagnetic fields
Jet lag
Watching violent/horror
    programmes and movies or TV
    reality shows that humiliate
    people or animals – these all dull
    the senses and stifle sensitivity

Junk and processed food
Factory-farmed meat
Overuse of computers, phones, TV
Loud music through headphones
Sleep deprivation
Unresolved anger
Stressful relationships

The more that we indulge in energy-enhancing activities, the greater our capacity to intuitively tune into animals becomes.

Explanations are essential

When animals do not understand what we, as their carers and guardians, are doing with them, relationships can unravel. Animals are often treated as if what goes on in a household does not concern them. However, discussing aspects of the home environment and forecasting a day's agenda is a good habit to get into with all animals. Although I have said earlier that animals know everything about us because they read our energy, the situation can become clouded by our own strong emotions and scrambled thoughts. Moreover, an animal may not be able to predict the likely outcome of a predicament and might need us to clarify this for them.

Another point to think about is that, depending on what is going on in our life, our worries can bombard and overwhelm the sensitivity of animals, who then become perplexed as to why the person or people around them are so unhappy. In this way, the animal becomes miserable by proxy. English bull terrier Wilf communicated to me that family problems two years earlier had upset him, and this was verified as the time when the mother of Wilf's carer had become seriously ill and subsequently died. Since then, things had taken some traumatic twists and turns, affecting Wilf via the people around him. Once I had explained to Wilf, via a soul-to-soul conversation, what had been going on, he became quite energised, bouncing around the room with a *joie de vivre* that he had not displayed in a long time.

Clearing the air is an important aspect of communication in order to avoid long-term problems. Sue, a veterinary dental nurse friend, fosters rescued dogs until such time as they can be found permanent homes. Woody is the family's resident canine, and Sue carefully prepares Woody before a fostered dog leaves. Sue senses that Woody is complicit in the arrangement, telling me, 'Woody understands his role in helping other dogs, because I do my best to keep him informed.'

With my encouragement, Wendy prepared her cat, Hector, for the disruption that would be caused by the arrival of builders. For several weeks, Wendy took Hector to her office whilst an extension was erected at home. She explained the programme to Hector each day and, when they got back, took him around the site to talk about the day's events. Wendy was sure this kept Hector chilled out during the upheaval.

It's vital too that people involved with animals – such as vets, ancillary staff, shelter workers and animal therapists – take the time to explain to an animal, using a soft loving voice, exactly what their intentions are and the potential benefits of their actions. Even if performed with the best will in the world, inconsiderate handling of an animal can result in lifelong phobias. When invading another being's space, we need to respect the differences between us.

- Verbally talk to animals about what is going on in your life. Explain your daily routine and what may be concerning you, but keep the conversation light-hearted. This helps prevent a backlog of your emotions swamping the animal. If you feel in low spirits, explain to the animal why this is so, and finish by saying 'I love you' with meaning and gusto. Then do something uplifting together that makes you laugh. Keep repeating happy moments.

- Try this when you have to go out: sit or stand by your animal and imagine the face of a clock. Then transmit an image of the hands moving round to your return-home time. If you prefer, show an actual clock. Whilst the animal has no idea what a clock actually is, by using such visual aids you are helping yourself to transmit information mentally in a positive way.

Confidence

The Universe will deliver to you whatever you resonate with. So if you think something is not going to work, this becomes a self-fulfilling prophecy. Wanting to telepathically reach an animal, yet believing it is impossible, are disparate and conflicting convictions. Trust in your ability to utilise your intuition. Doubt places a block on this sensory mechanism and prevents a clear messaging channel from forming.

Sometimes, the reactions and comments of others can undermine our confidence. However, conversely there can be a danger of our becoming over-confident, whereby we no longer focus on serving the animal's best interests, but on those of our own ego. When we become at ease with our communication abilities, we are more liable to want to share our stories with others. James, a local plumber, declared over a cup of tea one day, 'I thought that I would sound silly if I mentioned having telepathic conversations with my cats and dogs. To think I ever worried about that seems ludicrous now.'

Animal Zen moment

As a consciousness adventurer, you gain astonishing insights into reality.

Believe in yourself whilst at the same time remaining humble, knowing that you are an eternal student of the cosmos.

Like-minded people

When it comes to animal communication, you may not always feel comfortable chatting to your circle of family and acquaintances about what you feel, sense and experience if they do not relate to animals in the same way. However, you are not alone and a growing number of people the world over are shifting their consciousness through contact with animals. A letter I received from a man called Andrew about his animal relationships ended with: 'It does feel good sharing this with someone who understands.'

Sharing our spirituality with like-minded people is important, so seek them out, because it will help you to make sense of the experiences you have. There are plenty of workshops, groups and associations to join nowadays, whether about the use of healing energy or interspecies communication.

Worldview

Something that I very much enjoy during a communication session is receiving an awareness of the world as an animal sees it. One day, whilst teaching at the fabulous British Columbia, Canada ranch of Liz Mitten Ryan, a renowned author and artist, I found myself standing by her herd of free-roaming horses when one of the horses – a handsome bright bay called Miro – invited me to touch him. Presently, Miro pricked his ears in the direction of a hilltop, whereupon the other horses did the same thing. On looking myself, I could not see anything but the hill and its vegetation. Without conscious effort and through the power of herd sentience, I was instantly sucked into their world, becoming aware that my vision now comprised of a shimmering shape, a bit like a jellyfish. My view of the hill was all-encompassing and in the centre of the shimmer was an animal form which, whilst not identifiable to me, was brown with long legs. After about thirty seconds, I resumed my own persona and the horses went back to their siesta. Ten minutes later, a deer broke cover from the hilltop and bounded off down towards the valley.

That day the horses reminded me never to say to an animal that is staring into the distance, 'Silly thing, there is nothing there,' and never to assume that animals view the surroundings as we do. Just before arriving at the ranch, I had a few days in which to visit the area around Vancouver, including Stanley Park, where I saw my first wild racoon. He was behind a wall, which I peered over to get a better look. Suddenly – *whoosh* – I was seeing the world as a racoon, experiencing how their vision is contained within a few feet from the body, and fuzzy, compared to my human sight.

Over the years, I have glimpsed the worldviews of all sorts of animals and birds, and find this the most fascinating of experiences. The first time it happens to you, it may be startling, but be reassured that you are always anchored in your own body. Relax and enjoy the experience, because it is a precious glimpse into animal consciousness. Each species has a different worldview, so your experience options are extensive.

What can you see when you blend with the world of an animal, bird or insect?

The story of Finn and his dolly

All sorts of things can transpire in a communication session. Bev explained to me that her black-and-white spaniel, Finn, was usually standoffish with strangers and would growl at them. Spreading a horse rug onto the barn floor, so that Finn would have a warm surface to stand on and for my feet also, I sat on a stool and explained to Finn why I was there. In return, Finn told me that as soon as he had seen and smelt me, he knew what I was about.

'Can I touch you?' I asked Finn, whereupon he moved across the rug, lay down and pressed against my leg. I placed a hand onto Finn's back and he closed his eyes. Bev looked on in astonishment that her normally aloof dog should be so comfortable with a stranger. Finn and I got down to the business in hand of interacting through a healing conversation. First of all, Finn told me about a joint problem in the right side of his upper neck and added that he was also getting headaches. When I pointed this out to Bev, she explained that Finn resisted having his head stroked or patted and, now Bev understood his body-language communication, she would get the problem sorted out. I felt that the problem had existed from birth, possibly due to breeder intervention. Indelicately pulling a puppy out of a bitch during the birthing process, and even rough handling when towelling a puppy post birth, can cause problems to occur in the vertebrae and joints. (The same sort of thing can apply to kittens and foals.)

As the session seemed to be coming to an end, an image flickered in my mind's eye. It was a small plastic doll, which I was able to describe in detail. 'It's my favourite toy,' Finn ventured. This was, however, news to Bev, who told me that Finn did not possess such a thing. I noticed Finn sigh as though in disbelief, so I suggested Bev have a think about it and let me know another time.

The next morning all became clear, when Bev looked out of her kitchen window. The previous day, a few hours before I had met Finn, his brother Sam had found a plastic dolly whilst the two dogs were out on a walk. Very proudly, Sam had strutted around with his find, which Finn had been desperate to get at. Sam, however, wouldn't give Finn a look-in, resulting in the two dogs squabbling. So the doll had ended up being placed on the garden wall and it wasn't until Bev saw it there that she realised what Finn had been referring to. His communication to me was a hint that the doll *could* be a really treasured toy to play with. What could Bev do but let Finn have his wish?

Animal insight

Instead of trying to think yourself happy, focus on actually doing things that you enjoy. This expands the mind, leading to greater perception through intuition.

Finn's story goes to show how complex an animal's way of thinking can be, and what a great deal there is to discover about this process. Horses are in many ways even more complex than the other animals that we share our lives with, so the following chapter is devoted to them.

5 The Horse's Voice

Horses beckon us to look beyond mere horsemanship, and discover how we may nurture each other's souls in the most symbiotic union possible.

Thousands of voices surround me. I hear them every day; even when I am passing through their community in my car, this does not diminish the crescendo of voice upon voice, communicating messages that link back through the generations to when time began. In the intervening years, time has been well served by these beings, yet ill used by humans. Timeless communication sits comfortably in my being, something which my soul recognises from an epoch of aligned existence, even though it is taking me this lifetime to readjust. In truth, timeless communication is authentic to the horse; the tragedy is that somewhere along the line humans as a species fell out of sync.

The voices that I hear belong to the wild, roaming horses, surrounding where I live. Domesticated horses communicate in the same way – with passionate souls, giving hearts and spirits that yearn for the freedom of wildness. This represents the heart's ease that our own soul desires.

On coming into contact with humans, the horse usually quickly gets to know that humans have taken a monopoly on the lines of communication. To humans, their way is the only right way, and so the horse either shuts down or in desperation becomes reactive, leading to admonishment. The message of the horse rings clearly, piercing the cosmos as a beam of enlightenment that bounces back to Earth in every eye, on each back, under all hooves, and through the entire herd breath. The message states: *we read energies, we are telepathic, we communicate soul to soul … are you listening?*

Throughout this book, there are numerous anecdotes about horses, but I have included this special chapter to cover some notable differences when communicating with horses, as opposed to companion animals such as cats and dogs. Like us, cats and dogs are predators, whilst the horse is a prey animal and therefore highly sensitive and super-vigilant. Other notable differences are that they do not live in our homes like pets do or interact with us in the same social setting; and we sit on horses' backs and ride them. But, although horses are a domesticated breed, they have not physically evolved to carry people or loads, and we make them overuse their natural paces of walk/trot/canter/gallop/jump. All of this means that great care should be taken to understand the horse's needs. Communicating with, and listening to, a horse, demands that we pay attention to the way of the horse. I have heard it said that inside every wild horse is a tame horse, but the reverse is true – inside every tame horse is the spirit of the wild.

Trainers and riders may talk about 'communicating with horses', but usually not in the way that interspecies communicators mean. As well as assessing the body language of the horse, a trainer or rider often uses his/her own body language to get the horse to perform a desired action or to stop a reaction. An intuitive approach may or may not be used. With horses, it is easy to get swept along by peer pressure and adopt the philosophy of a rigid training method. Far better is to build up a relationship based on the horse as an individual, allowing your intuition to guide you in this respect. When we do this, we nurture a connection with the horse as a unique sentient being – and with all that entails. When we say: 'I am intuitively and telepathically tuning into you. In this moment I seek nothing from you other than a soul-to-soul connection. Tell me about yourself, how you feel, what I can do for you.' – *that* is communicating with a horse.

The horse as a *who* not a *what*

When I wrote in an article about the importance of getting to know *who* the horse is, not just *what* the horse is, I was inundated with messages heralding an increasing shift in awareness. Comments included: 'we sorely need this to happen', 'knowing the being inside the horse's body is vitally important', 'we are called to see the horse in a new way', 'if you ignore the who, then you demean the horse', 'with sentience neglected, the horse is dominated', and 'all my life I have waited for things to change for the better – hooray, the time is now!'.

As hearts and minds open, the horse is being embraced within the new consciousness and the old way of training and handling through domination begins to fade. For my part, I have long promoted the concept of the horse as a soul being. This much I know: when the horse becomes a *who* instead of a *what* to humans, then attitudes towards the horse will also evolve in the mass psyche. Which is a day dreamed of by the horse nation the world over.

When we listen

Setting an intention to share healing messages with horses can become the catalyst for a mutually rewarding relationship, as Bob from Texas quickly found out. He told me: 'Your book *Horses Talking* has changed my whole outlook and ways that I have been dealing with my horses. I see them now for who they are, and what their individual needs are. Since I began to do this they are more willing to interact with me. It's amazing. I was brought up old school, "breaking horses" and making them obey or else. I have now thrown out that mentality for good.'

My heart sang to hear this, and to know that horses were being helped. Bob then went on to inform me that he was using the philosophy with his grandchildren to very good effect as well – an intuitive approach is beneficial with all species.

Communicating our behaviour

Much said has been said about the horse's attribute as a mirror of human behaviour. This is both true and untrue. A horse is a mirror of his past or current emotional distress or physical pain, as well as his experiences, all of which affect the horse's response to challenges and human contact. In total, these things influence how a horse reflects our energy. The only horses capable of authentically mirroring us are those that enjoy a natural life with a herd, and are not overworked or in pain.

We think of a soul mate as being our perfect fit, but a true soul mate reflects back to us honestly the attitudes, actions and reactions that may be holding us back. When these flaws are attended to, the process can change our lives for the better. Time and again through my work, I come across horses acting as a barometer of the person's life, with the horse's health and wellbeing affected by what is going on. Horses offer soul-mate wisdom, but in order for us to reap the benefits we first need to investigate what reflections of ourselves we are offering them.

Horse Zen moment

Wind in the tree tops, a luminous sky, aromas travelling in the air. That is a fruitful day of learning. Our business is contemplation, curiosity, awareness and friendship.

It saddens me when horses are isolated from their own kind, unable to touch other horses, sometimes even to see them. This way of being is alien to horses, who need to integrate with each other. Perhaps this sort of horse management reflects a person's subconscious separation from the whole, which actually goes against our own basic nature. Horses repeatedly mirror back the lack of integration that people can suffer from.

A moment in time

Horses act in the moment and respond to us in this manner, but they do not live in the moment for they are influenced by the whole of time, including past and previous relationships (horse or human). Horses can also anticipate and understand future repercussions. Accurately understanding horse behaviour is paramount to our being able to communicate effectively with them, yet many myths about horses are taught as facts – but this is thankfully changing with the increasing advent of equine, science-based teachers.

I put it to biologist, equine ecologist and author Mary Ann Simonds that, when watching free-roaming horses, I have noticed that the herd mainstay, who is always an older mare, is often physically positioned in the middle or at the rear of a herd, rather than at the fore; therefore, it is surely a misconception that horses form relationships through leadership? Mary Ann agrees, telling me:

As social beings, friendships and strong social bonds are more important to horses than leadership. In herds, horses that form functional bonds are more likely to survive longer than those with unstable relationships. Leadership is usually based around spatial respect, but each horse can be equally important in horse society. Horses have social facilitators rather than leaders, often mares who create cohesion and cooperation among herd members. Awareness can vary as much in horses as it does in humans and not all horses are as responsive as others. More reactive horses need another horse in their life to make decisions.

Free-roaming horses can please themselves about how they spend their day. In such herds, which wander freely across plains, over mountainside and through valleys, we get a glimpse of the glorious unfettered spirit of the horse. Lack of free expression is why problems occur in over-confined horses or groups that are kept in too small an area. Intuitively tuning in with a horse means not only understanding the language of the horse's soul, but also the essential needs of the horse. Otherwise we risk standing in front of a horse to ask for mind-boggling messages, when the horse is looking about himself, saying: 'Why are you missing the blatantly obvious?'

I dream of a time when horse carers will as a matter of normality tune in with horses telepathically for the good of all. With the worldwide escalating interest in this topic, the curtain has risen and the new era is here. And you are centre stage in this awakening, with the ability to do a great deal of good to help horses too!

The 'natural' myth

I prefer to align myself with equine professionals who are not promoting methods or selling systems, but who instead consider the overall welfare of the horse. Justine Harrison is a qualified equine behaviourist, and I discussed with her the overuse of the term 'natural horsemanship'. Justine had this to say to me on problems which can manifest in horses through training methods:

Sadly, it seems the term 'natural' has been hijacked in relation to horse training. Too often, so-called 'natural horsemanship' methods are not natural to the horse at all. Techniques such as chasing a horse in round pens and the harsh use of pressure halters, ropes and sticks rely on the use of punishment and negative reinforcement, and as a result create very high levels of stress in the horse. They may appear to be quick fixes to problems, but horses trained this way can suffer from long-term side effects and health problems brought on by chronic stress. Behavioural problems, such as fear of humans, conditioned suppression or aggression, can also stem from attempting a 'quick fix'.

Behavioural science has repeatedly proven that a much more effective – and in my opinion much more ethical – way of educating horses is to use positive reinforcement methods, i.e. reward-based training. A willing, relaxed horse learns much more effectively than a stressed one.

Like Justine, I often come across horses who have been traumatised and depressed by inappropriate training. If a horse displays 'behavioural issues', the first thing that should be done is to call an experienced equine vet to examine the horse, in case he or she is in pain or sick. Training should only be considered when this has been done and we are absolutely certain that a horse is physically well. Even if a vet says your horse is not in pain, it is worth asking a person qualified in musculo-skeletal therapies to make an assessment. Relevant websites are on page 235.

Trusting instincts

A question that is commonly put to me is: 'I seem to have an instinct as to what is wrong with my horses if I slow down and listen to my inner feelings. Is this process something I can work on to improve? If so, how?'

We can all improve our intuitive skill with horses by trusting our instincts and acting on them. The more we do this, the more clearly we hear messages from horses and the more confident we become in acting on them. Things can go badly wrong when we turn a deaf ear and a blind eye to our sixth sense, which is the receptor for input from a horse.

When Amy started to train her horse, Rocky, he would have periods of turning into a ferocious beast. A veterinary examination concluded that nothing was physically wrong with Rocky, the opinion being that this was a young, opinionated horse who simply needed firm handling and hard work. Something niggled Amy inside, though; hence she brought me into the loop. Treating Rocky, I was concerned when I picked up several areas of physical blockages, and subsequently Rocky had a bone scan and X-ray, which highlighted a slight abnormality that did not however overly concern the vets. After some physiotherapy, Rocky improved but then reverted to body-language communication to express that something was wrong. Nonetheless, Amy continued to be told that Rocky was just a badly behaved horse, who required a tough jockey to ride out the bucking.

Amy tearfully called me, saying, 'I am beginning to lose faith in my intuition, because I am told by the experts that I'm wrong. I feel under so much pressure to move away from what my gut feelings are telling me.' There will always be differing opinions based on levels of expertise, and as a result I encouraged Amy to seek advice from senior orthopaedic vet Dr Chris Colles, who specialises in thermography, and he identified on camera the blocked areas that I was sensing. Dr Colles came up with a treatment plan that included osteopathy with my colleague, internationally renowned animal osteopath Tony Nevin. Her intuition vindicated, Amy resolved to always have the courage to follow it.

When Monique called a vet to her lame horse, Björn, she was told that the problem was laminitis, but Monique's intuitive connection with Björn told her this was a wrong diagnosis, so she asked another practice for a second opinion. X-rays showed foot problems that required remedial shoeing – which gave Björn immediate relief. Like Amy, Monique told me that she too has learnt to be confident about her intuitive responses when listening to her horse.

Our gut feelings are responses to the sensory input that we are receiving. It is important to act on them rather than allow ourselves to be swayed and intimidated by others, who can so easily spoil the trust that your horse places in you. We should always believe in what the horse is telling us.

Horses live on a different plane to us, yet they have become intertwined with our lives. Ben wanted to know how to improve his relationship with Mistral. 'Do you talk to Mistral?' I asked Ben, who told me that of course he did.

'How?' I persisted, to which Ben continued, 'Well, I say hello, tell him he's a good boy, or that he is being pushy. And I talk to him when we work together, using my voice to give him aids, such as "walk on" or "canter".'

I explained that Mistral needed to understand what was happening workwise, and that this did not mean just from a human viewpoint, such as 'go over there, do this over here'. Instead, the horse needed to be kept informed across the fullest sense of the communication spectrum. After all, the work would not be taking place without him. So I suggested that Ben should communicate why he wanted the schooling exercises performed and what benefit he hoped they would both gain from them. This would mean Ben showing his respect to Mistral as a key player in the partnership. As I explained this, Mistral nibbled Ben's ear to reinforce his communication of 'Listen to her, please!'

Depending on where we are, sometimes we may speak out loud to our horses, and in other situations it may be more appropriate to communicate mind to mind. The important thing is instigating a soul-to-soul dialogue, and during this we need to keep making intuitive cross-checks so that we can modify our stance whenever we sense the horse communicating a problem. Then we ask these fundamental questions: 'How can I help you? What have you to teach me that I have overlooked?' If we don't tune in intuitively to ask horses what they think or feel, then we are not on their wavelength. If we listen to the communication being transmitted to us, then we have the best chance of establishing a meaningful rapport with the horse.

Horses as observers

Horses frequently demonstrate to me that they are aware of the significance of things that we may not consider important. Dutch warm-blood horse Zeb transmitted the message to me: 'Ellen needs help.' On asking Zeb's guardian, Nicky, who Ellen was, Nicky looked flummoxed, before declaring her astonishment that I should ask such a question as I knew nothing about their local area. It turned out that Ellen was a horse whose rider Nicky had given a lesson to the previous day, and it had in fact crossed Nicky's mind that the horse was looking a bit stiff.

With resolute concentration, Nicky placed a hand onto Zeb's neck and silently communicated that Ellen's rider would be alerted to her horse's need. Half a minute or so later, Zeb shook his head and Nicky turned to me, commenting, 'I said to Zeb I will pass the message on about Ellen. I'll do my best to get her the help she needs ... but you know what people are like. And that is when Zeb shook his head!'

Even so, it would have been very satisfying for Zeb to have got his message across – all horses seek this sort of success with us.

Maddie and Sabine

When communicating with horses it is imperative not to overlook their individuality and to be prepared to make allowances accordingly, rather than trying to put horses into categories. The following story is a good example of horses operating on varying levels of the communication spectrum.

It was a glorious Easter day when I drove across a meadow to meet Iain and Kim, and their horses Maddie and Sabine. Maddie was first in line for a session with me – except that today, when I entered that communal place where information is exchanged, there was a void. I sensed it was because Maddie was a horse who kept things to herself; sure enough, eventually information started seeping through like water oozing out of cracks in a wall. It was fascinating to receive Maddie's memory of a fall in her youth, as though remembering it myself – a jump ahead and the rider on my back taking me to the obstacle crooked. Realising her mistake, the rider was yanking my head round by hauling on the reins, pulling me down onto my left shoulder, my neck twisted. The imagery then faded from view.

An attachment surfaced relating to when Maddie's best friend, twenty-seven-year-old Normie, had become terminally ill and been put to sleep in the paddock. Before this had taken place, Maddie and Sabine had been moved further away, but strangely on their return Maddie had not seemed upset. From what she was now communicating the distress had been internalised, her way of dealing with trauma. However, I sensed that there seemed to be something else needing to be said – but the communication door had slammed shut. I was about to end the session at that when Kim asked me whether anything was being communicated about a life-or-death situation. Looking at Maddie I wondered whether a private individual like her would want to discuss such a topic.

She did go on to enlighten me, though; not in great swathes of information, but with cryptic statements. The trauma had been to the head and neck. There had been an excruciating and debilitating headache. Particular pressure was felt on the left side of the face and neck. A description was imparted of the head feeling disassociated from the rest of Maddie's body, and a desire to pull her head off and throw it on the ground. There are some who might scoff at a horse making such a graphic statement, but they can, and do, express their thoughts and opinions in all manner of ways. Kim confirmed that my narrative made perfect sense, as she would soon reveal.

'That's enough for now,' Maddie said as she moved round in a circle and let out a short, low-pitched expletive of a scream. Kim anxiously asked, 'What on earth was that?' I was able to clarify that the sound was the release of tension coiled inside Maddie, hitherto unable to be expressed in the way that we humans can through sobbing. Maddie's scream had been emitted in a self-controlled way, like everything she does, whereas with other horses I have heard this sound rent the air. This was all very dramatic – what on earth had been going on?

A year earlier, Iain had come to check on the horses and found Maddie with blood trickling from her nose, particularly the left nostril, and her condition rapidly deteriorated. The stricken horse was rushed to the local veterinary hospital, where investigation showed that a common air-borne fungus, called aspergillus, had infected the guttural pouch on the left side, causing a plaque to form that had eroded the wall of the carotid artery. The situation was so dire that Maddie was given an hour to live and a specialist veterinary surgeon was called out to ligate the bleeding artery. There are a plethora of nerves in the face and neck, and damage to any of them could have resulted in facial palsy or fore-limb lameness; death during the procedure was also a possibility. Thankfully the operation was a success. After what Maddie had been through, no wonder she had so many bottled-up emotions, culminating in that scream.

I turned my attention to Sabine. As soon as I stepped towards her to introduce myself, she started to chat nineteen to the dozen. In fact, Sabine threw so many images, thoughts and words at me that they flew around like confetti. Unlike Maddie, who had communicated as if peeping out from behind a door, Sabine bundled up all the memories of her past and tried to release them in one go. The onslaught came at lightning speed and consequently I had difficulty grasping anything, as it seemed that Sabine was ready to share every incident of her life. As Sabine was twelve years old, I joked that it would mean my being there for a very long time.

'Slow down,' I transmitted to Sabine, 'and tell me things that are the most important and relevant to helping you.' After this request, Sabine took me back to the time when she had been a foal in France, bred to be a racing trotter. Her initial exuberance was stilled, and the images being transmitted wavered. Sabine could not elaborate about changes in those early days, because she had no concept of what these had been about, but her life was disrupted many times. From my own experience, I suspect what happened is that a few days after giving birth the mare was transported, together with her foal, to a stallion. This is commonly done in racing circles and is called mating during the foaling heat. Depending on where the stallion is, the journey can be long and arduous, and is always very stressful for mare and foal – both can succumb to illness as a result of this debilitating practice. It was poignant that, as I was in rapport with Sabine about this foal period of her life, she emitted two sounds like a foal's distress call to her mother.

After the weaning process, Sabine communicated that she had been sent to a place that she hated, owing to her not being given an adequate diet and being overworked until she collapsed. Considered a horse that did not try hard enough and labelled a no-hoper, Sabine was sold. From thereon, her history was chequered, with images floating around me like the patterns created in a kaleidoscope. As I talked, translating Sabine's messages, she would from time to time curl up her top lip in my direction as if to say: 'I am very happy that you can hear what I am saying.'

Iain made an interesting observation. He had watched the horses' sessions very closely, having himself been through counselling. It seemed to Iain that what I did with the horses was similar, except of course going about it in a different way. Telepathically, I had invited the horses to talk about anything that was bothering them or that they needed to offload, but in their own way and in their own time. A human counsellor uses verbal cues to do this. What had astounded Iain was seeing the horses releasing emotional baggage. The human process of letting go of deeply entrenched issues is a long, protracted process, which can involve seeing a counsellor every three or four weeks for a couple of years or more. Incredibly, the horses had let go in an instant.

I read a comment somewhere to the effect that our fears cause us to try to hold on to habits and behaviours even when they no longer serve us. In my experience, this is not true with horses and other animals. Given the chance, they will let go and move on in their lives, with the proviso that their lifestyle is supportive and enables them to do so. In this respect, as with so many other things in life, horses have much to teach us.

Things worth knowing

- As a prey animal, the horse is reactive and can be unpredictable. This is not a fault with the horse, just how it is. The more natural the lifestyle and considerate the handling, potentially the happier the horse can be.

- Horses are very sensitive to human energies. When touching a horse or holding a rope or reins, you are sending an energy message about what you are feeling and thinking. Your emotional state will either disturb or reassure the horse accordingly.

- Horses need to be with their own kind, so that they can touch each other. If group problems occur, the space in which they are being kept may be too small, the grazing too sparse, or the dynamics of the group not working. Horses make choices about whom to bond with based on personalities and age. Suggesting to a horse that it becomes 'kinder' to another horse or to stand up for him/herself will not make any sense. Looking at management changes is the option.

- For optimum health and wellbeing, horses need lots of time outside, with shade and shelter from weather and constant access to water. Equine vet friends tell me that horses forced to spend long periods inside, especially during the day, become immune-system depleted, prone to more illness, disease, soft-tissue and joint problems, with slower recovery rates. Full spectrum daylight stimulates the circadian rhythm in the brain as well as the pituitary – the master gland that regulates bodily functions. Sunshine is healing for horses as well as for people.

- Communicating with a horse who spends long periods in stables or stalls demands that we appreciate just how depressing and debilitating such living conditions are. It is our responsibility to the horse to make lifestyle improvements on the animal's behalf. There are extenuating circumstances when a horse is kept inside for veterinary reasons, and in these cases a stable where the horse can stick its head out of the door into daylight is highly desirable.

- Hitting a horse is poor communication. Our intuition responds by shutting down, until such time as we choose to be a healing rather than a hurting person. In her book *Enlightened Equitation*, Heather Moffett writes: '... I often ask audiences whether they would hit their dogs the way they might hit or kick their horse. No, they would not hit their dogs or kick them. Why? Because a dog would yelp. I am certain that it is the muteness of the horse that has been his undoing throughout history, and still is, even in this day and age. If he could cry out in pain, many riders would think twice before hitting horses.'

- Horses know what people think about them. A three-year-old thoroughbred, who was not doing very well in racing, communicated that he knew he was a disappointment, but didn't know how to perform any better. Even eating his food – was it the right way, was it the wrong way? Did he eat it well enough? We need to always be aware that horses read our minds and our hearts. It costs us nothing to be kind and considerate.

- Be consistent, realistic and logical with horses. If, for example, the horse is a miniature breed, then communicating an image to him or her of leaping over a six-foot-high fence is going to be received as a rather ridiculous notion. Remember also that horses are made of blood, flesh, bone and nerve endings, and through what they are asked to do can experience discomfort as well as mental and emotional distress.

- Stay in your neutral zone and breath calmly (see page 41).

A check list of problem signs

Being a horse communicator requires competent skills in reading body language.

Signs of physical pain in horses

Shying

Bucking

Rearing

Spooking

Nervousness

Wind-sucking, crib-biting, weaving

Constantly alert

Sudden change in behaviour

Aggression with humans and/or horses

Mount/dismount problems

Ridden or schooling problems

Withdrawal from the herd

Withdrawal from people

Losing condition

Poor eating habits

Lameness

Pointing one or both front feet

Tripping

Unlevel gait

Holding neck upright or low

Holding ears back

Taut facial muscles

General body tension

Areas of heat, swelling or sweating

Not being able to roll right over

Not lying down

Excessive time lying down

Not wanting to be touched, either at all or in certain areas

Not wanting to be handled

Moving away when approached with a saddle or tack

Suddenly avoiding being caught for work

Back dipping when the saddle goes on, or rider sits on saddle

Lethargy

'Dead' look in the eyes

Signs of emotional disturbance in horses

Spooking

Nervousness

Constantly alert

Wind-sucking, crib-biting, weaving

Constantly alert

Aggression with humans and/or horses

Withdrawal from the herd

Withdrawal from people

Losing condition

General body tension

Air of depression

Not wanting to be handled

'Dead' look in the eyes

Lethargy

Not showing signs of a personality

From the lists above, it can be seen that there is some overlap with physical and emotional pain signals. With any of these signs, advice from a vet should be taken before seeking help from other professionals. Horses operate on a level way beyond the limitations of our language. To understand them, communicate with them, hear and help them, we need to employ our intuition.

Be on the side of the horse

Spoken language and music can both influence our thoughts and even override our intuition, meaning that we become out of sync with what horses are communicating. If you want to know whether a horse trainer/handler is truly empathic, try watching a video/film of them with the sound turned off or wear earplugs at a show. The removal of extraneous input prevents any hypnotic influence being exerted over us and allows the unfettered sixth sense to do its job, channelling to us the truth of the horse's situation. We have power over illusion and, when we trust our intuition, we are shown the truth of the matter.

I remember being excited by the prospect of watching a famous trainer teach, but even so, I was determined to observe the horses closely because they always show me whether the words spilling from a person's lips come from the heart or are for self-aggrandisement. Whilst the trainer spoke in superlatives, a mare showed signs of hind-limb lameness, and the rider pulled the mare up, wanting to leave. The trainer sent the rider off to get pain medication, and was droning on about not giving horses the idea they could stop work by having a sore leg; the horse had to know that the rider was boss. The trainer's words and his actions were not congruent, and when I tried to make a fuss no one paid any attention, even shushing me, so I left the clinic, not being able to stomach what I knew would ensue. After four days of relentless work the mare was in a very bad way and would never be the same again.

By sheer coincidence, I was having supper in a place nearby when the trainer came in and I was able to make my feelings known, notably about his lack of empathy. A reply would have been of interest, but the trainer just stared at me before turning on his heels to flee my presence, boots clicking on the wooden floor. I had spoken out as a horse with a voice would ... and the man was totally out of his depth.

I watched another trainer start off a session by making the horse bow. It was not a stretch-the-nose-down-for-a-carrot type of bow, but on having its legs rapped with a stick, the horse knelt on the ground with the head grotesquely bent under the chest, an uncomfortable action for any horse to endure making. Due to the equine mute state, abusive humiliations like this take place, including making a horse sit like a dog, or lie down so a person can sit or stand on the horse's body. Neither intuition nor soul sense is working when domination is calling the tune.

Acknowledging that horses communicate on unseen levels brings with it the responsibility that we change our ways from hurting to nurturing. The horse's plea is that we all speak out on the horse's behalf. A unison of human voices creates the ripple of change needed to improve the welfare of horses. We should never be afraid to do what's right when the wellbeing of a horse is at stake. If we look the other way, the wounds we inflict on our soul will hurt us intensely, as well as doing the horse a great disservice.

In which Victor introduces Duke

Horses are adept spiritual messengers, a quality which often comes to the fore when we communicate with them. I found myself calling him a unicorn as soon as I clapped eyes on him: Victor, a white horse with an air of spiritual grandeur, exuded sage wisdom. From the off, Victor delved into complex topics in an attempt to help his person, Georgie, even though she had booked me to assist Victor overcome problems of his own. Whilst making notes during a lull in the proceedings, I heard Victor state: 'Duke is here.' With that, I telepathically sensed a large brown dog sitting by the horse, but facing Georgie.

'Who is Duke?' I asked Georgie, at which she gasped and went white as a sheet, before blurting out, 'Duke was my dog. He was stolen.'

Through means known only to a horse, Victor had created an opportunity for Duke to manifest himself that day in spirit form. With Victor by her side, Georgie tearfully told Duke's story. A Rhodesian ridgeback aged nine, Duke had been in the garden one hot

> **Horse Zen moment**
>
> Your vision becomes clear only when you look into my heart with the eyes of your soul.

summer's day whilst a heavily pregnant Georgie took a nap indoors. After an hour, Georgie had got up and, wandering into the garden, discovered to her horror that Duke was missing. A search party was immediately instigated, but Duke was never found and eleven long years had passed since that terrible day.

We needed to hear Duke's version of events. He revealed that he had been stolen by a local man, working nearby as a gardener. The man, who had always hated Duke, and wanting revenge for being barked and snarled at, had seized his chance that fateful day. With no one around, some drugged meat had been thrown to the dog, before Duke was put inside the man's van. Later Duke was sold as a guard dog in another city and found himself chained up in a backstreet compound. Missing his home and the people who had loved and cared for him from a puppy, Duke conveyed that his health had gone into a rapid decline and less than a year later he had died in his sleep.

'Please tell Georgie that I am alright now, I *really* want her to know that,' Duke impressed upon me. 'It is a message that I have long wanted to pass on, but the opportunity didn't arise until this day. Tell her to let go of the shock and the hurt. It really is OK.'

Throughout this exchange, Victor had stood stock-still, eyes looking ahead but not focussing on anything in particular. I knew that Victor was fully aware of dimensions blending together, for he was the catalyst for this mystical occurrence. As Georgie and I discussed Duke's message, I sensed his presence receding, like a light dimming. There was no loss of power to the light – it simply could not be picked up so clearly. Duke had peacefully returned to wherever he had come from.

It was an overwhelming session for me that day, as well as for the client; yet another piece of evidence that the soul has an eternal life, which can communicate with those still residing on Earth.

... Basil brings in Zoe

Something similar to the situation with Victor occurred when I went to see a special horse friend called Basil. Basil requested some healing, then pointed his nose downwards and announced that Zoe was with us. In the straw, I 'saw' a cat shape, but Basil's person, Mel, could not think who this spirit cat could be. Then it dawned on me.

A couple of weeks earlier, an acquaintance had contacted me to enquire when I could go over, because their elderly Tonkinese cat had gone missing. The cat had been sleeping under the engine compartment of a visitor's car, but the visitor had driven off without noticing that the cat was there. The cat was called Zoe. Once I had worked this out, Zoe communicated her recollection of events. Tumbling off the car a short distance from home, she had made her way into a nearby field and lain injured in the long grass. With darkness falling, a predator had sniffed her out and ended her life.

'She needs healing,' Basil communicated, whereupon I switched to directing energy towards Zoe. With that, the cat converted from a weak presence into a strong one and then vanished like a puff of smoke. It was to tell her story, which she knew I would pass on to her people, that Zoe had come. Through his spiritual radiance, Basil had created a portal for this to take place.

... Ed introduces Wilfie

Not all the animals that horses draw into the healing communication circle are deceased. Halfway through a session with Dale's pony, Ed, the soul energy of horse Wilfie joined us, yet I sensed that Wilfie was very much alive. Wilfie and Ed, it turned out, had lived together a couple of years previously and the healing communication session had created an opportunity for the horses to reconnect in a way that was more than simply sending out telepathic messages to each other. Through the healing link, Wilfie's essence had transported itself to be there for the mutual benefit of both horses.

... and Portia mentions Hector

As I channelled healing energy to Paso Fino mare Portia, communication flowed between us about her various ailments, but after a while there was a peaceful silence. Portia stared into the distance, and I became engrossed in tracking energy patterns as they moved around the mare's body.

'Hector.' The name came clearly, but without preamble or accompanying image, which left me floundering rather. So I repeated the name in my mind to Portia, adding the question – who is Hector? Portia pointed her nose at a place to her right, whereupon I picked up the presence of a dog sitting there. He was looking at me expectantly. 'This is Hector,' Portia said. I could 'see' enough to know that Hector was a spaniel-type dog and that, like Wilfie, he was alive somewhere, having joined us in his soul body. Frustratingly, neither Hector nor Portia alluded to what the actual point of the visit was. Portia's person, Kirsten, was adamant that she did not know of such a dog, even though I strongly felt that the canine was somehow linked to her, and the imagery of Hector then faded from my telepathic sense.

Twenty minutes later, Kirsten announced: 'I think I know who Hector is.' It turned out that Kirsten's brother and his partner had just had a baby … and they had a sensitive spaniel called Hector! With that statement, Hector briefly reappeared to communicate how he needed reassurance and attention, as he now felt neglected. As with the other horses, Portia had been able to facilitate the possibility of a soul transporting itself to our vicinity. Kirsten promised to get in touch with the couple and pass on Hector's plea to them, and I was able to go home, relieved that the mystery was solved.

Incidents like this inspire me to meet as many horses as possible, so that I can indulge myself in sharing their glorious ability to reach the heights of the Universe.

A rose by any other name

The following story will ever live in my heart as an example of why horses need us to be communicators in the truest sense of the word.

The first thing I noticed was the distinct lack of brightness in the grey mare's eyes, a haunted look I have seen far too often in the voiceless. I was with Ginger Ann, who three years earlier was found in a skeletal condition, with her sickly newborn foal lying in the mud beside her and dying and dead horses around her. After they had been taken to a place of safety, the foal was put onto a drip and Ginger Ann was treated for her wounds. For some unknown reason, when he was only three months old, the foal was taken from Ginger Ann, who then found herself at Festina Lente in Ireland, a renowned learning centre for special needs children. It was only later that the facility learned about the premature weaning.

The staff started to gently work with Ginger Ann, but after a year she was considered to be 'stuck': something was holding her back from fully integrating. When I entered the scene two years later, it was quickly apparent to me how deeply traumatised Ginger Ann still was, and, touching her shoulder to channel healing energy, I asked for nothing in return. Twenty minutes or so later, I sensed a faltering voice: 'They starved me. They bound me with ropes, they raped me. They abused me. They took my foal.' Steam rose above Ginger Ann's back, as she revealed her anguish.

Stupidly I jumped to conclusions – that the guilty party were the people who kept the ponies before the rescuers arrived – and started to expound on this to those watching. It was when Ginger Ann flipped her head to grimace at me that I knew I was on the wrong track. I had broken the golden rule of not making assumptions when animals talk to you, and gave myself a mental rap over the knuckles.

Horse insight

When we make a soul-to-soul connection with a horse, we embrace an untarnished essence that lies deep within us. This is our rite of passage from unconscious behaviour towards horses, to intuitive awareness.

This time I listened properly. It was the rescuers who Ginger Ann viewed as her abusers. Yes, she had been starving in the field, but she did not comprehend what had happened to her next. I talk in Chapter 4 about the vital importance of explaining procedures to animals, and this was a case in point. The ropes which Ginger Ann referred to were the ones tied around her to pull her into the rescuers' lorry; the 'rape' related to veterinary internal examinations, and what she considered abuse was her being given injections and medicines and having her body scrubbed. Well-meaning as everyone was, no one had even considered for a moment the necessity of talking to Ginger Ann about what they were doing, and why.

Taking such a young foal away from its mother is terribly cruel for both parties and, not surprisingly, Ginger Ann asked me: 'Where is my foal? I never got to say goodbye.' Through invoking the gracious, all-encompassing power of healing energy, I sought to reunite Ginger Ann with her foal, wherever he now was. In that moment, something extraordinary took place. With eyes closed and head hanging down, Ginger Ann started to sway; swinging from one side to the other, the momentum increased to the point where, with a shudder, she almost fell over, and the watching staff rushed forward in concern. The emotional pain, grief, and stress of bad memories were gone, but Ginger Ann had something more to tell me: 'I want a new name.'

We were intrigued as to what Ginger Ann would like to be called. Earlier, I had taken a walk in the gardens attached to the facility, so mentally I ran through the names of plants I had admired: *Jasmine, Honeysuckle, Ivy, Pansy, Daisy, Iris, Poppy* ... Ginger Ann stood unresponsively before me. I then mentioned my favourite flower, to which the mare responded by curling her head around my body, pulling me towards her. 'Her name is Rose,' I announced.

An official naming ceremony was planned and, on the appointed day, staff and children gathered roses from the garden and, singing the new name, scattered the petals onto Rose's back. In the commemorative photos, Rose looks positively glowing. Jill Carey, chief executive officer of Festina Lente, gave me her take on the proceedings: 'On the day of the healing communication, my sense of what happened was cathartic. Rose seemed exhausted afterwards and I recall that she drank a lot of water. The next day, I observed the benefits for Rose. She did not have her usual edginess, high level of anxiety or fear. Rose has proved to be a wonderful horse who is much loved.'

The renaming of Rose reminds me of when healer Emma Simmons came across a chestnut mare in poor condition at a dealer's yard and promptly took her home. The nameless horse was stamped with an export number, an abattoir her intended destination before the dealer took her. The chestnut mare locked eyes with Emma and communicated the name 'Amber', followed by 'Phoenix'. Emma recalls:

This beautiful horse, which had been labelled as waste, had a name for herself, which honoured and valued her spirit and, in that moment of connection, I learnt what it was. The twists of fate that had brought her to me held the energy of the Phoenix rising from the ashes to a new life – fiery, mysterious and defiant. All of this the horse proved to be.

Emotions get buried deeply within horses – tuning into them intuitively can be the catalyst for a new beginning in more ways than one.

The ultimate communication

Animals' eyes have a depth of honesty, which is why they are so mesmerising. The retina has the second largest electrical field of anywhere in the body, after the heart (the brain is in fourth place). Life-force energy radiates from the eyes and the saying that 'eyes are the window to the soul' is never truer than with a horse. Stand by a horse and feel the life-force energy radiate from that animal's eyes. When you do this, what does your intuition say to you about what the horse is thinking and feeling? Make a note of any changes when you place a hand onto the horse's neck and say: *I know you as a unique being and love you for that. I will help you all I can.*

The collective consciousness of the world's horses reaches out to us. This chorus of information is available for us to connect to any time we so choose. Such a union leads to self-discovery of the highest order, as we find ourselves not just at the heart of the herd, but blending into the creative process that has given rise to our Universe. All this the horse communicates, when we take the time to listen.

Through making a soul-to-soul connection, horses connect us to our true essence.

6 Healing Thoughts

**Healing energy operates on the same vibration
as intuitive communication. The healer,
as well as hearing the animal's messages, is
an observer of the magnificent benevolence of
an all-encompassing love.**

As I enter a barn to offer healing to a horse with a leg injury, a small black and white dog scuttles away to hide, looking around anxiously as he darts by. My client explains that the dog is hers, but that he never ventures close to other people owing to his mistreatment before being adopted. Because the horse is standing calmly, I decide to sit on a stool so that I can point my fingers more comfortably towards the injured knee. Healing energy flows through my hands into the horse, and I merge into the healing dance, which is like experiencing the breath of creation.

A rustle in the straw, accompanied by a movement, disturbs my reverie. Glancing down, I see the little dog that I had noticed earlier. He is by my leg, not looking at me but paying rapt attention to my hands, his black button nose quivering ever so slightly. Telepathically, I greet the dog warmly and hear him ask me if he can share in the healing bubble that has been created. 'Of course – come,' I reply. The dog places his front paws onto my thigh, then, scrabbling a bit with his short back legs, climbs up to lie across my lap and facing the horse. The horse, the dog and I are joined together in a loop of loving energy, and for the rest of the session the dog continuously licks my healing hands. Such experiences are more precious to me than the most costly manufactured item could ever be. They are gems embedded in my soul.

When we channel healing energy, we communicate to any animals in our vicinity that we are offering something of special benefit, and it is not unusual for a variety of animals to gravitate towards me when I am in healing mode.

Everyone is born attuned to the universal source of healing energy, but the ability to work with this energy often lies dormant in people until their intuition nudges them to activate a connection to this resource. When we feel the need to touch a person or animal in distress, our heart sending out love, this is a call from our healing core. Our hands are incredibly sensitive and, through touch, we can read the energy field of another being. Healing is about restoring balance mentally, emotionally and physically. And I like the way that Deepak Chopra, author of numerous books about spirituality, puts it in one of his 'tweets': *Healing is a return to the memory of wholeness.*

Healing notes

- Healers are thought to act as a conduit for beneficial energy coming from a universal source, which flows between the healer and the recipient, the benefits of which can be felt on many levels. Healing energy works throughout the whole being, not just in one specific area.

- The use of healing energy is safe for all species, ages and health conditions. You can offer healing to the newborn, as well as during the transition that we call death.

- Healing can be offered anywhere, any time, and offers a sense of peace. During times of illness or emotional need, healing can be given every few hours.

- It is helpful to use healing as a preventative measure, not just when problems surface.

- Sending healing energy from a distance through the airwaves is a very effective way of helping an animal that you are unable to be with in person.

- Animals naturally understand healing energy, what it does and how it works. It is a soul-to-soul connection.

- Intuition will kick in during healing, giving you insights into what is going on with an animal.
- Healing energy can work when everything else has failed. However, it is not a magic cure-all and should never be used as a substitute for veterinary advice or care.

Note: *Healing should not be attempted by persons suffering from depression, as this condition sends out discordant energy, which other beings, including animals, will want to resist.*

Preparation for healing

For healing to be effective, we need to prepare ourselves on an energetic level, in a similar way to tuning in for intuitive communication. This includes:

- Calming the mind through regular meditation and deep breathing exercises (see page 42).
- Respecting and nurturing the body, including paying attention to our diet. Body energy rises or lowers according to what we eat and drink. Certain foods and drinks can overstimulate the body or cause sluggishness, whilst other things we ingest are found to have a beneficial effect on cells. Keeping abreast of what helps improve health and wellbeing is something I like to do for myself.
- Spending time in nature.
- Regular gentle exercise to boost our energy field.
- Listening to relaxing and soothing music.
- Creative and artistic pursuits.

What to do

- The use of healing energy is a 'doing with' process – not a 'doing to' treatment. Light touch or holding the hand above the recipient's body, accompanied by loving thoughts and the sense that you are connecting to a powerful source, is what activates the flow of healing energy.
- You can channel healing for as long as the animal is happy for you to connect in this way.

- Healing energy can be channelled through the chakra system, with animals having eight major chakras whilst humans have seven. The eighth and most important major chakra in animals lies over the shoulder area. This is the healing start point.

- A short burst of healing can be very effective, so if you do not have much time a few minutes is helpful, provided that you do not feel rushed.

- If the animal moves away, then assume that he or she has had enough on that occasion.

My books *Healing for Horses* and *Hands-on Healing for Pets* cover the topic of using healing energy with animals in depth.

Feeling stuck when trying to resolve problems in an animal relationship? Channel healing energy to awaken your intuitive senses.

Tactile communication

Being a channel for healing energy is not an intricate process, and it is as natural to undertake as intuitive communication. The two modalities go hand in hand, as both operate in the zone of unseen energy and combine a variety of different strands of information.

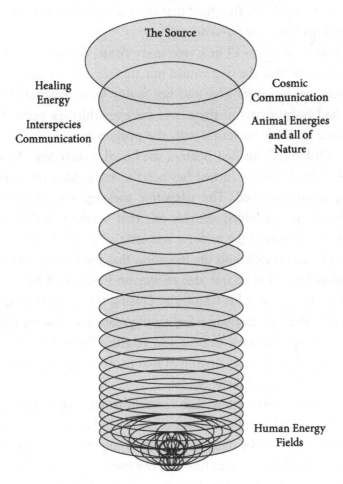

Through a healing connection we aim to raise our consciousness
and reach the Source of all that there is.

Healing energy operates on the same wavelength as intuitive communication. Practising healing raises our energy vibration to the resonance of animals, so that our intuitive communication with them is enhanced. You can tune into an animal's signature soul-voice energy through making a healing connection.

An exchange of energy

Because it works on the same wavelength as interspecies communication, when we send healing energy to an animal we often receive messages in exchange. These may come either from the animal in need or from others that we are involved with. Shirley's healing experience was also the first time that she realised that communicating with her dogs was even possible.

Red Bearen was very ill in a veterinary clinic, the vet having stated that he thought that the dog would not survive and should be put to sleep. Needless to say, Shirley and her family were devastated as Red Bearen had been a part of their lives for over thirteen years. Shirley went home to come to terms with the prognosis and, as she lay on her bed thinking about Red Bearen, she heard a voice say: 'Send him healing.' At that, Shirley turned her head to see golden retriever Bree standing beside the bed. The telepathic message was coming from Bree's direction. Intuitively, Shirley felt that sending healing to Red Bearen was the right thing to do; it was after all a gift of love.

Shirley concentrated with the intention that the healing was to help Red Bearen recover if he was able to stay on Earth or, if he wished to pass away, then to ease his transition. During this process of spiritual connection, Shirley described a feeling of great calm descending upon her, together with a wave of heat and tingling throughout her body. After falling asleep, Shirley dreamt of Red Bearen, running around and wagging his tail as healthy as can be.

On waking, Shirley knew that something was happening to Red Bearen and asked her incredulous partner to call the vet, who, to their amazement, said that he must have been wrong with his diagnosis. All of a sudden, Red Bearen was fine and the joyous couple were asked to collect their dog and take him home.

A year later, Red Bearen became ill again, so Shirley booked to see the vet the following day. That night, Shirley channelled healing energy to Red Bearen whilst holding him close to her. It was with a healing link that they both fell asleep, their spiritual bodies melding one with the other. With a start, Shirley awoke in the middle of the night, her hands still on Red Bearen. The difference now, though, was that she could not feel a heartbeat. Red Bearen had just slipped away, his body still soft and warm to touch. This time the healing energy had formed a bridge for his peaceful transition to heaven.

Shirley ended her story to me with the words: 'Since that first time, I now hear my dogs talk to me every day. When looking into their eyes, I see beautiful souls and know I am a lucky woman.' Me too. Whenever I am with animals, I think of how very fortunate I am to be in their amazing presence and this spurs me on to continue learning, both from them and about them. I learn about me too, because through each interaction I progress in some way, sometimes imperceptibly and at other times more noticeably.

Friday's healing story

As the story on page 133 about the timid little dog in the horse barn illustrates, when we ooze with healing energy, animals reach out and say, 'I'd like some of that, please,' which is what happened to me in Spain. It was my first teaching trip to that country, arranged by musicians Berti and Debbie. When I walked into the couple's house, Simba, a mastiff crossbreed, telepathically communicated to me: 'I knew you would come.' Sitting by Simba was his sister Leia, who reinforced the welcome with, 'Good that you are here.' I noticed that Leia's soul-voice was soft with a flowing resonance to it like flute music, whereas the resonance of Simba's communication was more like a string instrument. The musical comparisons that came to me as I stood by the dogs were particularly interesting for me, because Berti and Debbie play in an orchestra. There was no doubt that my journey was going to be worthwhile and that I was going to learn a lot from these animals.

Simba was having some sessions of physiotherapy, so I went along to watch, and after he had come out of the hydrotherapy machine and was being dried off, an assistant called Tanya offered to show me around. I was glad of this, because for several minutes I had sensed that an animal close by was calling me for healing help. On following Tanya through a door at the end of the corridor, I noticed a pale ginger and white cat lying on a padded chair, sunning himself under a therapeutic heat lamp. Drawn to the cat, I bent down and my hands were instantly sucked towards the feline body, as though pulled like a strong magnet. Healing energy automatically flowed between me and the cat, and I detected an almost inaudible purr rhythm, which rose and fell in response to fluctuations in the energy connection. 'That's good, very good,' said the cat and, stretching out a front paw, flexed the claws in pleasure. The cat's name, I learned, was Friday; he lived at the animal physiotherapy clinic and suffered from paralysis in his back legs.

After a few minutes of silence, I again sensed Friday's soul-voice, this time seeing his words bobbing along in my mind as though watching a karaoke machine. White, almost transparent words were displayed to me on a pale grey background. 'Please pass this message on to my people,' Friday communicated. 'I have so long wanted to be heard.' He continued: 'Thank you for not thinking that my life was worthless and not throwing me away. Thank you for caring about me. I have never known love before from humans, and it is the most beautiful thing to be so loved. Thank you for loving me.'

When I passed Friday's message on to Tanya, tears rolled down her cheeks – and mine too, I might add. Tanya explained that Lucia, the physiotherapy centre owner, had been driving home one evening when she had come across the injured cat by the roadside. She took it to a vet, who did what he could to repair the shattered bones. The cat's life was saved, but its use of its back legs was not regained. It was a Friday when Lucia had found the brave, little cat and that was how he had come by his name. Friday proved to be a feisty, happy cat. Initially, Lucia had taken Friday home with her, but her other cats did not appreciate the newcomer and, as he was disabled, it was not a good idea to have the cats start scrapping over territory. So he went to live at the physiotherapy clinic, with his very own chair and heat lamp.

Animal insight

Become a spontaneous healer, allowing healing energy to radiate from you wherever you go. This allows shades of light to illuminate other beings as well as yourself.

As I pondered over the profound message that Friday had transmitted to me, he spoke again, saying that he liked dogs. Then he communicated in pictures and quickly I realised that I was seeing the world through his eyes. This is often how we can pick up communication from animals – a sort of parallel-worlds conversation takes place. I 'saw' the profile of a short-haired brown dog and, as I did so, a strong feeling of loss and sadness overwhelmed me. Friday was grieving for the loss of a canine friend.

I asked Tanya who the dog was that Friday was showing me. The story that unfolded was a very sad one. When Lucia had first taken Friday in, she had been working at a clinic owned by someone else, where there was also a resident, rescued, disabled dog called Abegondo. Friday and Abegondo became inseparable best friends, playing, eating and sleeping together. When Lucia decided to open her own clinic, her boss became angry that she was leaving. He told her that she could take Friday with her, as she had found him herself, but not Abegondo. Lucia begged her boss to let Abegondo go with Friday, knowing how it would break the hearts of both the cat and the dog. But in his anger the man was resolute and uncaring about the repercussions of his selfish diktat. The dog would stay, the cat would go.

There are times when an animal communicator's job is to try to explain why humans do things, knowing that these actions will cause great anguish and hurt to the innocent. How could anyone tear apart the friendship of these two innocent animals, who had led compromised lives and who had found such comfort in each other's paws? It was suffering heaped onto suffering.

'Come,' I whispered into Friday's ear, as I bent closer to him, 'through the healing dance I will connect you with Abegondo, and you will sense his energy, as he will sense you close to him.' For ten minutes or so, I held my hand gently on Friday's back and, as the healing energy flowed, I prayed for him that he would find peace and Abegondo too. During this procedure, Friday invited me to join him in sending out a message into the world – that destructive energies on this planet be replaced by a loving approach to all beings. As Friday transmitted the words to me, I repeated them out loud. When I had finished, Friday moved from the chair, adeptly pulling himself along with his front legs to drink from a bowl of water, before eating from an adjacent plate. Having healing gives you an appetite.

That evening, after I had said, 'Good night, doggies,' to Simba and Leia, I heard Simba reply, 'Thank you for helping the cat.' It brought a lump to my throat, and I quietly sat down by these wise souls who somehow, through the universal consciousness, were aware of what had transpired that day between me and Friday. Just when I think I am progressing quite well with my intuitive understanding, along comes an animal to show me that I have to strive a lot harder in the awareness stakes.

Animals as healers

All animals have healing qualities and the paws, hooves and wings of kindness have touched many people's lives. Some animals have a particular aptitude in this respect. Virginia McKenna's personal assistant, Sarah, told me that during the stressful period when she was helping to nurse her mother through a terminal illness, one of Sarah's miniature long-haired dachshunds became particularly anxious and wanted to be cuddled all the time. Sarah was sure that in her own way the dog wanted to offer comfort and support. When things settled down, both dogs became their normal happy selves again.

When my friend Pauli got sick with a high temperature, she telepathically explained the situation to Whisper, her young Jack Russell terrier, saying he would have to wait for a walk until her partner returned from work. Pauli also communicated that she needed to be tranquil and could not cope with Whisper running around wanting to play. Whisper seemed to nod at this request and quietly went to lie in his bed. Later, when Pauli shivered with stomach cramps, Whisper jumped up to lie along Pauli's stomach, greatly easing the pain.

Brian was terminally ill with cancer and being cared for at home by his wife and family. Brian's dog Layla, a cocker spaniel-Labrador cross, would wander in and out of his bedroom and sit by him. The day before Brian died, Layla ran into the room and, clambering up onto Brian's chest, lay across him. The family knew then that time was running out for Brian. Layla was saying her goodbyes as well as comforting Brian. Layla's heart would have been over Brian's heart when she lay on his chest, and hearts have healing vibrations. There is no doubt in my mind that Layla was offering Brian healing to help him be peaceful for his journey into the light.

Another acquaintance, marketing executive Emma, remembers her childhood healing cat, Sam, who would always appear if Emma was upset. Sam would then rub his face on Emma's, wiping away her tears, during which she would hear Sam ask, 'What's the matter?' This encouraged Emma to share her tribulations with him and, as soon as Emma felt better, Sam would go off to do something else. All the cats that I have shared my life with have displayed healing abilities in their own individual ways and currently Lilly is the household exponent. When her brother, Teddy, got a blade of grass stuck down his throat, I had to wait overnight before taking him to the vet for the irritating object to be removed. Lilly licked Teddy's throat until he calmed down and then, with her paws softly touching Teddy's neck, she slept by him. Lilly knew that something was amiss, where the problem lay, and offered pussycat healing.

Pam's horses were quick to offer their healing help when she was living in Hawaii and had just had a row with her partner. Distraught at the realisation that the marriage was over, Pam drove to the paddock of her two independently minded ex-Polo ponies, who usually left Pam alone as she worked around them. Sitting down under a tree, Pam closed her eyes to consider her marital situation. Soon she became aware of a warm breath on her leg and, opening her eyes, saw one of the

Animal insight

Don't underestimate the healing power that runs through paws, hooves, fins and wings, as well as hands.

mares, Tia, sniffing her carefully and slowly. Rojo, the second mare, was standing right next to Tia. Pam realised that the horses had picked up her anguished thoughts and drawn close to heal her broken heart. For the next half an hour or more, the two horses stood over Pam like mares protecting a foal, until she finally stood up. Then the horses solemnly followed Pam to the gate, accepting the tearful hugs that they would usually disdain. Says Pam, 'No human friend could have given me the perfect emotional support, which those mares gave me that day.'

The caring nature of animals can shine through even when they are not directly involved with a person in need. The first time I met pony Thomas, his young rider, Katie, was intrigued when he communicated that he was sending healing energy to an injured man with a badly damaged leg. It transpired that the partner of Thomas's groom had fallen off a roof whilst repairing it. This accident and its repercussions are something the pony can only have known about from thoughts present in the groom's mind. Even so, Thomas knew that help was needed, so he did what he could to join the circle of healing surrounding the unfortunate man.

On another occasion, Thomas started pinging out a rather bizarre message to me relating to another person's thoughts. The message 'Remember the laundry' was accompanied by images of fabric flying through the air. Apparently the stable helper had been fraught about laundering travel bandages, as Thomas's things were gathered together ready for a show. This worry seemed to become imprinted in Thomas's psyche, going round and round in his mind as it had in the woman's. A zap of healing energy set Thomas free from that negative cycle. Each of Thomas's communications, from pathos to humour, demonstrated the wide range of surrounding activity that animals can access.

The invitation

Earlier in the year a horse sent me an invitation to go to him for healing. That particular horse, Lusitano Tetuã, who features on the front cover of my book *Horses Talking*, communicated to his carer and rider, Patrick Kempe, 'Margrit needs healing. Bring her to me.' Tetuã was spot-on, for I was feeling rather run-down, and the horse knew this, even though I had not consciously sent out a plea for assistance. So, of course, I rushed right over when Patrick got in touch to pass Tetuã's message on to me.

It was novel to be the receiver of healing from a horse rather than the giver and, stepping towards Tetuã, I placed my hands onto his neck, to which he responded by shutting his eyes, dropping his head and entering a horse meditation. For my part, I absorbed Tetuã's spirit as the healing energy began to flow into me, which I thoroughly enjoyed. After a while, there was a cessation, at which point Tetuã turned his head towards me and pressed his forehead to my chest. It was a horse blessing and the words I sensed touched my soul: *May the light which you share with me always protect you.*

By the next day, my sense of wellbeing had much improved, and now I know where to go for more healing help if I need it.

Jodi's love

Lisa came to one of my classes and told me an incredible story about her dog, Jodi, a huge Malamute-German shepherd cross, who had been rescued, aged six months, from a life of abuse. Four years later, Lisa hit a rocky patch in her own life, and the situation came to such a terribly low ebb that Lisa decided to commit suicide. On the day in question, Jodi sat at the end of the sofa, intently watching Lisa as she wrote a goodbye letter to her family.

Lisa explained that she was not crying at the time, because it all seemed so surreal that she felt rather matter-of-fact about what she intended to do. When Lisa got to the part of the note where she had to decide who to leave Jodi to, the dog got up and made a move towards Lisa. Gently Jodi placed one of her massive paws over Lisa's heart area and stared into her eyes. Jodi communicated this clear message: 'Do not abandon me, no one could love me as much as you or have the connection with me that you do. I love you.'

Lisa picks up the story:

An intense sensation of peace entered me through Jodi's paw, as she communicated these words to me. After this initial message, Jodi told me that together we would get through the hard times and that things *would* get better. She was right; quickly things improved and I am so grateful to be alive today. Jodi saved my life that night, ten years ago. Although Jodi has now passed away, I can still smell her at times and know that she continues to look after me.

Multiple healing hands

Getting together with like-minded people is of great help to any animal. Whilst teaching at the Mounted Police Academy in Brussels, I noticed that Asia, one of the mares, was very troubled. A year earlier, Asia had given birth to a colt foal that had unbelievably been taken from the mare after only a few weeks, whilst she was at a stud farm. Ever since that time Asia had lashed out at people. I called the class of over twenty people together, asking them to take part in a group healing, touching Asia where their intuition guided them to channel healing energy to help with her emotional rebalancing.

Everyone present gathered round Asia and, when we had finished our group healing, the mare looked sedated. It was only then that Caroline, one of the police riding instructors, came up to me, exclaiming that in our mission to help the horse we had all forgotten that Asia bit and kicked … yet surrounded by healing communicators she had stood like a lamb. The next morning, Asia's regular rider could not believe what he found; instead of an angry horse lashing out at everyone, he was greeted by a laid-back, gentle horse. Many healing hands gathering together produce powerful energy.

In which Ryley leaves a legacy of fun

Animals can be very responsive to healing energy sent from a distance, but it is lovely if I eventually get to meet the animal, as happened with a Maltese terrier called Ryley. The relationship started with an email from Tracy, asking for healing to be sent to gravely ill Ryley, who had been diagnosed with terminal heart disease, medical treatment having failed to improve his condition. Having read about my work in the New York *Daily News*, Tracy turned to me for assistance. I offered to see Ryley when I came to New York three weeks later, but he was getting worse by the day and not expected to survive much longer, so healing from a distance was the urgent option.

How healing can help depends on many factors, but it always reaches the soul level, offering peace. Tuning into an emailed photo, I transmitted healing to Ryley, then sent a message to Tracy explaining what I had done. Several hours later, Tracy got in touch:

> I can't thank you enough – there is an immediate change in Ryley. Before I even had opened your email (due to the time difference), I was thinking that Ryley is so much better. From his lying by our bed gasping for breath, unable to move and seemingly dying, we awoke to find Ryley in good spirits with bright eyes. He is playing and the coughing and wheezing are so much less. I know there is no promise of a cure, but I am just so happy that he doesn't seem to be suffering.

As a result, Tracy was able to bring Ryley to my class and it was wonderful to feel his body respond under my hands, when I demonstrated a healing treatment. There followed a hilarious incident, which I will always treasure as a wonderful cameo of meeting Ryley. Tracy invited me to lunch and of course Ryley came along too, trotting along in fine fettle. We spotted several appealing eateries, but were refused entry because we had a dog in tow. In a side street, we passed a tiny restaurant and, on peering through a window, noticed two chairs and a tiny table just inside the door, well away from the main section, which was down a flight of steps. We pushed open the door of the restaurant, heralded by a 'bing-bong' bell noise, and sat down on the two chairs, with Ryley placed on Tracy's lap and my lightweight scarf draped over him as camouflage until the waiter had been.

The waiter took his time in coming, though, and Ryley wanted to look around, so he pushed the scarf edge aside with his nose and peered out like a babushka. The bing-bong from the door bell went again ... and again and again and again. Every time that either myself, Tracy or Ryley moved, the door bell chimed, and we realised that we were sitting in direct line of the automatic trigger beam. An irate proprietor came stomping up the stairs and demanded to know why we were sitting there making the door chime, instead of going down to the main part of the restaurant. Tracy was waiting for a knee operation, so she pleaded an aversion to stairs as the reason.

All the time that this was going on, I was silently saying to Ryley, 'Help us out here, buddy, don't move again until we say so,' and the weird-looking hump on Tracy's lap remained immobile. As the proprietor walked away with our order, Ryley bobbed his head up and, to our horror, the door chime was set off yet again, but

Animal Zen moment

If every person allowed themselves to become a healer, there would be no need for healing.

luckily we were not thrown out. Daring each other to ask for a doggy bag made Tracy and me near hysterical, as we were lunching on soup, and we were sure that Ryley got the joke too as he poked his tongue out at this suggestion.

For the next seven months, Ryley enjoyed life with his family, getting to know two kittens whose games he loved to join in. Once I have met them, it is usual for animals to transmit telepathic messages to me when healing help is needed. So it was that one afternoon I felt Ryley linking to me and therefore contacted Tracy to ask after the dog's health. Commenting that my timing was impeccable, Tracy asked me to keep Ryley in my prayers, because he was struggling owing to his heart having enlarged further. I held Ryley in my healing thoughts, sensing his physical energy weaken with each passing hour.

The next morning, Tracy came to the agonising decision that it was time to let Ryley go, because of his increasing breathing difficulties. Taking Ryley into her bedroom, Tracy told him how much he was loved, and that he had given the family more than could be put into mere words. Now it was time to give Ryley the gift of peace, and Tracy hoped that what she intended was in his best interests … but if only she had a sign. At this Ryley jumped down from the bed and sat in front of the door, and when Tracy called his name Ryley refused to come. Instead he lay with his paws stretched out and head held high, looking at the door. She explains: 'Ryley was saying to me, "I can't come to you any more, it's time for me to go."'

That night, Ryley returned to Tracy in her dreams, showing himself as a fun-loving puppy. Ryley made everyone who met him feel happy, and that is a great legacy to leave behind on Earth.

Lance chill outs

Animals can be canny about the benefits of healing energy, something which I found to be particularly true with chatty cat Lance. Not many details are known about Lance's early years, as he had one day wandered into James's life and chosen to stay. Lance had sensed that James would offer him a home where his every whim would be pandered to in return for the abundance of his feline ministrations.

Animals can direct our hands to where healing energy can help them, and Lance was a master at this. 'I'll sit like this and you put your hand there,' he directed. 'Now, I'll move around and you put your hands here. Ah yes, like that, let me move my paw out of the way ... now stay with your hand in that position for as long as you like.' During our meeting, Lance made sure that most of his body got touched and he made it clear that he was loving every minute of his healing session. All the time I worked with

Animal insight

The currency of healing is unconditional love and a spiritual attitude. Animals sense whether we are spiritually rich or poor.

Lance, he purred, not a 'listen hard or you will miss it' kind of purr, but a roaring king-of-the-jungle expression of supreme contentment. His body became hot and sticky under my hands, and I took that as a good sign of rebalancing. The skin is the biggest organ of the body and one through which we can, using our touch, detect cellular changes.

For Lance, having the opportunity to take on board healing energy certainly did shift something and the evidence came quickly. The next day, James had thirty-two people round for a lunch celebration. Normally Lance would have disappeared upstairs at the sight of such a throng, but this time he hung around, draping himself across the back of the sofa so that his magnificence could be much admired. It was a turning point for Lance, and visitors continue to remark on how much more relaxed he is after our healing union.

Healers of the future

In a society where we often hear stories in the media about disruptive teenagers, it is heartening to come across young people following an enlightened pathway. Where possible, I like to encourage such youngsters to develop their spiritual talents. I noticed thirteen-year-old Sophie intently watching what I was doing with a horse called Ollie and, as she seemed mature for her age and her mother was in agreement, I invited the girl over to touch Ollie as I channelled healing energy. Very quickly, Sophie reported sensations of tingling in her fingertips and a pulse of energy under her hands. 'Wow!' she said, beaming over at her mother. Sophie had not read any of my books and had no idea what I was doing, so the more she accurately described healing energy sensations, the more I knew that before me stood a future healer.

After I explained that healing and tuning in intuitively are inextricably linked, Sophie was keen to try it for herself. I suggested that she ask Ollie a question, which was not about herself but something that Sophie would like to know about him. I explained that the answer to her question would come quickly, almost simultaneously with the question being posed.

PAWS UP

You can send healing to an animal that is not with you by visualising the animal in your mind, or you can look at a photograph. Either way is just as effective. At the beginning of the session, say the animal's name to establish your focus.

Sophie concentrated then hesitated, adding that perhaps she was mistaken about what she was sensing. Self-doubt can creep in when we first start communicating in this way, but soon passes with practice. Then Sophie accepted the communication: 'I asked Ollie how he got his scars, and he told me about an accident with wire. It's weird but I can see the place in my mind. It's a car park.' Ollie seemed delighted. He nuzzled Sophie, snorted and yawned, 'Yes, she got it right.' Sophie whispered to her mother, 'What I felt with Ollie just now is really cool.' I am told that this phrase is an accolade from a teenager. Ollie will have considered it equally 'cool' that Sophie tuned in with him, both on a healing wavelength and intuitively.

No matter what age a person is, young or old, healing energy is available for everyone to tap into. Healing is not an elitist activity – it does not cost anything to lay a hand on an animal and allow the flow of beneficial energy to help on whatever level is possible. It is a wonderful connection to make and, whilst you do so, allow your intuition to give you feedback from the animal about the sensations that you can feel under your hand. Perhaps there is a temperature change under your hand, or tingling. Maybe you feel the directional movement of the healing energy. Whatever you sense is you working in spiritual partnership with the animal.

The next chapter covers how to establish a communication relationship when an animal is not actually with you, which can also be combined with sending healing from a distance.

7 From a Distance

There are no barriers to sending and receiving information through the energy highway. You can just as easily reach an animal in a different country as you can connect to one in the next room.

The communication option that people may find the most puzzling is getting in touch with an animal which is not actually present. You too may be wondering how it can be possible to tune into an animal that is many miles away. However, the likelihood is that you have already connected to animals from a distance without even realising it, or you may have had an experience whereby you sensed consciously that you were energetically adjusting to an animal that was not with you. Just think how powerful these sorts of connection can be when acknowledged and consciously worked with.

It may seem incredible that I don't need to see an animal in person to be able to do my work, and I am frequently asked questions such as, 'How do you know you have contacted the right tabby cat called Kitty/zoomed in on the Charlie horse in question/connected with the correct dog called Buster?' I believe that my sincere intention to connect to a specifically named animal, associated with a geographical location and the person who has consulted me, is what takes me to the electromagnetic blueprint of the particular animal. Even if an animal is not named, I can still reach the individual, experiencing the sense of being whizzed along an astral plane until his or her essence is before me. Every being has an individual energetic call sign that we can isolate amongst the billions of signals constantly being emitted. No one can really explain how it is possible, but it is, and I feel that we draw closer to the day when physicists will be able to describe how these things happen.

Tips for tuning in from a distance

- Animals can connect to us from a distance without any conscious effort on our part, because when there is a window of opportunity animals may pop across a message for our consideration.

- As soon as you start thinking about the animal, the communication process has begun and you are ready to actively send and receive messages.

- It helps to be in a quiet place in order to communicate from a distance, although with practice it is relatively easy to blot out surrounding distractions. I can be speaking whilst simultaneously transmitting messages or listening to an animal's input, compartmentalising different aspects of my consciousness.

- Keep your message short and simple, upbeat and positive. Long messages fizzle out before they reach the recipient. The way it seems to work is that we are able to utilise a defined energy portal, a bit like popping a note into an envelope. Even a few words carry with them a multitude of meanings, charged with the power of your thoughts, emotions and the important transmission of your loving support.

- Allow your gut feeling about what is going on with the animal to play a key role in interpreting the messages you receive from them. This is your intuition guiding you.

- When animals know that we are talking on their wavelength, including from a distance, improvements to their wellbeing can be observed.

- When away from an animal, send news reports about what you are doing and when you will be returning. In situations where the animal is not with you, such as when it is at the veterinary clinic, send messages of support and include details of when you will be collecting him or her.

Photo connections

Tuning in from a distance via a photograph of the animal is a method that can instigate a deep connection. To gain experience, have a friend provide you with a photo of one of their animals, and start with a whole-body shot. Look at the photo of the animal and, using your intuition to guide you, see which part of the body you are drawn to. Ask yourself why this should be so, and listen to your intuition for answers. Do you sense pain in that area, is it the site of an old injury, or perhaps a more recent muscular/joint problem? When you are more confident, try working with a photo of just the animal's head or face.

Move on to allowing your mind to shift into blending with the animal's thoughts. What is currently important to the animal and why? Ask if there are any concerns that the animal needs to pass on to you, including how he or she feels about life in general and whether there any changes that need to be made. Discuss your findings with your friend to ascertain what information can be verified. In this way, you will gain practical knowledge about how to work remotely, as well as building up valuable intuitive confidence. You can also use photos to tune into any of your own animals who are not with you for one reason or another. When using a photo to send a message, whether the animal is your own or is cared for by someone else, envision surrounding the animal in a pink ball of light as you communicate.

Animals calling

It is not unusual for me to receive sudden messages from animals that I am involved with, who happen to be many miles away. This happens especially if I am feeling happily emotional, because at such times our intuitive awareness becomes heightened. An example of this occurred when English, senior-citizen cat Thomas interrupted my focus whilst I was watching live TV coverage of a royal wedding in a hotel room overseas. As Kate Middleton was making her marriage vows to Prince William, Thomas telepathically butted into my awareness, transmitting 'hello', together with an image of his distinctive face, mouth gaping in a meow. At first I was alarmed, wondering whether Thomas was ill, so I sent my love, coupled with a message that I would check in later. After the ceremony was over, I called Thomas's people and thankfully learned that the puss was fine. There was nothing in particular that Thomas had wanted to convey that day; it was just one of his typical social link-ins. Forevermore, I will link that historic occasion to a cat calling me just because he could.

On other occasions, the message can be absorbed as knowledge rather than through hearing actual words. Whilst I was driving close to a client's home, one of her dogs appeared in my psyche to transmit information that she felt unwell and what the problem was linked to, impressing on me that she wanted the message urgently passed on to the client. Subsequently, the dog was taken for veterinary examination to ascertain what was going on, and a thyroid malfunction was diagnosed.

One of the saddest situations of an animal calling me involved Eric, who had been referred for healing to help with a tumour and who had subsequently been given only a few months to live. Eric went into remission and, even though a few years had gone by, his family decided that they wanted to take part in a drug trial and the visits to me ceased. An anguished plea for help reached me from Eric; whatever was happening, he wanted it to stop. Upon contacting Eric's people, I learnt that the dog had become so distressed by the drug regime that he had to be muzzled and sedated during the procedures. No wonder that Eric felt under attack. From time to time, I still receive plaintive *help me* messages from Eric, and at those times I know that he absorbs healing peace from me.

I have found that one of the many benefits of my communications with animals from a distance is when they subsequently have an improved relationship with the people in their lives. After I tuned into a horse in France called Florenzo, his person, Caryn, noted: 'Funny thing is, that since Florenzo has talked with you, his eyes pierce right through me, and he now watches me with a very strong presence.' Florenzo understood that Caryn had asked for my help, resulting in his problems being identified, and this increased the level of trust between horse and human. Best of all, Florenzo now knew that Caryn could intuitively hear him.

Tea and biscuits with a pig

It's important when tuning in from a distance to take seriously all the information that you receive and investigate what changes can be made in order to help the animal that has communicated with you. Small changes in an animal's environment can have a great impact on the animal's emotional and physical wellbeing. Just like humans, animals have personal requirements that are extremely important to them and, if these aren't properly addressed, the animal can become unwell.

One of my contacts, animal communicator Niki Senior, was contacted by a Mrs Taylor for a telephone consultation about her pot-bellied pig, Freddie, who had become listless, but for which behaviour the vet could not find a physical cause. On tuning into the pig, Niki picked up Freddie's thought patterns, but the energy Niki received rather surprised her. Instead of the lethargy she had expected, Niki was sensing a cheeky, mischievous disposition.

Asking Freddie to describe what was happening, Niki learnt that the pig felt abandoned because, lately, Mrs Taylor hadn't been spending as much time with him as Freddie needed. An image flicked through Niki's mind of an overgrown garden with broken, discarded clay pots and straggly plants hanging over sticks. Bizarrely, Niki then saw in her mind's eye a woman sitting in an old cane chair and drinking a cup of tea, with a biscuit tin at her feet. As Niki concentrated, the initial image of the overgrown garden evolved into a picture of horticultural health, with onion sets and potatoes planted in the ground, and sweet peas climbing up stakes. The session was progressing most strangely.

Freddie showed Niki another picture: it was of him and Mrs Taylor taking morning tea together, and Freddie explained that during these sessions he would get a biscuit or a piece of homemade cake. From Freddie's awareness, Niki next sensed a hazy light around Mrs Taylor's lower back. During a discussion of her findings, Niki heard about terrible hip pains, which the elderly woman was too scared to seek medical help for, in case there was a diagnosis of the bone cancer that took her mother's life. Owing to her discomfort, Mrs Taylor had come to neglect the thing she loved most, aside from Freddie – namely her garden. These days, she even avoided going to the local shops, because of her fear of the gossip about how neglected the plot had become.

Animal Zen moment

We are all travellers wending our way through the intricacies of planetary consciousness.

After Mrs Taylor learnt of Freddie's plight, things improved apace. She agreed to a medical examination, during which nothing more sinister than a treatable trapped nerve was diagnosed, and gardening assistance was advertised for. Most importantly, Mrs Taylor made time to share a morning tea break with Freddie again. As a result, Freddie quickly returned to his old happy self, making mischief and snuffling around the potato plot.

'Could I just ask one thing?' Mrs Taylor said when she gave Niki the good news. 'How did you know about our tea breaks together and the biscuit tin?' To which, of course, Niki was able to reply: 'Freddie told me.'

Animals have lots to tell us when we tune into them on their wavelength, not only making our life far more interesting but teaching us about their needs. When we listen and make necessary adjustments, then life becomes easier for all concerned.

Billy gets the message

Linda told me about a fascinating experience she had, after hearing that you can send telepathic messages to animals that you are not actually with:

> I was working at my brother's company, where one of the cleaners was an elderly man called Denis. After his wife died, Denis adopted a Jack Russell dog from a shelter and named him Billy. Billy settled in very well with Denis, but quickly developed a habit each evening of going up to the spare bedroom to snooze. One day, Denis mentioned that he was very disappointed about this tendency, as he longed for Billy's company. Having met Billy on several occasions and formed a bond with him, I decided to experiment tuning in with the dog from a distance. So I sat down and focussed on telepathically sending a message to Billy, saying that Denis felt lonely and would love Billy to be with him in the evenings.

> When Denis came into work the next day, I casually asked how Billy was and whether he had gone to the spare room? Imagine my amazement when Denis replied 'No' and explained that Billy had stayed with him all the time. This was not a one-off either, because each evening thereafter Billy continued to accompany Denis. Of course the old man was thrilled. Furthermore, when I met up with Billy again, I got a sense from him that our message exchange was to remain a secret between us. As soon as he had got my communication, Billy had understood the importance of the request, including Denis's need to feel that Billy had himself chosen the old man's company.

I was able to explain to Linda that Denis had not been transmitting a clear invitation to Billy due to his emotional turmoil. The man would have had images of isolation in his mind, which Billy would have seen as an instruction to stay away and so he had obliged, even though he too needed company. When Linda had intervened, her telepathic message to Billy was sharply defined and that made all the difference. Billy then understood the reality of the situation and everyone was happy.

Dream connections

During sleep our soul body can float free from the turmoil of the day's activities, which the brain is busily processing. Whilst the brain is sorting and filing away life experiences, through the subconscious the soul can explore other dimensions and connect to messages from animals both past, present, or even those we will meet in the future. Sometimes, I wake in the middle of a dream, having been given words. Quickly, I write down these gems of spiritual wisdom before I go back to sleep, hoping for more. These messages are all communications from distant realms. From the regular correspondence that I receive, it would appear that this is quite a common occurrence. Here I present a couple of stories about communications coming from those we have yet to meet.

The award-winning maker of the film *Wild Horses in Winds of Change*, Mara LeGrand, has a dog who originally connected with her in a dream. Whilst she was asleep one night, a small, caramel-coloured dog appeared to her and called out a desire to be with Mara. The connection with the dog was so strong that, on waking, Mara made it her utmost mission to seek out this canine, looking for the animal everywhere that she travelled to. Whilst in Seattle, Mara came across a five-month-old female Shih Tzu, which had been placed for adoption and, on seeing her, Mara recognised the dog from the vision. Mara told me, 'I knew instantly that this sad pup was the little dog in my dream and needed me to rescue her.' Naming her Mamiko, Japanese for *little flower*, Mara tells me that Mamiko has blossomed into the happiest of soul mates.

Many years ago, I started to see a cat in my dreams, a small grey and white cat that I intuitively knew to be male. I looked up the meaning of cats in dreams – the book said that to dream about cats is generally considered an omen of misfortune. Oh dear, I thought – I was about to move house after a divorce and the change I faced was daunting enough. On the first day in my new home, I heard a scratching noise at the front door and, on opening it, there before me was the cat who had communicated with me in my dreams. He belonged to neighbours, but some months later those people moved away, leaving the cat behind. From then onwards, the cat lived with me and for the next fifteen years, until he passed away, the cat was a fantastic teacher of psychic attunement. More to the point, he was the most wonderful companion at a time when I needed help. In this instance, dreaming of the cat was definitely not an omen of misfortune, but of fabulous things to come.

Meant to be

I am often told by people how a horse seems destined to enter their life, with a communication bond forming between them before they even meet the equine. Tandy fell in love with a five-year-old, black Tennessee Walking Horse called George, but he was way out of Tandy's price range. Unable to get the horse out of her mind, Tandy installed a link on her computer, so she could watch a video clip of him as much as possible.

When George was sold, Tandy sent out thoughts for a good home for him, but she continued to watch the video. Some months later, to her surprise she noticed George again being advertised for sale, but at a much lower price than previously. When she left a message, the seller called Tandy back a few minutes later, saying that he didn't know why, but he hadn't replied to any of the enquiries until Tandy's. Having become smitten with George via the internet, the man had purchased him not knowing anything about horses. At first all went well, but when George started playing up, the man hadn't known what to do about it – hence the sale.

Tandy almost fell out of the truck, when she saw the state of George. He was in a dirt pen on a wind-buffeted hill with no water and no shelter, just a heap of black, mouldy hay. George was so weak, he could barely walk and, apart from starving, he was worm-ridden and a skin fungus covered most of his body. Carefully, Tandy loaded George into her lorry, then cried and prayed all the way home that he would survive the hour-long trip. During the first week, whilst the vet battled to stabilise George, Tandy was terrified that the horse would not live, but with her utmost love and care he thrived and also learnt to trust people again. Tandy wrote to me: 'I have cried a river of tears, happy and sad. I have never been so firmly touched by God before in my life. I still have a hard time believing George is here safe with me for the rest of his life. But he is, and I love him to bits. Even if I live to be a hundred, I will never stop being amazed by the miracle that is George.'

Standing by George whilst he was eating, Tandy read aloud from what I sent in reply: 'During those troubled days, even though he had never met you, Tandy, George had been sending you messages.' As Tandy spoke these words, George stopped chewing and looked her straight in the eyes. Tandy heard George say, 'It's true.'

Missing animals

Once we have become competent in tuning into animals from a distance, we can move on to using our skills to help locate missing animals. To play a pivotal role in reuniting an animal with its home is very rewarding indeed. Although animals have a highly developed sixth sense, which they use to orientate themselves, our high-tech world and man-made structures have created an electrical fog for them, often confusing the magnetic fields which animals instinctively use to navigate. Similarly, dogs and cats use their advanced sense of smell to orientate themselves, but chemicals used on the land obscure scent trails. Traffic adds another perilous factor.

Missing-animal work is notoriously difficult, because the animal may have been chased and not paid much attention to his or her surroundings when running away. Moreover, on connecting with the

animal, he or she may emit clues that do not appear to make much sense, such as repeatedly describing tree roots or the interior of hole. It can be problematic to distinguish the animal's thoughts of where he/she would like to be, from what has actually been seen on the journey, as well as from what prevails in the current surroundings. It is also widely acknowledged among professional animal communicators that it is very difficult to ascertain whether a missing animal is still in the physical body. If death has come suddenly, the animal may not realise for a while that he or she is out of the physical body. The reverse of this can happen through an animal being very scared: we can mistakenly interpret that fear as the animal having left the body. Also, if we sense blankness, we may assume that the animal has died, but it could be that connection with us is being rebuffed.

When communicating with a missing animal, asking 'are you still in your physical body?' rather than 'are you still alive?' is preferable, because the spirit lives for eternity, so the animal would always answer yes to the last question. Sometimes an animal chooses to move homes due to dissatisfaction or lack of interest, and others may simply be seeking an adventure. Helping to find missing animals requires practice and great attention to detail; making numerous cross-checks with them will help to clarify your interpretations. These are some of the things that work for me:

- In your mind's eye, conjure up a map of the area where the animal went missing, and allow your intuition to orientate you. As though you are using a telepathic compass, consider whether the animal seems to have moved north, south, east or west from the original location.

- Send a beam of light from the top of your head to the animal. Imagine attaching the beam to the animal, then loop it to the animal's home or other place from which it went missing. If physically able to move, the animal will receive an energetic boost to help guide it home. It's always worthwhile to send a telepathic beam, because whether the animal is in the physical body or not, it is very comforting to have that connection made.

- Combining in a team effort enhances beneficial energy. When searching for an animal, gather together as many people as you can to send out thoughts and locator energy beams as a group. This provides a powerful lifeline signal for the animal to use, if at all possible. Avoid nagging any animals remaining in the household to bring their friend back home. They will already be doing what they can.

When my friend Mel contacted me to say that Dinky, one of her cats, had gone missing after being spooked whilst peering out of the front door, I quickly managed to locate his personal signal. Dinky had never ventured from the house before, as his outside time was spent in a secure garden area with another cat. I sensed that Dinky was not dead or injured, just extremely frightened, and that he was not far away either. On working out in which direction Mel's house lay to where Dinky was ensconced in his hideaway, I used my telepathic compass to attach a beam from the cat to home. It is important to regularly focus on such a beam to keep it energetically charged. Sure enough, two days later, a bedraggled Dinky arrived on the doorstep and was very grateful for supper and the reunion with his cat pal.

Gus

Joan Ranquet, author of *Communication with All Life*, shared with me the story of the time she helped to locate a dog called Gus, after being contacted by his person, Barbara. A Bernese Mountain stud dog with a fancy pedigree, Gus was being transported from the Virginia area to upstate New York for a big dog show. Gus had been collected by his new show-dog handler, Amy, and during the journey Amy had stopped at her home to spend the night. After Gus was let outside to stretch his legs, something had startled him and, in his panic to get away, he had knocked Amy over, breaking her arm, before disappearing into the darkness. Amy's home was on the edge of a huge forested area and so it was assumed that Gus could not be found, but wanting to try every avenue Barbara got in touch with Joan to see if an animal communicator could fix the problem.

When Joan first checked in with Gus, he was confused about where he was, but showed her pictures of his hiding spot, an abandoned barn on a hill with surrounding outbuildings and a small house in the distance. In his travels to this resting spot, Gus indicated that he had been alongside a river in a wide valley that had lots of homes on the other side of it. Letting Barbara know that the place where Gus was situated smelled distinctly of fire, Joan asked if the dog handler's home was near a campground. This produced the somewhat stressed response from Barbara: 'Don't you know there's a ban on burning?' Joan replied that as she lived all the way across country, no, she wasn't aware of such a restriction.

The next day, Barbara called Joan back, a tearful convert. She had found the river and the valley as described, and the highway had taken Barbara all the way up to a campground. They still weren't having fires there, yet Barbara could detect the distinct odour of fire. After following the smell she found the one farm in all the northern part of New York State given permission to burn during that sweltering summer. The farm owner was burning dilapidated barns and, on asking if she could walk around, Barbara found signs in the one barn still standing that a dog had bedded down in a corner.

On searching behind the building, Barbara heard rustling in the bushes there. Not daring to set her hopes high, on crawling through the undergrowth, Barbara discovered Gus. After staring at her for what seemed like minutes, with a flash of recognition Gus came bounding over, as Barbara opened her arms to welcome him. Joyous yelping from both woman and dog resounded far and wide, a testimony to the power of communicating with animals from a distance.

Tiger

Making contact with an animal that has been missing for a long period of time can also sometimes lead to a fruitful reunion, as this next story demonstrates. After her cat, Tiger, had been missing for two years, Angela asked animal communicator Mia Sampietro to connect with him to try to find out what had happened. Angela at that time was on holiday in England, whilst her husband was at home in America. Mia relayed to Angela the sense that Tiger was still alive and that he had gone missing after falling down a deep ditch. A short while later, Angela called back ecstatic with joy. Angela's husband had received a call from a vet twenty-five miles away, who had Tiger with him. He was in a poor state, hungry, thin and bedraggled, but otherwise OK and, luckily, as he was micro-chipped, it had been easy to locate Tiger's family.

After Angela returned home and was reunited with Tiger, Mia was asked to again communicate with Tiger to see if details of his time away could be filled in. Apparently, when he fell Tiger had suffered from concussion, and thereafter remembered little about his past. He had been too frightened to show himself, only coming out at night to hunt for food and journeying many miles in a confused state. The communication link with Mia had jogged Tiger's memory and given him the courage to be seen, and thus to be found on that very same day.

Narfee

If alive, a lost animal will be connecting to us as we search for him or her. Narfee, a small fluffy dog, found André in the bush when he was serving in the army in South Africa. After that, no matter what conflict André was involved in, Narfee stuck close by. Having left the army, André was driving in a remote area, when he had an accident and his car was a write-off. Thankfully, André was uninjured, but, running off in fright, Narfee disappeared. Having been through so much with André during his army career, it seemed inconceivable that Narfee had now gone.

However, André quickly knew that Narfee was still alive, because he was picking up on her thoughts and feelings. For three weeks, André and his sister, Tammy, drove around the area where André most strongly sensed Narfee's presence, but they could not find her. There came a turning point when a man came out of a property to flag down their car, saying, 'I found a stray dog a few weeks back that is going berserk as you cruise slowly by. Could she be yours?'

It turned out that after the accident Narfee had been taken in by these people, and that every now and again the dog would become hysterical to be let out. Then, just as suddenly, she would slump back into a corner to tremble miserably. Eventually, the people made the connection with the dog going nuts and a certain car appearing. What a jubilant reunion that must have been to behold; and Tammy told me how, once she was safely back home, Narfee fell asleep with André's shoelace in her mouth.

Luzie

As with Narfee, when cat Luzie went missing, she got in touch telepathically with her people, but in this case her reunion with them almost didn't take place. As I unpacked my things in my bed and breakfast accommodation, my senses soon started to react to something unseen. Was that a soft footfall close by? Where were the telepathic flickerings coming from, and who was transmitting them?

On turning round, I found myself face to face with a black and white cat, peering around the door into my room. I knew that the cat had been attracted to my presence, sensing a human who could converse on the wavelength of animals and offered healing, although at that moment it was not obvious to me why my help was needed.

Nevertheless, we chatted a bit about things that I cannot adequately describe in words, because they involved an instant transfer of wisdom and knowledge, a conversation that takes place in what I call 'the overlap mode'. This is when two beings communicate and the messages that flow between them are instant, as if piling one on top of the other and blending together. There is no time for thinking about what you are receiving, only allowing the knowledge to be absorbed in your soul. It is easy to miss these rapidly transmitted energy exchanges if we become distracted by our analytical processes.

Looking at my watch, I told the little cat that I needed to find somewhere to eat, and it was when she turned to leave that I noticed the odd gait in her back legs, which was causing her walking difficulties. I immediately thought how strenuous it must have been for the cat to climb the steep flights of stairs to visit me. 'See you tomorrow, and if you like I will give you some healing,' I offered. The cat looked up at me before shuffling away. It was a deal.

The next morning, after a delicious breakfast of home produce, I took a walk around the beautiful property situated in the Westerwald region of Germany. A blue sky with a few white clouds scudding over the tree tops, contrasted with the green of rolling valleys fringed by jostling wildflowers. Presently, from within a barn where he had been artistically carving some branches, Winfried appeared. He ran the accommodation with his wife Beatrice. On asking him about the cat, I was told that her name was Luzie and she was estimated to be around six years old, her exact age unknown as she originated from an animal shelter.

Almost a year to the day before my visit, Luzie had gone missing. Normally Luzie did not go out of sight for long, so Winfried and Beatrice had begun to look for her almost immediately. At the end of the day, the whole village was alerted, but no one had seen the cat, and an extensive and thorough search did not reveal her whereabouts either. Stressful days followed, during which Winfried and Beatrice both sensed that Luzie was alive and close by, but in big trouble. After a few more days, Winfried picked up a telepathic connection from Luzie; she was sending out a communication that said: 'I am here. I am alive.' Attached to the message, however, was the information that Luzie did not have the strength to return home, and there was no clue as to which direction the energy beam came from.

The days of searching were drawn out until hope started to fade of ever finding Luzie. On the fourteenth day, in floods of tears, Beatrice gave away items of cat food to a neighbour, convinced that Luzie must now be dead. Winfried sensed Luzie tuning into this act and told Beatrice, 'Now Luzie knows that we are giving up hope, she will make a last-ditch effort to come back. I think that it will be tomorrow.'

The next morning, there was a strange noise in the kitchen, accompanied by a pitiful, heart-rending howling. Winfried and Beatrice were shocked to find a badly injured, emaciated and soaking wet Luzie dragging herself through the cat door. She was paralysed from her mid back downwards and was pulling herself along by her front legs, paws bloodied and raw from the supreme effort. On seeing the people that she so loved, Luzie increased the bloodcurdling wailing: 'Help me ... help me.'

Animal insight

When you feel a bit down in the dumps, think of all the messages flying around in the stratosphere. Grab some of them out of the airwaves; what animal is connecting to you and from where?

The vet diagnosed impact trauma. Although no bones were broken, the lower spinal nerves were crushed and the pelvis twisted. It seemed that Luzie had been hit by a vehicle – a terrible misfortune in such a quiet village. As her story unfolded, I sensed that in the first instance of shock Luzie had dragged herself into a dark hiding place, where she had passed out. In an attempt to facilitate recovery from trauma, cats can shut down non-essential activity, and this was what Luzie had done. It had been a wet April, so Luzie could lick rainwater, and insects provided an occasional snack. Luzie knew that her people were searching close by and had communicated to them, 'Don't give up hope for me. I will try to get back to you.'

It is quite incredible that despite losing so much body weight and with every bone in her body clearly visible, Luzie eventually found the strength to drag herself home, a marathon journey as the cat fought for her survival. When Luzie finally did make it, though, Winfried and Beatrice noticed that her eyes were clear and bright, expressing a desire to live.

After four days of strong pain medication, Luzie started to regain some use of her back legs. Three weeks later, she was able to move around the house, albeit in a wobbly manner. To help her muscles recover, Winfried and Beatrice performed daily physiotherapy exercises on her. As I remarked that I would like to help with healing energy, Luzie appeared around the corner of the house and made straight for me. Plumes of purple wisteria draping over archways nodded their approval as Luzie said, 'Yes, please.'

In a pool of sunlight, I knelt down and softly placed my hand over Luzie's back; she made no attempt to move away. When my knees ached and I momentarily took my hands from her back to adjust my position, she did not leap up as I expected her to, but instead rolled onto her side. As I continued healing, Luzie transmitted images to me of the terrible accident: a car driver not knowing that an animal had been struck by a wheel, the shocked crawl underneath a building, slipping in and out of a coma, grotesque pain. These things flashed before my mind's eye like thunderbolts. Luzie communicated the horror of knowing how close home was, yet being unable to reach sanctuary. Luzie's willpower to survive had been her strength. On the fifteenth day came the window of opportunity. The pain, although still acute, had become bearable enough to attempt movement. Vitally so, because through her inner wisdom, Luzie conveyed to me that she knew her weakened state meant that time was running out for her. She would go home that day or never.

PAWS UP

Each day, send a message of support to animals around the world, rather than just saving up communication from a distance for 'special occasions' or when you are in dire straits. Other beings are constantly caught up in environmental pollutions, devastation, conflicts, cruelties, neglect and factory-farm horrors. If we are to be authentic interspecies communicators, we will readily encompass all life forms within our intuitive portfolio of talking and listening

I watched Luzie move off towards a bush where a buzzing insect had attracted her attention, before turning right and clambering up onto a low wall, where she sat staring across a meadow. It seemed to me that after the healing session Luzie's movements looked stronger. A couple of weeks later, an update came from Winfried and Beatrice, reporting that Luzie was indeed generally less crooked and walking much better, and that she was now nimble enough to run.

Whenever animals share their lives with us, we will have some fantastic experiences, many of which will be pleasurable, and a few traumatic. There is, however, a time for all earthly relationships to end, and in the next chapter I explain how we can communicate with those animals who have passed away. Even if we were together for only a short time, a reciprocal agreement has already been made that we can always keep in touch. This is the unbreakable bond of love.

8 Beyond the Here and Now

Absorb the meaning of every moment you spend with the animals in your life. These times last forever in our hearts, so that our animal friends are with us for eternity.

When cherished animal companions pass away, a large measure of the anguish that we inevitably feel comes from our no longer being able to see or interact with them physically, or touch them affectionately. That door has irrevocably shut, and there may seem to be no way that we can ever recover a semblance of the relationship that once brought so much pleasure to our lives; only the sting of emotional and mental pain is left in its wake.

But it does not have to be this way. Through a great many unusual experiences of my own, I have discovered that the soul energy of all life forms, human and non-human, continues elsewhere after abandoning the physical body. In fact, one of the laws of physics is that energy cannot be destroyed, only converted from one form to another. As all living beings are energy forms, this is a property of energy that they too must surely obey. This means a soul that has left the Earth plane, whilst invisible to us, is not lost to us. Whilst none of the former physical interactions remain possible, the vibrancy with which animals live on in spirit form means that we can connect with them in the afterlife.

On countless occasions when I have been present at an animal's physical death, I have felt a surge of energy in my hands, a tapping or spiralling sensation under my palms, or a subtle change in the surrounding atmosphere if I have not actually been touching the animal. During this process, I communicate with the departing soul, sending healing love for a peaceful journey to the afterlife. The communication of energy varies with each animal (or person), owing to the soul signature of every individual being unique – like a fingerprint. And I believe that there is a Source somewhere that knows each soul as an equal part of the whole, contributing to continuing existence. Once, when I was holding a departing rabbit, in the moment that I sensed the soul entity leave the body, it seemed to reverse and that energy filled my whole body. I took this as symbolic that we are one being. This is why I find myself saying to the animals that I meet: *You are me and I am you.*

How will we know when an animal is with us in spirit form?

There are certain things that can signal the spirit of an animal is close by. Trust your instincts. If you sense something going on around you, or have a sudden flash of inspiration about an animal that you used to know, review the information coming to you. You may sense subtle movements of air across your body, particularly your hands, face and legs. There may even be sensations of soft footfalls or a paw touching you, or you may even 'see' the animal.

'Physical' signs

As a member of the holistic team helping Jess with her various ailments, I had known the collie cross for nearly four years. When Jess became terminally ill with cancer, I went to her home an hour before the vet arrived for her final visit. One of my services is to counsel people through the bereavement process and perform a special Earth-leaving ceremony during euthanasia, which was what Jess's people, Min and Steve, had requested. The ceremony is a celebration of lives shared and a time for honouring the soul about to depart into celestial realms.

I gave dear Jess a final hands-on healing treatment, as Min, Steve and I talked while we waited for the vet to arrive. Min asked me how she would know if Jess came back in spirit form, and I mentioned signs based on my experiences over the years. Min was convinced that these were implausible. And it's true that there is no guarantee an animal will choose to come back in spirit form to say hello; even if it does happen, it can sometimes take a while, months even, to occur. Yet at other times, the re-visit can happen very soon after the animal has passed on.

Less than ten minutes after I had sensed Jess's soul body spiral upwards from her physical body, Min cried out, 'What's happening here?' Waving her fingers to demonstrate, Min explained how she had suddenly become aware of a gentle waft of cool air across her face: Jess had come back to commemorate the start of her life everlasting with a soul kiss.

Robin was devastated after the death of her black cat, Bluto, but only weeks later he proved himself an accomplished communicator from the afterlife. When I connected with him, he made us both laugh by saying that in his new life he was like Merlin the magician, able to travel anywhere, invisible yet powerful. Based on this communication with him, I assured Robin that Bluto would soon make his presence known to her too, and I didn't have to wait long for confirmation.

Two days later, Robin told me how she had sat outside and sent a message to Bluto, thanking him for coming to talk to us, before going to lie on the couch, where she closed her eyes but remained awake. After a while, Robin felt paws walking on the sofa next to her face, and so she opened her eyes to see if they were those of her current feline companions. Instinctively, though, Robin knew the footfalls didn't belong to them, for the pressure was too light and delicate to be physical. It was Bluto, letting Robin know that he was there. Robin broke the spell, however, by asking Bluto to sit on her chest like he used to, at which he disappeared; for future visitations, she learnt to allow Bluto to do his own thing.

An image of an animal appearing in your mind's eye

Occasionally and for no apparent reason, an animal appears to me in my mind's eye. This is particularly true of animals that I have worked with, who may come to touch base or give me a message to pass on to their past human guardians.

Feelings of warmth in your heart area

You may get a curious feeling of warmth around your heart, accompanied by memories of the animal.

I had a surreal experience many years ago, whilst travelling to London on a train. My upper body flushed with heat at the same time as memories of a childhood dog called Patch filled my mind. These memories were so vivid that the scenes seemed to be occurring in real time – which I knew was because Patch was on the train with me in spirit form.

Sudden sensation of being enveloped in love

Grief-stricken after the death of her dog, Logan, Lorna described to me how she had placed her hand onto Logan's body during which a powerful feeling of peace had come over her. Lorna's sobbing stopped and she knew that this incredible sensation was the result of Logan's love.

A brief flash of light in the room, like the pinprick of a star, or an orb

I once saw a light hover at the top of a Christmas tree, but it was a few moments before I remembered that there were no electrical decorations on my tree. Maybe I was having trouble with my eyes, I thought, and gave them a rub. It was only when the light held my gaze and was then combined with the awareness in my mind of a much loved cat, who used to share my life, that it dawned on me what was going on. The spirit of the cat had come with his glad tidings and bountiful memories of shared Christmases past.

These sorts of precious sensations may be fleeting or may last for quite a few moments. Treasure them when they occur, and acknowledge that the animal is with you as your intuition hones in on the wonderful energetic presence. When you sense something, avoid asking for more; enjoy what is possible under the circumstances, bearing in mind the fact that the animal has made a great effort to cross the inter-dimensional barriers of time and space. If we treat what is offered as trivial or as though it is inadequate in any way, we are effectively removing ourselves from the communication circuit.

Animal Zen moment

Change walks alongside us. It is part of us.

Animal messengers travel through the dimensions of time and space to be with us. We do not have any control over this process and cannot make it happen, but when the meeting does take place we are invited to enjoy every second of it.

The right track

When connecting to other people's animals in the afterlife, it is essential to ask for information in order to verify that you are on the right track. Ratification can come in any shape or form. I could 'see' spirit dog Basil standing on a pile of magazines, which seemed like a rather confusing clue until his person explained that she was an advertising executive for a glossy publication. Cat Jasper filled my mind with his piercing yellow eyes, as he showed me three cats that he had joined in the spirit world, two black and one cream. The description fitted cats who had once lived with his person, and convinced her that I was connecting to Jasper.

Animals who have passed away will often get in touch with third parties in the hope that their message will be passed on to loved ones. After studying some of my articles, Lisa was inspired to send an internet link to a piece called 'A dog's last will' to the manager of a veterinary clinic. She hoped that the words would help comfort clinic clients whose dogs had died. When manager Sarah replied and said that her own dog, Puzzle, had just been put to sleep, Lisa strongly felt that her contact with Sarah was not a coincidence.

Because she had met Puzzle a few times, Lisa felt intuitively drawn to instigate a communication session with the pooch. As she had never discussed the subject of animal communication with Sarah, who was very much a non-believer when it came to certain spiritual topics, Lisa was initially reluctant to pass on the information that came from Puzzle. She had the strong impression, however, that Puzzle wanted her to do this, so she bit the bullet and sent off her notes. The information was so evidential to Sarah that it gave her food for thought, as well as bringing her a sense of peace. After all, that was what Puzzle had wanted.

The black poodle

Taking part in meditations can help improve our intuitive awareness, so that we are better able to tune in and communicate with animals in the afterlife. The message that Katharina received was not just comforting evidence, but revealing in terms of how animals see their own roles on Earth. Over supper at a lovely country inn, Katharina told me how, as a child, she had been given a small black poodle by her dog-breeder grandfather. The poodle was called Batschi and became Katharina's best friend and constant companion, but unfortunately, when the time came for Katharina to leave home to further her education, her father was not keen for Batschi to remain in the house. The grandfather, therefore, found an elderly woman who was very pleased to take Batschi to live with her. Time and again, Katharina would agonise over whether the right decision had been made in sending Batschi to another home. She even wondered whether she should have taken the dog to live with her in her student lodgings, even though she knew in her heart of hearts that it would have been impossible. Batschi died whilst Katharina was away studying, after which Katharina experienced a painful, fluttering sensation in her heart whenever she thought about Batschi, or saw a black poodle.

Twenty years later, Katharina took a course in animal communication and was surprised to discover it was possible talk to animals by intuitive and telepathic means. A workshop at a later date covered the topic of communicating with animals in the afterlife and, intrigued by this prospect, Katharina took a photo of Batschi along to the class. Even after all those years Katharina felt guilty about having left the poodle, so finding out how he had felt about what happened to him was very important to her.

During a meditation that the class took part in, a little black dog revealed himself to Katharina. It was Batschi. In that moment, like a cloud lifting, it dawned on Katharina that Batschi had in fact always been with her. Throughout the intervening years, Batschi had been guiding Katharina and giving her strength to cope with life's problems. There then followed an intense outpouring of love from Batschi, which came without judgment or blame. Shocked at this revelation, Katharina thought, 'I gave Batschi away and yet he gives me eternal love and help. How can I forgive myself?'

When we are emotionally blocked by difficult or conflicting feelings, it can be helpful for someone else to tune in on our behalf. Another woman in the class, who wanted to practise her communication skills but who knew nothing about Katharina or Batschi, looked at the dog's photograph. This is what the woman told Katharina: during his time with her, Batschi had loved their long walks together, but his important life-task had actually begun when he went to live with the old woman, because he was required to fill an empty place in the lady's heart. The wonderful time that Batschi had spent with Katharina had given him the ability to fulfil his healing role.

Animal insight

We are never truly alone. Energy vibrates all around us, including from beings who have previously lived on Earth. These divine guides shower us with radiant love.

Katharina's story is astounding for two reasons. Firstly, it provides evidence that communicating via a photo of a deceased animal really does work, and, secondly, it confirms the potency of love. Love is a very powerful energy, creating its own communication network. The love that Katharina shared with Batschi meant that they were eternally linked. And this same love helped an old woman to feel loved in the last years of her life.

When we love an animal a promise is made to us and it is this: *My soul will always be linked to your soul. I am with you always.*

Ghostly images

Animals can detect invisible entities that live in other dimensions than ours. If we establish an intuitive connection to animals when they become aware of these beings, we can tune into what they are sensing. I remember sitting listening to music many years ago with my cat Casey asleep on my lap, when I sensed a presence in the room. Simultaneously, Casey woke up and stared, wide-eyed, over my shoulder. Casey tipped up his head and kept moving backwards, until he flipped over and plopped onto the floor by my feet. I had 'seen' what Casey had: an angel form had appeared behind me and drifted over my head. Casey had visibly reacted to the movement, but the fact that he was not overly upset by the phenomenon led me to believe that seeing such things was probably a regular occurrence for him.

When Vizsla Isla passed away, her canine companions Phizz and Ellie were grieving, and so I visited to help these two dogs through their sorrow. I intended to help them with healing energy and by allowing the dogs to express their feelings. Phizz gravitated towards me first. However, after a few minutes I sensed Isla's spirit form appearing in the corner of the room. As it did so, and before I could verbally express what I was picking up, Phizz leapt to her feet. With hair standing on end and staring at the space where Isla's spirit was manifesting, Phizz barked furiously. Then, cocking her head quizzically from side to side, Phizz seemed to make sense of the apparition, her body relaxed and the barking stopped. Turning round, she went to lie by Ellie, who, interestingly, had looked on passively throughout the outburst from Phizz. Animal responses are always varied, which is why we should never assume one animal is going to behave like another.

Through the crisscrossing of inter-dimensional time zones, the spirit forms of people can also be drawn to animals with whom we have opened up communication connections. While I was sitting on the floor with dog Max and his guardian Joanne, there was a lull in our mutual conversation until the name Judy popped into my mind.

'Who is Judy?' I asked Joanne. At this, Max sprang up from the floor and peered behind me, tail wagging and a look of anticipation and joy on his face. The reaction was incredible to behold. To all intents and purposes the dog was staring into space, but I sensed the presence of a woman. Joanne had no idea who Judy was, so I asked Max, who immediately informed me that the woman had doted on him at the shelter from which he had been rehoused some years earlier. Judy had obviously passed away since that time, but her loving presence was palpable and, after a minute or so, this faded from my senses. Simultaneously, Max stopped staring behind me and came to settle by my side. For a moment or two, Max threw the odd look towards the spot where Judy had manifested, his ears rising in the manner of a dog expecting a treat to be offered, but eventually he lay on his side. From reading his thoughts, I knew that Max was remembering the woman who had shown him consideration and kindness when his life was otherwise empty.

My friend Doris contacted me to talk about the time she observed her young Maine Coon cat Simba suddenly start to act as if chasing something. OK, so cats (and dogs) can sometimes enjoy a mad five minutes tearing around the house or garden, but Doris noticed that Simba's activity appeared to have a purpose to it. He had started by intently watching a place in the room, although neither Doris nor her partner Nic could see anything there. Then Simba started to run in hunting spurts, focussing on a particular spot. Leaping forward as though catching something, Simba flipped the invisible playmate into the air before cavorting around, all the time watching the ground. Simba performed every action that a cat would do with a mouse; indeed, throughout his antics, Doris had the strong impression that a spirit creature was in the room. The mouse would, of course, be having great fun with Simba, because as an energy form it was invincible.

As he had access to outbuildings and fields in which to roam whenever he needed to play, Simba had no need to entertain himself by hunting imaginary things. The property is a two-hundred-year-old converted farm building, which used to house animals on the lower floor and people on the upper level. No doubt a ghost mouse was passing through what was now the living room, and Simba was enjoying the interaction with it. I would have loved to eavesdrop on what cat and mouse said to each other as they played, both in different spheres but neither noticing.

PAWS UP

To send a message to an animal in the afterlife, form the words in your mind and the animal will automatically pick them up. You may or may not sense this happening, but have confidence that it does.

Dealing with grief

The process of grief hits us all hard after the loss of a much-loved companion. Unresolved grief and the pressure of strong emotions can create a barrier to intuitive awareness. If we have other animals living with us when one passes away, care must be taken to devote time and attention to these remaining companions. Otherwise, they can often feel neglected if the person cannot move on with their life. This is a great shame because every animal is worth getting to know for their individual teaching, but we need to be a willing participant in order to learn. Here are some suggestions to help you overcome these sorts of blockage.

Your grief

Talk out loud to animals about what is troubling you; bottling up emotions radiates a disturbing energy cloud. Explain everything in as much detail as you can, because the animal will understand the sentiment behind your words. Then it's important to tell these animals how much you love them, and that they are not second best compared to the one no longer with you. Every life is as valid as another and we all need to feel valued. In your communication, let the animals know that you are working through your grief towards a goal of contentment.

An animal's grief

Animals react to the emotion of grief in a similar way to us. They can feel sad, shocked, lonely, misunderstood and unsettled. We should help animals cope with bereavement, otherwise they will think that we are not sensitive to their needs.

Gently place your hands onto the grieving animal's body and imagine golden light flowing from your fingertips. Whilst you channel this peaceful healing energy, tell the animal that you understand how he or she feels and that you will always be there for them. Do this as often as possible until the situation eases. Avoid swamping the animal with feelings of pity, though; be positive about your combined future.

Signs from the afterlife

After the loss of a much-loved animal companion, people sometimes tell me that they had hoped for a sign of the animal's spirit essence drawing close, but that this has not been forthcoming. What can they do to tune in?

- Being outside in nature, as described in Chapter 9, instigates a healing process, allowing our awareness to become clear. When we allow our mind to freewheel, it can get into sync with the unseen world, of which our animals are a part. Our sixth sense then comes into play and information starts to flow, with evidence presenting itself that we are not alone.

- Communications from the afterlife can come unexpectedly. Trying to force a rapport can have the reverse effect, leading to frustration and disappointment. Going about our life and allowing things to happen naturally is a much better option.

- In times of need, we can send out a message to an animal that has died, asking him or her to draw close to us. When in a crisis, we will always receive spiritual support and can sometimes experience a feeling of great peacefulness after we send our message.

A dog sends balloons

If we are open to signs of the existence of an afterlife, this can result in our having some intriguing experiences. Helen was heartbroken when her boxer dog, Riley, passed away. During their life together, Helen and Riley had spent a lot of time on the family canal boat, which he had loved more than anything. A couple of weeks after Riley's death, Helen went for a trip on the same boat, during which there were many canal locks to negotiate. On getting off the vessel to work one of these locks, Helen was astonished to see three balloons bouncing down the towpath towards her. It was utterly bizarre, because this part of the canal was in a remote area with no nearby inhabitants, and nor were there any walkers or cyclists on the towpath.

One of Riley's favourite games had been to play with balloons, when he would go absolutely bonkers chasing and bursting them. On seeing the balloons, Helen told me that a calmness descended over her, for she knew without a doubt that they were a sign from Riley to say that all was well with him. I have absolutely no idea how a dog managed to send balloons from the afterlife, but then nothing surprises me about the signs that we can receive, both from animals and people.

Moving objects

Sometimes signs involve objects being moved around, as happened to Marika a week after the death of her dog, Trixie. Marika had thrown her sandals haphazardly down on the floor by her computer and gone to bed. The next morning, Marika, who lives on her own, was so stunned by what she saw that she felt faint. The sandals were lying side by side, with one of Trixie's favourite dog treats placed neatly in front of them.

I myself have experienced objects changing positions, apparently activated by beings in other dimensions, and – like Marika – I have wondered how this could be possible. I can only conclude that there seems to be a system of parallel worlds in existence and every now and again they overlap and interconnect. Animals, I am convinced, view this sort of thing as perfectly normal.

Unexpected visitations

One of my associates, Lyn Purden, was devastated when her husky, Zena, passed away suddenly from kidney failure. Lyn is the founder of Friends of the Strays of Greece, and Zena had come from a shelter in Aegina. About a year after Zena's death, Lyn and her husband, Mark, were back visiting their house in Greece. As always, they were very busy with their charity work, helping abandoned dogs, so Zena was not foremost in their mind.

Yet, during that visit, Lyn had a dream, which she told me was so vivid, she truly thought that she was awake. In the dream, Zena was on

the other side of a frosted-glass door, trying to get to Lyn, who found that no sound would come out of her mouth when she tried to call the dog. Because of this, Zena started to walk away, whereupon Lyn found her speaking voice and managed to call out: 'Zena, come to me!' This had the desired effect: Zena came through the door.

Lyn explained to me: 'It was not imagination, I could actually feel Zena's fur ruffling under my hands. But as I explored this incredible reunion, Zena suddenly disappeared backwards, like retreating down a tube, and then she was gone. I woke immediately and told Mark all about it, crying with joy because I really had touched Zena. Mark said I had eyes like saucers and was grinning from ear to ear, laughing and crying at the same time. Only on returning home, did I realise that this experience had occurred on the exact anniversary of Zena's death.'

One day in my twenties, while I was mourning the death of a soul-mate rabbit, Flopsy, I felt a distinct pressure on my chest as I lay in bed. Involuntarily, my arms closed around what was there – the shape of dear Flopsy. Sometimes a visitation can be so unexpected that we are blown away. After the death of a horse that I was particularly fond of, complex business negotiations in my career at the time served to distract me from pondering over my loss. Months later, whilst in a meeting, I found myself registering the unmistakable smell of horse. No one else in the room seemed to notice so I carried on shuffling my documents.

Later, I would describe to a mentor how, out of the blue, I heard a voice say: 'Thank you for the biggest apple,' and how I intuitively knew this to be a communication from the horse. Stunned, I left the conference for a while to compose myself, because I still remembered how, hours before the horse died, I had taken him an apple, saying: 'I have brought you the biggest apple from the tree in my garden.' Consequently, what happened on that and numerous other occasions has contributed to my perception of life and death.

There are those who may say these sorts of anecdote are simply the figments of overactive imaginations; the animal was not really there and it was wishful thinking. However, such sceptics can spoil our relationships. My advice is to believe what you know to be true and ignore that which would diminish your reality. Live your life as *you* experience it, for this is what animals guide us to do.

Guiding paws

It is not unusual for me to pick up the presence of an animal in spirit form, which has come to guide a terminally ill animal into the afterlife. Miniature schnauzer Katie was gravely ill with an enlarged liver and I visited her twice to offer healing peace. On the second occasion, as I knelt beside her, I heard a voice say, 'I'm here and my name is Katie.'

'Yes, I know your name is Katie,' I said, wondering why the dog should say such a strange thing to me at this point.

'No, I'm white Katie,' came the rapid reply, together with the misty impression of a dog standing behind the one lying under my hands. Ah, now this was becoming clear – there was another dog in the room. The spirit dog explained that she had drawn close to act as a guide for sick Katie during her imminent transition into the afterlife. When Katie's guardian entered the room, she told me that in her youth she had had a mostly white (speckled with a few brown markings) Jack Russell terrier called Katie. How wonderful that the link had come full circle and the two Katies would soon be playing together.

There may be several spirit animals from different species surrounding a departing animal, but however many are present, they will be aware of each other. A few minutes before thirty-six-year-old horse Frosty passed away, he rallied and pricked his ears forward, whinnying loudly as though in response to a call. On following Frosty's gaze, I saw the paddock ahead full of spirit animals, including horses, ponies, donkeys, dogs, cats, birds and even a lion. The March rain clouds parted, and a shaft of sunlight shone directly onto Frosty's forehead as he was welcomed by the throng. What an entourage to lead an old horse into the heavenly realms!

> **Animal Zen moment**
>
> Time is memory. Or anticipation. It is where I am now. Here in this place.

The time traveller

I find it really exciting when I work with an animal, and something especially sublime takes place. Criollo pony Chico is a very pretty red dun colour with a distinctive dorsal stripe. When tuning into him, I quickly learnt that he was a decisive individual who liked to investigate new territories. I also discovered that his curiosity extended to transporting his soul body to be with his rider, Alexa, when she was elsewhere.

From Alexa, I was intrigued to hear of a recent occasion when, together with friends, she had been sitting in a chapel, silently thinking of a man whose life-support machine was being switched off after a serious accident. In a burst of recognition, which Alexa described as like a light going on, Chico's presence filled Alexa's head, bringing with it an awareness of great magnitude. 'He's there,' Alexa heard Chico say, and with that the pony's presence faded as quickly as it had arrived. The message that Chico had brought allowed Alexa to know that the man the group were praying for had arrived where he was meant to be – seemingly a place to which Chico was also somehow linked.

As I listened to Alexa's account of what had happened that day, Chico butted into my mind with a communication. Two days earlier, Chico told me, he had energetically projected himself to stand behind Alexa whilst she unloaded items from her car, and when Alexa turned around she had fallen over. This was verified by Alexa, who had had no idea she had literally bumped into her pony. I suggested to Chico that he perfect his time-travelling technique a bit, and I am looking forward to my next meeting with him to hear how this is coming along.

Into the future

Through their attention to energy, animals demonstrate an ability to read future events, such as predicting extreme weather, the development of cancer cells or whether someone is about to have an epileptic fit. But even more incredibly, it seems that on occasion animals can predict when their life on Earth is destined to come to an end. I surmise that they are so in tune with the workings of the Universe that they are perhaps able to 'read' some sort of blueprint in action.

When one of my doggy friends, seventeen-year-old Mia, became very ill after a stroke, Blue, the male in the pack of six, lay by her bed throughout the night. The next morning, Mia was taken back to the vet clinic and passed away there; and the dogs remaining at home acted in a strange manner, mooching about morosely. These particular dogs are used to one or more of their group leaving the house for a few hours or even days, as they are all competition or therapy dogs. Normally there is no change in their behaviour, yet on this occasion they clearly knew that Mia was not coming back. Yet how did they know? Animals possess advanced sensory abilities, reaping information about which we remain ignorant. Through activating our intuition, we can make advances towards being as aware as our animal friends.

Will they come back?

The subject of reincarnation is a complex one. Many years ago, I begged for a much-loved, deceased cat to come back to me in the form of another feline, but I gradually came to the realisation that what I had learnt from the relationship was complete. The friendship had shaped, changed and evolved me, and I needed to move on and learn something else from a new animal companion. Yes, there is pain aplenty when a soul mate passes away, but it is a small price to pay for the

Animal insight

Animals urge us not to waste time, rather to enjoy each moment that we spend with them, because life on Earth is not an endless sojourn.

outstanding and unique experience of having shared precious time with them. The way I see it, by sharing my life with varied animals, I learn as much as possible about myself and about what I am capable of.

A needy animal can always benefit from the love that an animal friend leaves permanently in our hearts. It may be an old saying that when one door closes another opens, but it is nevertheless true. I have even known animals to send messages from the afterlife to inspire people to take in a newcomer. Our past furry friends want us to share our love and to spread it around, so that love is everywhere and no animal is ever neglected or unloved.

The connection to past animal companions does not diminish with time, for they are part of the fabric of our spiritual progression. Enmeshed in this is how we relate to the world around us, including nature. Listening to wild talk has great value for our spiritual development, as well as being essential if we are to become the most competent interspecies communicators that we can be.

9 Wild Talk

There is an instinctive bond between people and other living beings. When we gravitate towards nature and begin to listen to the voices of the wild, our natural love for these forms will help to sustain life itself.

The word 'wild' can mean many things. Looking the word up, I found definitions relating to fifty-one different topics, many of them concerning humans ('wild parties', 'wild card', a 'wild' sport, 'not wild about cheese', 'wild financial schemes' and so on). To my way of thinking, applying the term 'wild' to unruly or bad human behaviour does a gross injustice to the sentience of animals, as well as to the cellular intelligence and beauty of plants. In this book, I use the term 'wild' to denote an animal living in a natural environment, or an animal which should be doing so.

To an animal, wild means being able to take care of itself without human interference. However, some animals have been domesticated over thousands of years, which means that they have adapted to living in human environments. Archaeology has placed the earliest known domestication of the dog at potentially 30,000 BC, followed by the cat at least nine thousand years ago, then the horse around six thousand years ago. Yet all domesticated animals retain the ability to respond to situations in accordance with the distant heritage of their wild ancestry. Nature as a force cannot be tamed or confined, even though some of her creatures can be. As wild animals share our planet with us, what can we learn from them?

A wild animal knows that survival depends on mental and physical awareness. We can adopt the wild animal's philosophy by becoming so thoroughly aware of our surroundings that situations are acknowledged and dealt with as soon as they occur, rather than unconsciously repressed. A knock-on effect of this attitude is our becoming attuned to the foundation of life. Animals sense that they are linked to a greater order, but only those living in the wild can truly experience the integration. Deep down this is what our own soul yearns for too: whenever we watch free-roaming beings, we subconsciously feel that in a similar state of no restrictions, in which we could simply follow our instincts and intuition, we would also be contented. This is why we often feel so good when out and about in nature; it is not a primitive or retrograde step, but represents our reaping the benefits of getting away from material things. When American biologist Joe Hutto spent eighteen months living with wild turkeys, it changed his outlook on awareness, and he declared in a TV programme that 'these birds are more conscious than we are'.

I'd like to explore here the analogy between the wild and spirituality. I see the human attraction to wildness as a metaphor for soul freedom. While humans have lost their connection to and affinity with the wild, animals retain this and are not therefore spiritually challenged in the same way. Wild animals do not have to fill their days with empty beliefs; rather, they follow their true nature without distraction from opinions or diktats. How many of us can say we live like that?

Becoming moral and considerate to all species is the natural consequence of tuning into the wild world. The future invites us to take greater note of the lessons and benefits to be gained from environmental attunement, even though it currently seems that human curiosity is bent on the production of ever more technology. As a species, we need to become motivated to make better use of our technologies, so that we move from being exploiters to protectors of the wild. But most of all, we need to use our natural innate intuitive skills, rather than just blindly follow the dictates of technology, because technology will never allow us to hear another being's soul-voice and thus the fundamental purity of existence is overlooked.

Wild animals are not cuddly toys and nor do they wish to live with us in our domesticated situations. I'm right up there with people who protest against the indignity and oft-times cruelty of confining wild animals in zoos, private collections and circuses. Recognising the right of animals to live in the wild teaches us to leave them be, free to follow their own way, and to overcome our species' overwhelming propensity to control, dominate and destroy for its own sake. Perhaps this acknowledgement is psychologically irksome to some people, stimulating them to kill for entertainment, sport or trophy.

Wild animals remind us that as a species we are not the be-all and end-all. These animals do not look at us and think, 'Gosh! There is a being who lives in a fancy house and drives a big car – I am impressed!' They have no concept of that sort of status, so if we get in the way of their family life or territory, we can get hurt or mortally wounded as a consequence. It is foolhardy to venture close to a wild animal's domain. We need to keep a respectful and safe distance, and when tuning in with wild animals, it is always essential to do so in such a manner that the animal is not interfered with or disturbed in any way. Our ancestors lived cheek by jowl with wild animals, but this kind of lifestyle can be fraught with danger; even experienced wildlife biologist Joe Hutto was attacked and injured by one of the group of turkeys he was researching, which hitherto had been a benign companion.

All life forms have a consciousness, not just animals. In their bestselling book, *The Secret Life of Plants*, Peter Tompkins and Christopher Bird documented scientific experiments on plants performed with a modified lie detector. The instrument would register when a plant's leaves were cut or burnt. When a plant 'perceived' it was going to be killed, it went into a state of 'shock' or 'numbness'. This possibly prevented it from undue suffering. So what on earth is going on with animals, if it seems that even plants have a consciousness? What vital pieces of information might we be missing in our everyday animal relationships? This is why making a habit of tuning in intuitively to them is so important.

Nature's invitation

On the retreats that I lead, people are usually visibly relieved to be told that they are barred from using computer equipment or phones for the duration. To be without such stultifying restraints to self-awareness for a period of even seven days is both therapeutic and cathartic. It can be seen in the creative writing and art that people start to produce as the week unfolds.

Elizabeth declared early in my last retreat that she could not draw, and indeed at first it seemed that she was unable even to make a start, her pencil hovering over a blank sheet of paper. I pressed Elizabeth's hand down as she held the pencil, and it produced a dot on the paper. Everyone can make a mark, I told her, and many marks become the detail of a drawing. After a week on the retreat, inspired by the surrounding wildlife, trees and plants, Elizabeth produced the most beautiful drawing, declaring, 'The thing I will most remember about this week is that I now know how to make my mark.' That statement symbolises the act of stepping into our spiritual shoes: nature and her wild living souls invite us all to make our mark in a positive way, so that we can realise our soul potential.

Nature is a majestic place, rich in information and significance, which is easy to miss if our intuition is not active. The world's ecosystem is complexly balanced through the existence of animals, insects, birds, sea creatures, plants and the environment as a whole. If one component is removed, everything else will collapse – including the human support system. Without wildlife, our planet would be a barren, soulless place to live. There is an intercommunicating order to the wild world, yet, as a species, humans all too often tinker with or destroy habitats, damage animal families and disrupt the balance of life – all selfish, non-spiritual acts.

Animal Zen moment

Sunshine is a warm caress of healing from the life-affirming sun. Bathed in the radiance of a clear moon, I lose myself in its cool stillness.

There are those who may question why we need to protect animal species considered 'pests', such as foxes, badgers or sharks, for example. A more pertinent question to ask is surely why we should ignore another species' fundamental right to live without pressure from human harassment? I have never understood the desire to kill or destroy wild creatures, instead of working on correcting our own species' inadequacies. Through a connection with all of Earth's life forms, harmonious nurturing energies develop, which helps safeguard our world for all, including future generations.

If we just trundle around, not paying much attention to our surroundings, our intuition slumbers. If you do the following things, this will help to keep you intuitively active, so that you can detect any communications coming your way:

- Wherever you go, pay attention to all forms of life. Scenes are made up of thousands of details.

- With your intuition fully open, listen to your inner self and take note of the feelings stirring within you in response to the life reverberating around you. Be aware of the unique vibrations of each animal, bird, insect, fish, tree and plant.

- Absorb the information that your heart and soul are processing from nature. What messages are being transmitted to you?

The grizzly

Over and again, when I take time to be in nature I find that wonderful things present themselves. Sensing a tree suck up water, a ladybird landing on my finger or seeing petals unfurl towards the Sun… there is always an interesting spectacle taking place. Tuning into nature's power can lead to absolutely incredible experiences, and the following story is about one that I had. It is not first and foremost a tale about life everlasting, but rather about how tuning into the energy of the wild allows us to experience such phenomena. Nature becomes a catalyst, creating a chink through which we can glimpse a tiny smattering of the unseen machinations of the Universe.

Something magical happened to me on a mountain. In between teaching assignments in Canada, I had a few days relaxation in the stunning Banff National Park and was fortunate to see many varieties of wild animals and birds, including moose, elk, black bear, coyote, osprey and eagle. A healing trip to a sanctuary for injured wild animals had brought me into close contact with two mule deer, a great grey owl and a bighorn sheep. Eager to see more wildlife, I decided to take the chair lift up to the top of the mountain at Lake Louise, which passes over flower-strewn meadows that are one of the best places on Earth to see grizzly bears in their natural habitat.

On arrival, visitors are directed to the visitor centre to view a short film about the wildlife viewing possibilities, as a well to be given a safety briefing. As I watched the grizzly bears in the film, I was overcome with emotion at the possibility of seeing one. While I sat in front of the screen, I was aware that outside grizzlies were lumbering around not that far away, oblivious to my existence ... or were they? There is part of all life in every cell and in every being, so in essence we are connected to everything. Suddenly, I felt the connection strongly, and I wondered if perhaps in some way so did the bears. After the awe of seeing black bears in Alberta, I had written down some words on a scrap of paper which were still in my pocket: *When two worlds meet, learning begins and our own behaviour can modify.* The world of the grizzly bears and my own were about to overlap, and I knew that in some way my concepts would thereafter be altered. Just how much though, I was not anticipating.

Excited by the prospect of seeing a grizzly, I unzipped my camera case before the visitor film finished, so that I was ready to take photos straightaway. The lights went up, the doors opened and my husband and I hurried towards the chair lift, where the attendant got us seated and sent us up the mountainside. The lift rises soundlessly and slowly for 2,088 metres. We had not gone far when I started to reminisce about my work with animals, which had led to this fabulous opportunity and the chance to safely see a wild grizzly bear. My heart raced with anticipation. In my musing, I reflected on how much my late mother, a healer herself, would have admired my adventures. I wished I could send her a postcard with the message: 'Having a wonderful time, seeing lots of wildlife. Wish you were here.'

The chair lift skimmed over tree tops and bumped past a pylon, towards the upper mountain slopes where we hoped to see bears. On glancing to my right, I was infused with the powerful and intense sensation that my mother was with me. It was not a memory of her;

rather, it was *knowing* that my mother was there and very much 'alive', floating in space beside me – which, I admit, is a strange notion.

After I had acknowledged my mother's presence, a conversation took place between us, a rapid dialogue of wordless information bouncing from one to the other. My mother reminded me straightaway that she was aware of everything going on in my life. Postcards were now superfluous. To be honest, I cannot transcribe the whole conversation that followed after this, because the form of it was more like an instant imprinting of diffuse knowledge that took place within me, rather than an everyday chat. I do remember asking a question, however: from her exalted place could my mother send me some extra special energy to assist with my work with animals? With her typical radiant smile, my mother said that she surrounded me with her love. And with that she was gone.

Turning to look back up the mountain, I wondered if I had missed a lot of scenery, so long had the conversation with my mother seemed to take. In reality, though, we had only travelled a few metres. Refocusing, I noticed a man clutching a video camera in the chair lift coming towards us. He was pointing excitedly downwards and mouthing, 'Grizzly!' A look of sheer wonderment was on the man's face: it was clear that he felt privileged to be seeing something wild, beautiful and awesome. I felt exactly the same way, when I too witnessed the spectacle of the bear's raw beauty.

Craning my neck, I saw the female grizzly bear foraging amongst the lush, nectar-rich vegetation below us. These huge herbivores need to consume 40,000 calories a day in order to put on sufficient weight to survive the long winter hibernation. In summertime, the Lake Louise mountain ski slopes' abundance of flowers and berries attracts the bears. As I observed this awesome spectacle of nature's wildness, and quickly took souvenir snapshots, I knew that the most meaningful images of this bear would be forever imprinted on my soul. In fact, what better food for the soul than to glimpse a free spirit?

The lift reached the docking platform, where a female attendant raised up the bar from across our laps, allowing us to get down. As I stood up, I put my hand into my jacket pocket to retrieve my camera case, but it was not there. Oh no, in my excitement and haste I had left the case on the bench in the visitor centre, rather than having stuffed it into my pocket!

Noticing that the lift attendant was holding what appeared to be a black cell-phone case in her hand, I asked her if she could call the office to report my loss. The attendant placed the black item onto the ledge on top of a wall, and, reaching inside a bag, pulled out a phone to call her colleague. I stared at the article on the wall – surely not? It looked very much like my camera case.

'I think that's my camera case,' I said, whereupon the attendant replied that it was impossible – she had taken it off an empty chair lift that had stopped before ours. Someone had left it there, although the young woman was puzzled that it had not fallen off the swinging seat as it travelled up the mountain, and that it wasn't accompanied by a person. No, she told me, if I was missing something, it could only be at the bottom of the mountain from where I had come.

For a moment, it felt like I was going crazy and I began to doubt my actions, let alone what my possessions looked like. After all, I had noticed the black object in the lift attendant's hand as soon as our chair had slowed down and she lifted our safety barrier. Yet ... the battered case was the same colour and make as mine and covered in similar patina markings. Perhaps there was someone else on the mountain that day, who by a sheer coincidence had an identical item. My head was buzzing; it felt like I had entered some weird dimension in which everything had become muddled up and where time was not orderly or linear. It was most odd.

My husband and I decided to walk up to the interactive centre, where we listened to a talk by a park ranger, before coming out to see the same grizzly moving along a distant slope. Even though she was now further away from my view, I was still as enthralled. Gleaning details from the ranger about the bear's age and family history made the connection seem more personal.

Arriving back at the chair lift to make our descent, I noticed the black case still perched on the top of the wall and, idly picking it up, I looked inside ... to find my spare memory card. Without a doubt, this was *my* case. The attendant appeared and told me to take it, because no one else had reported the item missing, and nothing had been handed in at the visitor centre either. How on earth, though, had my camera case got onto a chair lift going up the mountain ahead of me?

As I slid my camera back into its cover, a flash of insight hit me. This was my mother's doing. Since her passing, she has made her presence powerfully known to me on several occasions, always in connection to my being involved with animals. That day, my mother had surrounded me with her love and in that intense moment had performed magic, by which I mean not a sleight-of-hand card trick such as conjurors perform, but a real miracle. Having known that I had left my camera case on the bench in the visitor centre, my mother had somehow transported it up the mountain. She had performed this feat through the realms of energy, the very same system that our intuition and healing hands connect to, and which emanates from an unseen source. A shiver ran through me at the thought. That day, I got a glimpse into just how powerfully the system operates and what it can achieve. What had triggered this, though? Without a doubt it was my deep connection that day to the wild-bear energy. I had on countless previous occasions, and in many different countries, sat on chair lifts and gone up mountains; they are one of my favourite places to meditate. Nothing even remotely like this had ever happened before.

We arrived back where we had started, at the bottom of the valley, where a member of staff engaged us in conversation, giving me the opportunity to mention that I had regained my lost property. On my recounting the story, the young man raised his eyebrows, saying, 'Wow, that's spooky.' Pausing, he added, 'You know, there's an awful lot going on that we don't understand – there is something very special out there,' and lifted his hands up to the mountain.

Through our connection to the energy of wild creatures, we too can experience that miraculous *something*. When an enchanting moment happens between us and nature, we know that we have walked together in a state of harmony.

Peace offering

The emotions and thoughts that can arise in wild places lead to feelings of soul contentment. When I put the question, 'What does being in nature give you?' to my colleagues in the animal world and others interested in the sort of work that I do, I was inundated with insightful comments, some of which I include here:

> 'Being in nature makes me slow down'; 'it's about belonging where I should be'; 'it brings us back to the source of life'; '... allows me to let go'; 'a feeling of inner calm'; 'refreshes me and gets rid of any stale energy'; 'where I find perspective and balance'; 'nature has a profound ability to heal'; 'connection with creator and creation'; 'a place for teaching and learning'; 'truth and wisdom'; 'where I can re-energise'; 'tranquillity'; 'being in nature is the most natural thing in the world. We all need to take time to stop and smell the roses.'

Marion poetically wrote: 'Sitting in the fields and watching my horses, chickens and other creatures that share our space takes me away from the weariness of day-to-day chores. My fields are my church. Animals and the Earth are my God.' And Matthew said: 'I feel immensely privileged to be in nature, be it furry, feathered, floral or greenery.'

The most common comment I received was: 'Being in nature gives me peace.' Let's always remember that peace is what all beings seek.

Getting in touch

Being in nature helps us to connect with our true self, an experience that is both revitalising and calming at the same time. The wildness of nature offers us a place in which our intuition can come fully alive, where we can hear wild voices and take part in wild talk. Contemplating the open sky and savouring the fragrances and sounds that travel through the air outside can make for a day of abundant knowledge.

- Nature provides us with the opportunity to feel whole and connected with all living things.

- Nature prevents us from becoming self-obsessed. We are all part of the dance of life and humans are not centre stage, even though they mistakenly place themselves in that position.

- Nature is a supernatural force and demands our respect, to match the sensitivity that other species possess. As the most dominant species on Earth, humans have a particular duty of care towards this planet and her creatures.

- Nature's creatures are significant beings, because they reflect our own needs and potential, in terms of developing our own consciousness and awareness.

I would like to share with you a few of my favourite quotes relating to the natural world:

'There is little that separates humans from other sentient beings – we all feel pain, we all feel joy, we all deeply crave to be alive and live freely, and we all share this planet together.' *Gandhi*

'We depend on nature not only for our physical survival. We also need nature to show us the way home, the way out of the prison of our own minds. We got lost in doing, thinking, remembering, anticipating – lost in a maze of complexity and a world of problems.' *Eckhart Tolle*, Stillness Speaks

And the famous British statesman Winston Churchill commented, 'Nature will not be admired by proxy' – meaning that we need to get out and experience it for ourselves.

Our intuition invites us to entwine with the cosmic manifestation of beauty, power, resonance, strength, spirit, energy, interaction, harmony, integrity, inter-dependence, perfection and completeness that is nature. And whose creativity no human can emulate without her leadership.

You are in the centre of Nature.
Live in full awareness,
communicating with the life around you.
Be the protector of this life,
for without it you are not complete.

Differences

Wild animals are very different to domestic pets, horses and farm animals, and therefore communicating with them also has some notable variations. An animal in the wild feels intrinsically part of the web of life, as opposed to many domesticated animals, including farmed, which we have isolated from integration with the whole, through preventing them from making choices or doing what comes naturally to them.

Animals living wild don't rationalise their behaviour, because it is instinctive. We can't give them verbal clues or train them to do things, and they pay scant attention to our body language. So whereas messages from our cats, dogs, horses and small furry pets are frequently about their interactions with us, communication with wild animals is mostly about their feelings, which are unattached to us, and any messages they transmit are either related to our spiritual growth or about humans creating environmental havoc. I have from time to time been requested to communicate with exotic pets, a euphemism for a captive wild animal. Commonly, the creature is unhappy and physically, mentally and emotionally depleted, because of its unnatural and restricted lifestyle. Far better is to share a home with a member of a species that has genetically adapted to live alongside humans over thousands of years.

The key to communicating with wildlife is to open yourself up intuitively and allow Nature's energy to infuse you, taking note of what you feel and what it means to you. If you ask Nature or wild animals questions about your material world, these will be ignored, so try just to 'be'. It's always possible that you might suddenly sense what it is like to be that animal, as I described happened to me in Chapter 4 when I blended with the racoon. A wild creature may inhabit your surroundings, meaning that you see it frequently, in which case a telepathic rapport may build up between you. The animal will only feel at peace,

Animal Zen moment

Always, there is the sound of living systems wrapping around and through us, which we hear by listening through our intuition.

though, if you respect his or her wildness, allowing your two worlds to overlap yet retaining independence from each other.

Mamma Roo

Around the globe, situations arise whereby the consciousness of caring people overlaps with the parallel world of an animal, in this case a member of the kangaroo nation. Mary Hitchcock, an animal communicator from Australia, sent me her moving story:

Driving home one evening on a moonless night along the winding roads of Tasmania, in my car headlights I saw a kangaroo standing by the side of the road. Kangaroos are renowned for jumping in front of cars, so I slowed mine to a crawl and it was then that I noticed a small bundle on the road. Pulling over to the side of the road, I got out of my car and was upset to find that the bundle was the kangaroo's baby, which had been hit by a vehicle. The distressed mother kangaroo was obviously in shock so I squatted down by her in order that I wouldn't seem so intimidating, and began talking in a soft, compassionate voice. After saying that I wanted to help and knew people at a kangaroo sanctuary, I asked Mamma Roo if it was alright that I attend to the baby. She was still for a moment whilst looking at me and then made a motion with her head, looking down at the form lying on the road, then back at me and again to the baby. Instinctively I knew that I was being given permission to go to him. As I stood up, Mamma Roo took two jumps back from the side of the road and stood watching my every move.

On picking the baby kangaroo up, his body felt warm and soft and I carried him over to the car headlights so that I could assess the injuries, talking throughout to Mamma Roo out loud, reassuringly explaining what I was doing, her ears going back and forth at every word I uttered. All the time, I was thinking how to tell her that, due to the terrible injuries inflicted, the baby wasn't going to make it. Softly, I said a prayer as I cradled him in my arms while his life ebbed away. Something quite extraordinary then happened.

Through my tears I felt a warm hand gently touch mine, and looking up found Mamma Roo standing very close to me, her paw placed onto my hand. In that instant, our eyes locked together, and I could see shining from hers the compassion and love she had for her baby. I also sensed her emotional anguish and overwhelming grief. That moment seemed to last for ages until Mamma Roo took a couple of hops away, before turning back to again look at me, whereupon I very clearly heard her say, 'Thank you.' These words came from her soul-voice in a way that I can only describe as an angelic gratitude.

Promising Mamma Roo that I would come back in the morning and bury her baby, I laid his body down in the grass so that his mother could be with him throughout the night and deal with her loss the best way she knew how. Kangaroos are family-orientated animals which live in mobs and tend to stay in the same location for many years. When a young kangaroo is hurt and nursed back to health by humans, it is important to release it back where it was found, so it can find a family member and be integrated back into the group.

The following morning when I returned Mamma Roo was still by the body. She watched the burial proceedings from a little way off and, as soon as I had finished, I told her that the body of her son was at peace in his own country, thanked her for letting me help and said how I wished things had worked out differently. Mamma Roo nodded her head, which I took to be a sign of agreement, before turning away and jumping off without looking back. I will never forget that night, for it holds a very special moment in my heart. The connection that was made between us will never leave me.

The kangaroo too will always remember. Inside each creature beats the heart of an individual who understands the workings of the Universe. Soul-to-soul connections, like the one which Mary experienced with the kangaroo, exist for eternity.

Hazel's walk on the wild side

I love rabbits and several have lived with me over the years. I met Adele on the set of TV series *Animal Roadshow*, when she brought in a rabbit called Rupert for me to be filmed with. Sometimes, as well as fostering unwanted pet rabbits, Adele took in wild bunnies. Adele had found tiny wild rabbit Hazel in a herb garden, covered in scratches, dehydrated and with both eyes stuck closed. Usually, it is best to leave wild bunny babies be, but Hazel was lethargic and barely moving. The vet advised euthanasia, because not only was the bunny so young, he also had a broken back leg. Being very experienced in rabbit care, Adele decided to try to save the little chap's life, making a matchstick splint for his leg, and hand-rearing him with suitable milk from a syringe. As a result, Hazel survived and the leg healed.

'We became completely in tune with the each other's intentions and had the deepest connection,' Adele told me. As he grew older, Hazel had a bizarre habit of running at Adele at lightning speed, then dashing up her legs and body to snuggle under her chin. The communication link between Adele and Hazel was so powerful that he used to hold direct eye contact, sending thoughts of his next move to Adele, who would position her body ready for him to run up.

Adele soon discovered that Hazel was scared of open spaces. When placed in the large garden areas constructed to house fostered rabbits, Hazel would panic and head for the smallest space to hide in. Several times, Adele tried to release Hazel back to the wild, but that only resulted in him running straight back to Adele, shaking. Through communicating with Hazel, Adele picked up that he had had the direst fright when carried out of his nest by a marauding predator and consequently Hazel did not feel secure in the open and was happiest in the house. The door to the garden was open daily, but Hazel never willingly ventured outside.

Although he was hand-reared and handled constantly, you could still see the wild heritage in Hazel. His senses were more acute than those of a domestic rabbit and he had a completely different routine to the others who lived with Adele, dawn and dusk being his most active times. Now and again, he would perform a display of dextrous acrobatic dances, incorporating mad back flips, crazy hops, enthusiastic skips and high kicks, all so delicately and precisely executed.

At the grand old age of ten, Hazel had a call from the wild. Leaping from Adele's arms as she held him on the doorstep, Hazel scooted off down the garden at great speed, before vanishing into the countryside.

It was obvious that Hazel knew where he was going, yet it was an astonishing act for a rabbit that normally refused to go outdoors. A few hours later, Adele spotted Hazel in an apple orchard behind her house, but, completely out of character, he did not go to Adele upon seeing her; instead, he promptly disappeared into the greenery.

Three days later, on the morning that her grandmother passed away, Adele was doing the washing-up in the kitchen, when a sudden image of Hazel in a golden ball of light flashed into her mind. She felt an urgent need to open the back door and, on doing so, there was Hazel – who ran forward and, on being scooped up, tucked himself under Adele's chin in his familiar way. 'Here I am,' an overjoyed Adele telepathically heard Hazel say.

Hazel communicated to Adele what going away had been about – that Hazel knew that his time to leave Earth was getting closer and he had wanted to revisit his wild place of birth. With his wish fulfilled, the angels had guided Hazel back to Adele, with whom he lived for a while longer, before joining Adele's mum and grandmother in heaven.

This story just goes to show how self-aware and conscious even the most common of species is, when they are given the freedom to act according to their nature. All creatures have supreme wisdom, responding to the rhythm of the cosmos rather than resisting it like humans mostly tend to do. No matter how seemingly insignificant or small, each animal, bird and insect communicates with us, teaching us how to enrich our life.

Bird brain

The sentience of wild creatures means that they telepathically communicate their intentions to each other, which they update as their plans unfold.

Rupert, a sable and white Sheltie, belonged to my friend Valery, and the dog's regular treat was chewing marrowbones in the garden. One day, glancing out of the bedroom window, Valery noticed two crows on the lawn near to where Rupert was eating his bone. One of the crows hopped to the rear of Rupert and leaned forward to tweak his tail hairs with its beak. Startled, Rupert looked round to find out what the offending tail pull was all about – and at that precise moment the second crow hopped onto the bone and pecked some marrow out of it. When Rupert turned back to his bone, this bird hopped off, allowing Rupert to continue to gnaw at his treat. Then the birds swapped positions, and executed the same procedure. One bird pulled at the dog's tail and, when Rupert looked round, the other bird pounced on the bone and had a quick peck. This ritual went on for several minutes and Valery said she could sense Rupert's indignation.

A few days later, a pair of magpies ganged up to do the same thing. Interestingly, when Rupert had a rawhide chew without the marrow content, none of the birds bothered. It seems clear that they were fully aware of what the dog was eating and whether it suited them for a meal, whereupon they developed a strategic plan of action as to how to steal a bit for themselves. By their actions, the birds illustrated teamwork, planning, foresight and above all a means of telepathic communication. So if you are ever called a bird brain, regard it as a compliment – it means being an adept communicator!

In relation to their size and delicacy, I find that proportionally birds have large energy fields. Having channelled healing energy to many injured birds I am always intrigued by the volume, intensity and speed

of the 'buzz' that they possess. From this information, I can detect a split second before a bird opens its wings to fly, or gasps a last breath. In the latter situation, there is a sense of evaporation, yet simultaneously an expansion, as the bird's soul energy joins the mass energy of the Universe.

It is comforting to know that Nature sends us help whenever we need it; it is just a question of noticing. Our intuition reveals what is going on around us.

Anne the elephant

Like many thousands of people, I was outraged at the brutal beatings that elderly and severely arthritic elephant Anne, the last circus elephant in Britain, suffered at the hands of a groom. Images of her agonies were released to the newspapers and the resulting uproar quickly resulted in Anne, an Asian elephant, being transferred to dedicated and expert care at Longleat Safari Park in the UK.

On the day that the photographs and film of the abuse surfaced, I sat down to send healing to the traumatised elephant. That night, I awoke in the early hours, knowing that I was connected to Anne through the realms of energy. I sensed her soul-voice, a sound that came in waves like the whooshing of an ocean on the shore. In reply, I communicated that humans with integrity and compassion were doing everything to help improve the situation and that soon Anne would be safe.

I wondered how Anne had coped during the fifty-four years since she had been captured as a baby for the circus. In her undulating voice, Anne replied, 'Through the airwaves I have kept in touch with the herd. I call to them constantly and they send messages of support.' This communication was so overwhelming in magnitude that momentarily it was like Anne's feelings were my own.

After Anne had been at Longleat for less than two weeks, I went to do some healing communication work with her. The staff involved with Anne understood her predicament and an intensive health and wellbeing routine had immediately been implemented. I appreciated that the situation was difficult for the keepers. Apart from the safety issues inherent in working in close proximity to a four-ton animal, their work with the elderly and traumatised elephant was thrust into the media and public spotlight. At that time, Anne still did not know them, just as the people involved had no inkling of her personality and mannerisms. A rapport needed to be established and friendships kindled. Elephant and humans were all concerned about what the new relationship might entail.

Introducing myself to Anne, I reminded her that we had already been communicating from a distance, which she acknowledged. With that, I touched Anne to offer healing peace and her immediate response was to turn to look at me, open her mouth in a yawn and roll her eyes. Tears sprang from those sad eyes and ran down Anne's face, wetting her cheeks: she was weeping. I took it as a good sign, for it meant that with the healing touch Anne was perhaps beginning to let go of her inner turmoil. Anne then retreated into a world of her own, and it was similar to those occasions when I have worked with people suffering from post-traumatic stress syndrome. Shock reverberates through every fibre of the body.

An emotional release

Later, Anne ambled around her paddock, where she moved over to a huge boulder and rubbed her back along it, before pushing against a log. Anne seemed to be thinking. She turned and aimed for a tractor tyre lying on the ground, which she lifted up so that it was on end. Then Anne smashed the tyre to the ground with her trunk, bending it in half. Such tyres are steel-lined and it takes a huge force even to compress them, let alone bend and crush one in this way. Anne lifted her trunk and trumpeted as if she were emitting a war cry, before attacking the tyre in the most aggressive way imaginable. For over half an hour, the tyre got stamped on, bashed, thrown around. A watching vet came over to me and said that he was observing an expression of emotional release in Anne as a result of the healing session.

Finally, Anne pushed the tyre towards the paddock fencing, which is made of thick solid metal to withstand large heavy animals leaning on it. Lifting the tyre by looping her trunk through it, Anne started trying to stuff it between the fence's bars. Watching this I sensed that Anne wanted the tyre – clearly a surrogate for the abusive groom she hated with a vengeance – symbolically out of her life.

The spacing between the bars was not wide enough to allow the tyre to pass through, but Anne persevered, until she had crushed it enough to wedge it between the bars. Standing back for a little while to gather her strength, Anne surveyed the stuck tyre. Maybe that was a symbolic moment for Anne – having been stuck for years in a life of captivity with no way out. Next, Anne powerfully surged forward and with one mighty push from her massive head the tyre fell through the bars with a resounding bang. Anne had forced the abuser and his abuse out of her life.

They say that elephants never forget, but I hope that through her healing release Anne has now forgotten the worst of the horror and is left with only a shadow of it, rather than a black cloud. After her sustained attack on the tyre, she stood swaying gently from side to side, emotion spent. Scooping up dust with her trunk, Anne threw it idly over her back. Those of us watching commented that the elephant was like a deflated balloon; something had shifted.

Since that time, Anne pretty much ignores the tyre. I have seen a huge improvement, not only in her physical health but in her emotional state too. The vacant look in her eye has been replaced with an inquisitive aura, even the sparkle of humour. It is obvious that not only does Anne now trust the keepers but she likes them, a bond having been formed between them.

Head keeper Andy says of Anne:

I find it difficult to define in words how my relationship with Anne works, because it is an instant and all-knowing rapport that we share. At first I found it difficult to read Anne, but now my intuition is attuned to her, meaning that I know how she is feeling and what she is thinking. I know that she reads me in a similar way. When I touch Anne, my hands also give me feedback from her body. There is something very special about this elephant which draws me at the end of a day's hard work to go and hang out with her, chatting about this and that, like mates do.

From the beginning, deputy head keeper Ryan used to express that his dearest wish was to hear Anne emit the famous elephant rumble sound, because then he would know that she was happy in her new environment. He didn't have to wait long before Anne made this sound, which I also love to hear. 'Teamwork is important,' mentioned Ryan, during one of our chats. 'Myself, Andy and Anne are subconsciously tuned in together. We are all totally focussed in each moment.' Having watched this team in action, I would say that they are definitely mastering the art of shared communication.

Being up close and personal to an elephant has been an honour for me, as well as a sharp learning curve about the best way to communicate with, and channel healing energy to, an elephant. Is Anne's life perfect? No, because perfection would mean turning the clock back to when she was a baby and not capturing her so cruelly for the circus. Then, she would have continued to be part of her family, learning from their wisdom, having babies of her own and teaching them all she knew, and eventually becoming a matriarch of a free-roaming herd. Through callous disregard for elephant sentience, none of that came to pass. However, Longleat is now Anne's place of physical sanctuary – if not her spiritual home.

Plans are rolling along at Longleat to construct a purpose-built elephant sanctuary with swim pools, heated sand pits, private woodland areas and play areas. It will be much appreciated by Anne and other rescued elephants, who I look forward to helping in the future.

At the annual meeting of the American Association for the Advancement of Science, held in Vancouver in 2012, scientists declared that elephants, as well as apes, whales and dolphins, should be given special protected status as 'non-human persons' – to be allowed to live peacefully in a safe environment and not be held captive for entertainment. All creatures deserve this, and I look forward to a time of commonsense and justice, when every single being is treated as a *who*, not a *what*.

Life in a concrete jungle

I was raised in a city, so I am familiar with the problems of noise pollution and the resultant dulling of natural sounds. But even in places where humans have created a concrete jungle it is possible to find wildlife and communicate with it. An example of this struck me when I was en route to Montana for a conference and had a stop-over in Chicago. With some time on my hands, I made my way to a shopping mall that was surrounded on all sides by freeways bustling with traffic. The car park for the mall was in front of the main entrance, which had a canopy over it. The wall to one side of the door

Animal insight

Humans haven't lost the connection to Nature, because it lies deep inside us all. What has happened in modern life is that people have forgotten how to link to that connection. Paying critical attention to Nature helps us to return to our inner wisdom.

was covered in ivy, where a chink of light glinted down on the foliage through a gap in the canopy. Something rustled. In the twilight, I could make out a pair of sparrows roosting for the night; I wondered where they would find sufficient food and water to survive in this city environment, but they obviously managed somehow. When I stopped to communicate good wishes, the result was a few startled looks as other shoppers rushed past me. To this day, I only remember these birds, not the interior of the store or what I purchased there.

We do not have to travel to unusual locations to see wildlife; it reveals itself in our gardens and window boxes. Yesterday I watched a snail going about its business. Snail, sparrow, rabbit, kangaroo, elephant or bear, they all have something elemental and valuable to teach us. Each experience lives within us for all time, so we need to be mindful of how we shape it into our soul. When we leave Earth, we take only our soul with us; that in reality is all we ever own.

From wild animals, I will be taking you back to domestic ones and offering insights in the following pages on caring for them mind, body and soul. This is an important aspect of being a fully rounded interspecies communicator.

Random Acts of Communication

Animals are constantly reading, assimilating, assessing and acting on information that they tune into intuitively and telepathically. They do this with integrity and without distortion. As our own intuition is like a muscle that needs exercising, and the more we do so the stronger it becomes, I have devised a programme inspired by nature, which I call 'Random Acts of Communication'. When this concept becomes part of our mindset, communicating with all life filters through to us as second nature.

* Every day is a piece of art, a reflection of nature's love for all life. Make a sketch or write something about nature's messengers. Making your mark in this way records your spiritual journey.

* Write a letter of appreciation to a place, plant, bird or animal that has inspired you in some way. Keep this note in a special place.

* Stop by a dog, cat or other animal in the street and ask: 'Hi, how are you?' A jolly greeting brightens their day.

* Share your smile, not just with passing strangers, but with animals too.

* Seek out a wild bird and talk to it about what you imagine it is like to have wings and fly high above people's heads. The knowledge you receive will set you free to explore new ideas regarding communication possibilities.

* Plant a tree in your neighbourhood. Fill your garden or window box with insect-attracting flowers or, if you live in an apartment, grow herbs in your kitchen. Plants lend their energy to your intuitive abilities.

- Sponsor an animal at a sanctuary in whatever way you can manage.

- Offer to connect with healing energy to the animal companion of someone you know.

- Listen attentively and deeply to all the animals that you come across, no matter what species.

Compose your own personal Random Acts of Communication affirmation list, as animals and nature inspire you to join the interspecies communication revolution.

10 It's Natural

Look after the wellbeing of animals – mind, body and soul.

What must it be like to live with others who do not hear what you say and who often misunderstand your behaviour and actions? Other people can understand our descriptions of problems or our concerns, and we can also make our own decisions about how to take care of ourselves, mind, body and soul. However, animals rely on us for help, and depend on our vigilance and understanding. An animal's health and wellbeing can change in an instant or fluctuate, as can ours. Because animals are complex characters, for whom many different things can go wrong, if you ever have any concerns about an animal's health, wellbeing or behaviour it is important to consult a vet as first port of call. We should never try to second-guess what a problem might be or try out complementary remedies at home instead of seeking a proper consultation with a vet, as the animal may be suffering from an ailment that needs urgent attention or it might be in pain.

Once a diagnosis has been made, we are in a much more informed position to consider the available options, such as whether to take a conventional or a complementary approach. In my experience, holistic vets generally offer more time for a consultation and take a detailed case history, asking questions which cover lifestyle, diet, personality and behaviours, as well as about the animal–human interaction. These vets can, if necessary, offer allopathic as well as natural remedies.

After one of my lectures to post-graduate students of animal behaviour at the University of Southampton in the UK, one of them, a young vet from Norway called Camilla, mentioned being inspired to develop her intuitive skills. 'It's crazy,' she told me, 'we accept, and are even taught, that animals have a sixth sense as part of their normal way of being. I have always thought that we are primitive in that respect and cannot compare to an animal, but now I realise that with a bit of effort and practice, people can also operate on the same wavelength.' Opening up to this level of communication will mean that animals in the care of vets like Camilla will have an improved chance of being understood.

To help you gather around you a holistic team of qualified people, this chapter includes information on the avenues available.

Each day make a routine mind, body and soul check

- **Show your interest** Ask your animal, 'How are you?' and listen to the feedback, either in the form of words you may be receiving, images in your mind's eye or gut feelings.

- **Intuition acting as a warning flag** Observe body language, which may indicate discomfort. Note any changes in behaviour, as these can be indicators of pain as well as illness or unhappiness. If we are actively on the lookout for problem signs, this will take the pressure off our animals, who might otherwise be trying constantly to give us nudges to pay attention to them. Instead, our intuition can flag things up to us.

- **What to look out for** Chapter 5 has a list of what problem areas to look out for in horses. Here is my list of signs in small animals that need to be investigated by a vet. These can include:
  - Any change in behaviour, e.g. newfound aggression, shyness, reactivity, circling, vocalisation etc
  - Crying, grumbling, lashing out, biting, scratching or snapping when touched, handled or stroked
  - Not wanting to play with animal friends, or snapping/lashing out at them
  - Withdrawing from contact with humans or other animals
  - Sleeping or resting more than normal
  - Dull eyes
  - Coat looking dull and feeling harsh to touch
  - Sore mouth or other dental problems such as bad breath
  - Panting or gasping for breath
  - Coughing

- Red/itchy skin
- Animal off its food or wanting to eat more than normal
- Drinking more or drinking less than usual
- Weight loss or weight gain
- Abnormal vomiting
- Diarrhoea
- Straining when going to the toilet
- Blood in the stools
- Lack of bladder control
- Walking or moving in a different way, including stiffness
- Holding a paw up in discomfort
- Reluctance to go for a walk/exercise
- Dog lagging behind on walks
- Reluctance to get into a car or climb stairs
- Animal crying out when moving or getting up
- Animal crying out, flinching or lashing out when touched
- Licking/biting/scratching/clawing at limbs or the body
- Falling over
- Huddling or feathers falling out for birds

... and anything else that you are concerned about.

Dogs are known to show signs of pain more readily than cats; and we have to be especially vigilant with older cats because, although they may naturally sleep more, if they are resting more than usual, this may be owing to discomfort from arthritis or other problems. With all animals, having regular check-ups with a vet is essential, as well as taking preventative measures to reduce the possibility of health problems developing. When someone asked me to chat to her cat, who did not like his head being touched and was hissing and lashing out, I suspected, even without tuning in, that this was a pain response. Sure enough, arthritis in the neck, which was giving him a sore head, was subsequently diagnosed. Keep checking in with your animal, so that you become aware of daily variations in mood, behaviour and movements, and your intuition will be able to flag up when attention is needed.

Being observant

Unfortunately, animal carers can give vets red-herring clues, when they offer up their own opinions as fact. To make matters worse, general practitioner vets do not usually have a lot of time in a consultation to dig deeper. The other problem is that they don't usually see ill animals in their home environments.

Clarissa told her vet that cat Yoda was coughing a lot. After listening to the described symptoms, the vet diagnosed asthma and prescribed medication, even though he could find nothing particularly wrong. When I visited Clarissa's house, Yoda did indeed cough a little, but only after he had groomed himself. I suggested that, as a long-haired Maine Coon cat, Yoda was perhaps reacting to hairs in his throat and maybe a hairball was forming. A holistic vet, who visited the house after me, confirmed that the cat did not need the medication. Daily gentle brushing of the cat was the solution instead.

In another case, a dog was brought to my clinic supposedly with aggressive behaviour. Mattie came muzzled, but intuitively I sensed that this was a sick dog, not a badly behaved one, and was drawn to blocked energy deep inside her skull. I noticed slight tremors around Mattie's eyes and a glazed look before she tried to bite. The family had never observed the dog's face closely enough to link these physical quirks with her aggressive outbursts; hence their vet going along with the suggestion that Mattie had become out of control. A second-opinion vet X-rayed the dog and, finding an inoperable brain tumour, released Mattie from her suffering.

Another client asked me out to help her horse, who had become anxious after a companion passed away. Or so she thought. As I stood with the horse, he threw at me the words 'metabolic syndrome'. Quickly, I realised that the horse's debilitated state was due to a serious illness, unrelated to the loss of the pony. Based on the woman's initial assessment of a grieving horse, I had been granted veterinary permission to visit him. However, once I had called the vet with my findings, he visited too and was able to confirm the horse's self-diagnosis. I was glad to have been able to help because the horse was physically very sick, but the woman had in all innocence put two and two together and got five.

It helps to take a step back, be observant and include our intuition. Whilst not infallible, this combination helps heighten our awareness in terms of what is going on with our animals.

Emotional pain

Animals can, and do, suffer from emotional pain, which may have a variety of causes, including grief, separation from friends, hospitalisation, loss of home or companion, change in family circumstances, lack of exercise and/or stimulation, incorrect lifestyle, environmental problems, abuse and neglect. Natural therapies and help from qualified behaviourists can help an animal to overcome emotional pain, provided that any lifestyle issues have been resolved. As with humans, emotional problems can be at the heart of physical diseases, and illness will also trigger emotional distress.

Signs of emotional pain

Lack of motivation
Lethargy
Unresponsiveness to other animals
Unresponsiveness to people
Over-dependence on other animals or people
Not wanting to play
Loss of appetite

If emotional pain is suspected, the cause should be investigated, including a check-up at the vet, as some of the symptoms of emotional distress are similar to those of physical pain. The use of healing energy, homeopathy, herbal remedies and acupuncture can be very helpful with animals who feel emotionally depleted. Keep the communication channels open, talk to the animal and say what you are doing to help. And don't forget to say: *I love you, I will help you.*

Dog-walking problems

People can create or aggravate behavioural problems in dogs on a leash. Certainly it is abhorrent to use spike or choke collars, because of the damage that they do to the trachea and the oesophagus, not to mention the pain and distress they cause. Even normal leather or fabric collars can create anti-social behaviour in dogs, as misuse such as sharp jerking can cause spinal problems in the neck area, which can lead to issues of acute and chronic pain. In addition, misusing collars can cause fear associations to be made by the dog, leading to unwanted, anti-social behaviour. One example of this is the application of tension to the leash, which then travels down to the neck and throat, causing discomfort. This is less common when an appropriate harness is used, such as a balance lead and harness. For example, if you are walking a reactive dog on a collar and lead, and you see a strange dog coming towards you, subconsciously you may shorten or tighten the lead, which will pull on the collar. This alters the dog's posture and causes neck pain, which raises stress levels, making the dog more liable to react. Using a double-ended balance lead and two points of contact on a harness avoids neck tension in the dog and improves body language towards the oncoming dog. A harness should be soft and well fitting, ensuring that no areas create pressure points on chest, shoulder or back nerves. Nerve irritation will lead to pain and resulting problem behaviour. However, there are several possible reasons why a dog may show anti-social behaviour on a leash, so always seek advice from a qualified dog behaviourist if you experience any problems in this area.

Maureen consulted me because her young pedigree dog was not doing well in the show ring. He would throw himself around and generally refuse to 'behave' in front of the judge. The dog communicated to me that when Maureen took him to shows she was filled with nervous apprehension, which travelled down the leash into his body. The dog was jiggling around, mirroring the woman's fears. Maureen admitted that this was true; she had a stressful job and suffered from health problems. In this case, I advised her not only to change to a soft, properly fitting harness rather than clip a leash onto the collar, but to seek help for her own anxiety too.

Dogs like to be with people and go on walks in their company, but dogs should be allowed to stop and sniff things, rather than be route-marched along or, worse still, made to run whilst the person is on a bicycle or skate board. These human habits can lead to dogs developing musculo-skeletal ailments. When dogs go out with us, they want to have a good time, and that means employing their highly developed sense of smell and being able to vary the pace, including making stops where they want. This is essential for both physical and mental wellbeing.

Animal behaviour counselling

Sometimes it's obvious what is going on with an animal, but at other times it takes a bit of working out. A 'behavioural problem' is an animal acting in a particular way because it is trying to communicate something. With expert help, we can usually sort these kinds of problems out. Adopting an intuitive approach will also help to determine what an animal is communicating, but we should remember that what may appear to be problem behaviour from our perspective may be perfectly natural to an animal. Be aware that an animal may not want to change its behaviour, and it is not the role of an animal communicator to convince an animal to change, but to act as a faithful translator of his or her communications. While our actual physical looks are not important to an animal, we may sometimes require an attitude makeover. It may be our actions, manner or outlook causing what we believe to be behavioural problems in an animal.

We must bear in mind too that animals respond to situations depending on their species' needs and requirements, as well as based on their individual past and current conditions and relationships. Separating puppies, kittens and foals from the mother too early can, and does, lead to problematic behaviour in later life. Foals should not be under six months old, kittens and puppies not less than eight weeks old. Weaning should be gentle and gradual, taking into account the feelings of the mother. With all young animals, considerate handling and socialisation with people is paramount, particularly with kittens and puppies. Lack of human attention at this stage can lead to behavioural problems in adult animals.

Some things dogs have to say about behaviour

Psychic skills were not needed to divine why German shepherd dog Fliss was tempestuous and chewed the house to pieces after her people left for work each morning. Correction of the habit would not be achieved by delivering a telepathic instruction. On my recommendation, a dog walker was employed, who took Fliss for long walks and consequently she stopped destroying the furnishings.

Some dogs like to live with other dogs, while others prefer a one-to-one relationship with the people in their lives. Many are OK about both scenarios. Monty is a Staffordshire bull terrier, who was four when I met him. The couple who had originally bought him as a puppy had started a family of their own and, after their second baby arrived, decided they had no time to look after a dog. An animal behaviourist, called Colin, happened to become aware of Monty's plight and took him to live with his other five dogs. However, Colin felt that Monty was not 'quite right' – hence his visit to me. When I asked what was wrong with him, Monty's reply actually started to filter through before I had time to finish the question. Monty didn't mince his words: 'I hate pack living.' As he let out a huge sigh, I detected a sense of relief in Monty that he had got through to someone at last, and that his troubles had lifted. Colin resolved to instigate immediate changes. His parents had just retired and they agreed to take Monty, who thrived with the one-to-one attention that allowed him to express his exuberant personality.

Holly is a jolly dog, a Pomeranian-Jack Russell cross. Her 'mum', Rachel, wanted to know if I could help her understand the reasons for Holly's overly protective behaviour. Holly preferred to pal up with females and she would sometimes aggressively snap and growl at men, even those she knew well and who were part of her family. Now that she was eight years old, the situation had become a self-perpetuating cycle, whereby Rachel and her husband, Brendan, anticipated Holly's antisocial behaviour, and so were subconsciously sending out the wrong signals. During the consultation, I explained that Holly was receiving anxious messages from them, associated with images of her biting, so that's what she felt encouraged to do. Brendan in particular admitted that he had become so wary of Holly's antics that he would tensely wait for them to occur. Holly no doubt thought that she was being a good dog, as she was paying attention to what she was being asked to do. Bombarding animals with thoughts can be very confusing for them, particularly when those thoughts take the form of mixed messages, which conflict with what we actually want to happen.

Positive thinking was needed, as it was essential that Holly be sent clear messages about the sort of behaviour that was acceptable. I explained to Rachel and Brendan how important it was to relax and hold images in their minds of Holly being calm. They needed to act in the moment, like Holly does, and stop linking their thoughts to past behaviour, thereby triggering a future pattern.

Of course, just as we need to make sure that we don't inadvertently trigger certain types of behaviours, we also need to be aware of safety issues when around animals who can behave unpredictably. All dogs and cats have their own unique personalities and do not act in a robotic fashion. Some animals are inherently more assertive than others, just like people are. To that end, for when Holly became overly bossy, I suggested training using distraction techniques and rewarding good behaviour.

What cats say

Suki is a three-year-old cat Siamese cat, who started to spray inside his home, despite being neutered. Having had several Siamese-type cats myself over the years, I know how sensitive they can be, as well as expert exponents of cat vocalisation. They have an opinion on everything, so I needed to know what Suki had to say to me about his unsavoury habits. He was quick to impart the information, once he realised I could hear him telepathically. It seemed that the new boyfriend of the family's teenage daughter lived in a house with two cats, and when this boy visited he wafted strange cat smells around from his clothes. The problem was solved by having the boyfriend change into freshly washed garments and well-aired shoes before he visited.

House cats can become depressed, because they miss experiencing the elements and lack enough varied activity in their lives. Burmese cat Benny became so unhappy at being cooped up all day that he developed severe auto-immune problems. Through healing communication, I helped Benny out, whilst overseeing the building of a large, secure, caged garden area that he could access at will from the house, and which incorporated a seat, patches of long grass, cat-friendly herbs, shrubs and even part of a tree. Benny's pleasure at leaping up the trunk to sit on a branch in the fresh air and feel the sun on his body turned his physical and emotional health around within a very short space of time.

And what rabbits say

Another time, I was asked to communicate with a rabbit called Saffy. She was very pretty, but the family she lived with were not won over by her attitude, namely her hissing and biting when handled. As soon as I met Saffy, I could see why she was behaving that way, for she was housed in a cage in the corner of a patio and let out rarely. I sensed Saffy's anger and bitter frustration at her neglectful, imprisoned life. I explained that rabbits do not make good pets unless they have access to a large area for their own enjoyment. As in Saffy's case, they will become anti-social and aggressive as well as depressed. This family did the right thing – admitting that they did not have enough time for Saffy, they sent her to another home, where she was able to join some guinea pigs in a large purpose-built area.

- **Rabbit tip** They should never be housed only in hutches. Instead, they should have access to runs, which need to be at least 4 metres long; not the tiny runs sold in pet stores (although you can add a few of these together to make up the length). Rabbits need to be able to do more than just take a few hops.

Consulting a professional behaviourist

Unfortunately, anyone can call themselves an animal, dog or horse behaviourist, and a great deal of harm can be done by people who are not properly trained in these disciplines. Problems can be made worse, any pain present overlooked, or the animal may become confused, depressed and even feel abused because its communication is not heard or understood. Thus it is important to seek help from an appropriately qualified professional if experiencing problems with an animal's behaviour, and in the first instance to always have a veterinary check-up for the animal, as there may be an underlying medical issue. For example, the dog who refuses to sit when asked may be deemed stubborn or wilful, but he or she may actually be in pain.

One problem with non-accredited trainers is that they may opt for a quick-fix approach, rather than try to ascertain the fundamental causes and emotions behind the problematic behaviour. I was called out after a so-called dog trainer had traumatised a sweet Doberman called Patrick. Patrick had taken an aversion to entering the kitchen, only doing so after taking a detour through other rooms. The trainer's solution was to force the dog through the kitchen by dragging him along. The result? A traumatised dog. Taking one look at the kitchen floor, I knew what the problem was. Shiny surfaces can be like an ice rink to dogs, their nails acting as skates if they try to cross them. Patrick explained to me how he had hurt his back months earlier whilst hurtling across the floor, which was caused by his legs slipping from under him. In self-preservation, there was no way Patrick was going to do that again. The solution was simple: the floor needed to be covered with some rugs, so that Patrick had safe 'stepping stones' on which to cross the room, and thereafter he was happy to again enter the kitchen.

Qualified behaviour counsellors work in veterinary practices or make home visits to help with domestic animal problems. They deal with a range of behavioural problems exhibited in companion animals, including aggression, destructiveness, toileting problems, marking, spraying, self-mutilation, vocal behaviour, nervousness, car travel, livestock chasing and generally being out of control. A consultation in your home should last around two hours or more, and a detailed history will be taken, including notes about species type, breed, genetics, age of pet, sex, and when the problem started. Diet is also discussed, as it affects behaviour. An analysis will be made to help the practitioner to work out what is going on, and the consultant should also liaise with the veterinary profession. Suggestions will be made as to how to manage the situation, followed by phone calls and further visits as necessary. Humans often need retraining in how to treat, and behave with, the animals in their care. By intuitively tuning into animals, we are encouraged to recognise when we are at fault and need to make changes to our management of their lives.

These websites give information on how to find professionally trained animal behaviour counsellors:

- www.apbc.org.uk
- www.coape.org
- www.animalbehaviorcounselors.org for the USA

What natural therapies can help a domestic animal?

Homeopathy

Homeopathy is a therapy that treats the mind as well as the whole body, not just the symptoms, and it is used by millions of people around the world, as well as in the treatment of many animals too. Organic farmers rely on homeopathic remedies as an effective, yet safe, alternative to drugs, as they leave no unwanted residues in milk, meat or eggs. Homeopathy relies on the energy of a remedy to work with the animal's individual vital force in order to aid the natural healing process, and homeopathic vets will take a detailed history, so that they can match the right remedy and dose to the individual animal. Homeopathy, as prescribed by an holistic vet, is safe for all ages and all species; it can help treat many conditions, including tumours, heart, kidney and liver problems, skin problems, epilepsy, a poor immune system, shock, grief, and chronic illness.

I am a great fan of homeopathy, having experienced the benefits for myself and for the animals in my life. Golden retriever Bobby's enjoyment of life greatly improved once holistic vet Nick Thompson had prescribed some homeopathic remedies for the dog's prolific hay fever and rhinitis. A general practitioner vet had treated Bobby's condition with antibiotics and steroids, which had not helped the problem and the dog had suffered badly for a couple of years. Bobby's excellent response to the natural remedies meant that the nasal discharge was reduced to 10 per cent of what it had been, and Bobby came off the steroids. His person reports how Bobby now has his bounce back.

Cats are also very responsive to natural remedies and Nick talked me through a case involving an ocicat called Ellie. She was being bullied by another cat in the household and, because they are house cats, Ellie became stir-crazy at not being able to go outside and do her own thing. This caused Ellie to stress-lick her back legs and belly until the skin was raw. Carefully choosing a homeopathic remedy to enable Ellie to cope with her resentments, Nick has helped Ellie reach the point where she no longer self-harms. A benefit for the cat's owner also transpired. The woman had lost her sense of smell and, incredibly, it was restored by just handling Ellie's remedy!

When the correct remedy and dosage are identified, homeopathy is also excellent help for horses. Thirteen-year-old mare Maya was in such a lot of pain from polyarthritis (a condition which causes

inflammation to most of the joints) that she was due to be put to sleep. Nick had an immune-system-boosting remedy made up from a sample of Maya's blood, and it was so successful that within two months the mare's condition improved considerably and she continues to have a good quality of life. Nick also practises acupuncture, which he uses from time to time to help Maya when she has a stiff muscle, a treatment she relaxes into despite being needle-phobic. Animals certainly know what is good for them.

Nick's intuitive skill was of real benefit in the case of German shepherd dog Gwen. Gwen was taken to Nick because she was intended to be a breeding bitch, but had twice aborted and was then showing signs of infertility. The general practitioner vet who had previously examined Gwen had no answers for the infertility problems, saying that it was just one of those things. However, when taking down her case history, Nick noted that every now and again Gwen would attack the other dogs she lived with, that she had been hypersensitive to noise since puberty and that her body was abnormally barrel-shaped.

Although Gwen did not display any of the normal hypothyroid characteristics, such as sluggish metabolism or excess body fat, Nick intuitively suspected a thyroid problem, so he took some blood to send to Dr Jean Dodds, a vet in the USA, who specialises in identifying hypothyroidism in dogs. Dr Dodds' sensitive thyroid testing equipment can highlight problems that other general labs often miss. The results of Gwen's blood test came back, verifying that she did indeed have a low thyroid function. Nick immediately supplemented Gwen with thyroxin tablets, and there was a rapid change in her body shape, mood and reaction to noise. It is hoped that Gwen's fertility will improve at the next mating.

These websites offer further information on the use of homeopathy for treating animals:

- www.bahvs.com
- www.holisticvet.co.uk for Nick Thompson
- www.ahvma.org and www.viim.org for the USA

For information on whether your dog could be suffering from hypothyroidism read *The Canine Thyroid Epidemic* by Dr Jean Dodds, (First Stone, 2011)

Note: *In the UK, it is the law that only a vet may prescribe homeopathic remedies for animals. In other countries without this restriction, I still advise people to use someone with veterinary training rather than a layperson, in order to safeguard the animal's health and wellbeing. There are some good self-help books available, which offer advice on easing minor conditions, once a vet has made a professional diagnosis.*

Herbs

Veterinary herbal medicine is as old as human herbal medicine and is used to treat a wide range of ailments, as well as to promote good health. Trained holistic vets can prescribe herbs for medicinal purposes as an alternative to drugs, as well as give advice on which herbs to offer pets in their food. When considering using herbs with animals, it is essential to take advice first from a holistic veterinarian about which herbs might be suitable, in order to avoid creating a fresh problem or making an existing one worse. Cats can be particularly sensitive to herb toxicity. Herbs should be grown organically to avoid chemical residues being absorbed into the animal's system. In the UK, only a vet may prescribe herbs or herbal tinctures for animals, but wherever you live always check with a specialist vet to avoid making your pet ill.

For further information, consult one of these websites:

- www.herbalvets.org.uk
- www.vbma.org for the USA

Acupuncture

When performed by a qualified veterinary acupuncturist, acupuncture is safe and can be very effective with animals. It is mostly practised on dogs, cats and horses, but many other species can benefit, including birds, rabbits and guinea pigs. Animals can be helped with acupuncture for a wide range of conditions, including joint problems, neck and back problems, muscle spasms, pain and inflammation, lameness, arthritis, nerve problems, paralysis, wounds, eye conditions, skin conditions and for pain relief after surgery or accidents. In female dogs and cats, acupuncture can help with urinary incontinence.

During an acupuncture treatment, very fine needles are inserted over specific points, but for nervous or sensitive animals a laser-stimulation pen can be used instead. I frequently suggest to clients that they consult an acupuncture vet. This is because I have found it so successful with my own animals over the years, and I like the fact that there are no side effects, only side benefits.

My colleague, holistic vet Cheryl Sears, shared some of her case studies with me. Twelve-year-old Labrador Jasper was diagnosed with elbow dysplasia in both front legs, when he was seven years old. Jasper responded very well to acupuncture and herbs. Jasper also suffers with inflammatory bowel disease, which responded to a constitutional homeopathic remedy. Jasper was doing well until the day a year ago when he was playing with a large dog who flattened him, and subsequently Jasper was found to have an exploded disc in his spine. After this, Jasper had very weak hind legs, which did not improve with conventional medication. Jasper's abdomen increased in size, and investigations revealed a very large liver and spleen, but no cause was identified, and cancer was ruled out. Acupuncture, at first weekly, then every two weeks as Jasper became stronger, has helped the dog lead a relatively normal life, enjoying his walks and going on holiday with the family. The acupuncture treatment has also helped to reduce the size of the liver and spleen. Cheryl told me that Jasper's energy meridians had been compromised by the injury to the spine and said that acupuncture allowed the energy (chi) to flow in a normal fashion and reduce any stagnation in the internal organs. After the injury, there was congestion of blood in the liver and spleen; following acupuncture the organs drained more efficiently and reduced in size.

Pepe is an eighteen-year-old, black, short-hair cat, who was referred to Cheryl for help with a fused lumbar sacral spine. Cheryl assessed Pepe as being in a lot of discomfort, for which the anti-inflammatory drug Metacam had been prescribed by the general practitioner vet. To help Pepe, Cheryl did acupuncture treatments weekly for five or six weeks, then gradually reduced the frequency to monthly for three years, along with the use of homeopathic remedies. This helped so much that Pepe was no longer on Metacam.

A year or so ago, Pepe showed signs of elbow arthritis, which increased his need for acupuncture and the use of a laser on the tender points to a frequency of every two to three weeks. More homeopathic remedies were also prescribed. More recently, Pepe was diagnosed with cancer around the heart, and he is now on a mixture of homeopathic medicines and the Metacam has been reinstated. Pepe is still with us and enjoying a good quality of life, with a hearty appetite and regular patrols of his garden. Cheryl checks Pepe over every two weeks and tells me that he comes out of his basket meowing and talking for England, then explores all over the consulting room. This story just goes to show how much holistic veterinary expertise can help an ageing animal.

For further information see:

● www.abva.co.uk
● www.hampshireholisticvet.co.uk for Cheryl Sears
● www.ivas.org

Note: *In the UK only a vet may administer acupuncture to animals.*

Physiotherapy, chiropractic and osteopathy

These disciplines aim to restore and maintain mobility, function, independence and performance. All animals can respond to these therapies, which are most commonly used with dogs, cats and horses. Conditions commonly treated include joint problems, lameness, neck/back/shoulder problems, arthritis, falls, after surgery or accidents and age-related weakness/stiffness.

The title of chiropractor and osteopath are protected by law in the UK, and those working with animals will have taken a recognised post-graduate training. However, anyone can call themselves an animal physiotherapist, so I recommend choosing someone who is a member of ACPAT (Association of Chartered Physiotherapists in Animal Therapy). Many chartered animal physiotherapists now have a Master's degree in veterinary physiotherapy, which is recognised worldwide as a measure of excellence. In the US, the letters 'PT' after a person's name is an indication of professional training in this field.

A hydrotherapy pool should only be used with dogs following a consultation with a qualified therapist, as there are conditions which can be aggravated, or even created, by swimming. Dogs who take part in agility or other sports can benefit from physiotherapy, chiropractic and osteopathy in order to nip any problems in the bud and keep them in tip-top condition. Horses greatly benefit from these therapies, as they are prone to musculo-skeletal ailments.

Vera, a friend's boisterous dog, tweaked her back when she was nine months old by rolling next to a radiator and getting a leg jammed under a pipe. After being freed, Vera seemed to be OK and no one thought any more about it – until I visited, that is. The first thing that I was drawn to was Vera's right hip, and a niggling gait that suggested discomfort. That is one of the great things about tuning into animals: we can pick up problems that would otherwise go unheeded. Without the right treatment, Vera could have ended up lame, so I thanked her for letting me know about her damaged muscles. A few days later, she had physiotherapy, which helped relieve the injury.

Similarly, agility dog Henry fell from a piece of equipment and twisted his neck on landing. The vet verified that no bones were broken and gave his approval for me to help Henry with healing energy, and an osteopath colleague treated Henry soon afterwards. Between the two of us, we have maintained Henry's physical wellbeing to the point of him going on to become an agility champion.

Cats are often overlooked when it comes to having treatment for physical ailments. As they go about their daily lives, injuries can result and cats can also suffer from ageing-joint problems. When necessary, physiotherapy and osteopathy can help cats maintain mobility and alleviate discomfort. Internationally renowned animal osteopath Tony Nevin was able to do wonders for a cat called Henley, who belongs to Di, a TV producer. When Henley's back legs became very weak, X-rays showed spinal degeneration and the vets said that not much could be done for his condition; it was just a matter of time before Henley would be put to sleep. Whilst Di was talking to her own osteopath about how upset she was at the prognosis, he mentioned Tony's specialism with animals. After a couple of treatments with Tony, Henley was active and leaping around again, even clambering onto the shed roof. Di was so taken with what osteopathy for animals can do that she and Tony have got to together to produce a TV programme about his work.

If you are interested in physiotherapy for any animal, visit:

● www.acpat.org.uk
● www.orthopt.org/sig-apt.php for the USA

Information on veterinary chiropractors is available via:

● www.i-a-v-c.com
● www.ivca.de
● www.animalchiropractic.org for the USA

For information on osteopathy for animals see:

● www.uksoap.org.uk
● www.zooost.com for Tony Nevin
● www.osteopathic.org for the USA

Healing energy

This topic is covered in Chapter 6 and if you would like to train in either pure spiritual healing, which is my speciality, or reiki, or are looking for a healer for yourself or an animal, the following organisations may be able to help you:

● www.thehealingtrust.org.uk
● www.sanctuary-burrowslea.org.uk
● www.collegeofpsychicstudies.co.uk
● www.healinginamerica.com

There are also a number of useful books on healing energy:

Margrit Coates, *Hands-on Healing for Pets* (Rider Books, 2003) and *Healing for Horses* (Rider Books, 2001)
Margrit Coates, *Animal Healing* (New World Music, 2007); an instructional DVD on how to channel healing energy to animals is also available
Christina Mark, *Energy Healing* (Watkins Publishing, 2009)

An animal is what it eats

Diet is one of the fundamental areas of pet care. Holistic vets encourage feeding pets fresh natural foodstuffs, both to help prevent illness and to improve the health of sick animals. We have become over-reliant on purchased pet foods, many of which contain additives and poor quality ingredients. Processed pet food is linked to health problems, particularly those of the skin and bowel. If we feed a pet dry food (kibble) and nothing else, or with just a bit of tinned food added, we are not giving him or her a healthy diet. This kind of food does not allow cat and dog digestive systems to do the job they are designed for – to process a variety of raw foods. Cats and dogs have sensitive taste buds, so how boring must it be for them to be given a bowl of dry food day in and day out? Fresh meat, preferably free-range, has the added benefit of cleaning the animal's teeth. Many holistic vets have easy-to-make recipes for pets on their websites.

Animal Zen moment

To be with you as a friend is to share life.

Problems related to diet can include skin conditions such as itching and irritability, arthritis, digestive and bowel problems, including pain and diarrhoea, as well as hyperactive and aggressive behaviour. There is also a cancer link to a junk-food diet. It is easy for us to help animals by changing their diet to natural food.

Major, a yellow Labrador, was brought by Steve for healing to see if it would help with Major's itchy skin condition. When Major came into my clinic, his body was so bloody and bald from constant scratching that I did not recognise his breed; he was mostly bald with a few hairs sprouting here and there. Extensive veterinary skin tests had been done and none provided a diagnosis, so steroids had been prescribed but these were not alleviating the condition.

The first thing that Major communicated to me was: 'Give me raw food!' There was nothing subtle about this statement, which Major blasted into my mind. On then learning that Major was fed only a packet, dry-food diet, I could understand his request. In fact, Major had been shouting loud and clear about what he needed to improve his health. He was digging up carrots to eat from the garden vegetable patch, breaking into the greenhouse to steal cucumbers and tomatoes, and taking fruit from the apple tree. Out on walks, Major would fastidiously select berries from hedgerows, pushing through prickly branches that he would refuse to go near if it was just to fetch his ball.

Through my connection with Nick Thompson, I suspected that diet lay at the root of Major's problem and advised Steve to look on Nick Thompson's website (see page 230) for recipes. Improvement to Major's skin was rapid, with his hair soon growing back. Cats can also suffer from dietary-related health problems and, for this reason, I feed mine according to raw-food principles.

For rabbits, feeding them only a dry diet leads to painful teeth problems, as well as gut disease. Muesli-mix foods are fattening. Rabbits need to eat grass, as the silicates in the blades wear the teeth down. They must have fresh, good-quality hay at all times, topped up with some fresh, seasonal vegetables, leaves and herbs. Their runs need to be moved around the garden to ensure a constant supply of fresh grass. Mown grass should not be fed to them, as it rapidly ferments, and the use of chemicals in the garden should be avoided due to toxic residues.

Also see:

- www.bahvs.com
- www.ahvma.org
- www.viim.org

Veterinary specialists

Just like in human medicine, there are consultant specialist veterinarians, who have qualified in post-graduate subjects, such as orthopaedics, soft-tissue surgery, dentistry, ophthalmology, dermatology, cardiology, oncology, parasitology, neurology, internal medicine, homeopathy, acupuncture, anaesthesia and intensive care. You are entitled to ask your general practitioner vet for a referral to someone on the veterinary specialist register.

Using a professional animal communicator

A reputable professional animal communicator will always seek verification that an animal has been seen by a veterinarian before taking on a commission. For any suspected medical issues, they should always recommend you see a qualified veterinarian. If you are seeking help with connecting to a missing animal, then this will not apply. It is advisable to work with someone who has lived with (or, in the case of horses, looked after) the type of animal that you seek a consultation for, otherwise some guesswork about the animal's nature may creep in. Avoid sending money to a website, unless you are absolutely sure who the recipient is. Check that the person you select shares your ethics and is on your wavelength when it comes to their food choices and whether they use products free from animal ingredients or testing, for instance. Do they eat animals or are they non meat eaters, as I am?

- When considering a practitioner, ask yourself whether you feel aligned to this person's ethos about animal communication in what you read about them or hear about their work. Have other people recommended them? Does the person offer a good selection of customer testimonials?

- It is important that you gel with the person, so have an initial phone conversation to allow your intuition to gauge whether you resonate with the advertised communicator. You might like to have a cursory chat to several people before making a final selection.

- When contacting a communicator, ask yourself where their focus is when talking about animals. On themselves? On you? On the animal? It's worth finding someone who is good at relating to both animals and people. Anyone displaying a large ego and suggesting they are the best, is most likely one to avoid.

- You should be talked through the process of making the communication, how the communicator works and how much it will cost. The communicator should share with you a brief overview of their background and training. Any questions you may have about them or the process should be readily answered. The person should not be gathering lots of background information from you about the animal's history; in fact, the less they want to know the better. This ensures they are not simply trying to read the situation based on what you say, but are genuinely going to connect with the animal with a blank sheet of paper, so to speak. After the session, you should be provided with a written copy of the communication, so that you can refer back to it as often as you wish.

Recommended websites

- Margrit Coates for worldwide workshops
  margritcoates.com
- Awakening to Animals annual conference www.awakeningtoanimals.com
- Carol Gurney, USA
  www.gurneyinstitute.com
- Joan Ranquet, USA
  www.joanranquet.com

Books on dog training and behaviour

John Bradshaw, *In Defence of Dogs: Why Dogs Need Our Understanding* (Allen Lane, 2011)
Barry Eaton, *Dominance in Dogs: Fact or Fiction?* (Barry Eaton, 2008)
Sue Reid and Elaine Downs, DVD *Barking Up The Wrong Tree?* (Animal Matters, 2011)
Sarah Whitehead, *Clever Dog: The Secrets Your Dog Wants You To Know* (Collins, 2012)

Cat and rabbit books

Vicky Halls, *The Secret Life of Your Cat: Unlock the Mysteries of Your Cat's Behaviour* (Hamlyn, 2010)
Sarah Heath, *Why Does My Cat ...?* (Souvenir Press, 2000)
Anne McBride, *Why Does My Rabbit ...?* (Souvenir Press, 2000)

Books about understanding animals

Marc Bekoff, *The Emotional Lives of Animals* (New World Library, 2008)

Marc Bekoff, *The Animal Manifesto* (New World Library, 2010)

Leslie Irvine, *If You Tame Me: Understanding Our Connection with Animals* (Temple University Press, 2004)

Books on natural remedies for pets

Richard Allport, *Natural Healthcare for Pets* (Element Books, 2001)

Richard Allport, *Heal Your Dog the Natural Way* (Remember When, 2010)

Ian Billinghurst, *The Barf Diet* (Ian Billinghurst, 2001)

Christopher Day, *The Homeopathic Treatment of Small Animals* (Rider Books, 2005)

Don Hamilton, *Homeopathic Care for Cats and Dogs* (North Atlantic Books, 2000)

George MacLeod, *Cats: Homoeopathic Remedies* (Rider Books, 2005)

Henrietta Morrison, *Dinner for Dogs* (Ebury 2012)

Kymythy Schultze, *Natural Nutrition for Dogs and Cats: The Ultimate Diet* (Hay House, 2003)

Martin Zucker, *The Veterinarians' Guide to Natural Remedies for Cats* (Crown Publishing, 2000)

Books about horses

Margrit Coates, *Healing for Horses* (Rider Books, 2001)

Margrit Coates, *Horses Talking* (Rider Books, 2005)

Margrit Coates, *Connecting with Horses* (Rider Books, 2008)

Peggy Cummings, *Connect With Your Horse From The Ground Up* (Trafalgar Square Books, 2011)

Sue Devereux, *The Veterinary Care of the Horse* (J.A. Allen & Co, 2006)

Marthe Kiley-Worthington, *Equine Welfare* (J.A. Allen & Co, 1999)

Heather Moffett, *Enlightened Equitation* (Enlightened Equitation, 2011)

Paul McGreevy, *Why Does My Horse …?* (Souvenir Press, 2000)

Heather Simpson, *Teach Yourself Horse* (Horse & Rider Magazine, 2004)

Amanda Sutton, *The Injury-Free Horse* (David & Charles, 2006)

Music for animals

I have collaborated on four CDs of relaxing music suitable for playing to pets and horses. These include the titles: *Animal Healing*, *Music for Pets*, *Animal Angels* and *Connecting with Animals*. A fifth CD, called *Animal Communication*, has my spoken meditations to enhance your intuitive connection to companion animals and horses. All are available worldwide from New World Music (www.newworldmusic.com).

Spiritual books for people

Martin Boroson, *The One-Moment Master: Stillness for People on the Go* (Rider Books, 2007)

Deepak Chopra, *The Happiness Prescription* (Rider Books, 2010)

Thich Nhat Hanh, *Peace is Every Breath: A Practice for Our Busy Lives* (Rider Books, 2011)

Thich Nhat Hanh, *The Miracle of Mindfulness: A Manual on Meditation* (Rider Books, 2008)

Simon Parke, *One-Minute Mindfulness: How to Live in the Moment* (Hay House, 2011)

Rupert Sheldrake, *The Science Delusion: Freeing the Spirit of Enquiry* (Coronet, 2012)

James Van Praagh, *Watching Over Us: What the Spirits Can Teach Us About Life* (Rider Books, 2009)

11 High Notes

Communicating with animals is about being part of a world different to our own. The variety of thought, action and attitude in that other world makes life more interesting, and the energy that animals bring to our lives lifts our mood in so many ways.

In the pleasure of a moment, joy creates joyous energy. To end the book, I share here a few special stories, my personal experiences of how animals draw us into their sense of fun.

A cat's humour

Teddy, a typical Siamese-type cat, likes to create havoc. Often, as I sit in my office, I will hear a howly wail and a crashing, tumbling noise. Teddy is taking something apart, perhaps to demand my attention, maybe for the sheer hell of it. Once he even ripped open a bag of horse feed and – almost unbelievably – ate some ... Then there was the time he ate the bread I had left out, ready to make myself a sandwich, meaning I had to leave for a day's horse work with only a couple of tomatoes to sustain me. Teddy's antics are akin to living with a hyperactive comedian.

When I leave for a trip away, I always tell Teddy where I am going, when I will be back and to be a good cat in my absence. There are often some interesting adventures to hear about on my return, and one in particular comes to mind. I had left the UK on the day that snow fell and, as I was up in a plane, Teddy was seeking entertainment while my husband, Peter, was filling bird feeders and breaking ice on bird baths to help our feathered friends survive this very cold spell. The heavy snow fall had also broken off tree branches, so there was quite a bit of tidying up to do. After a couple of hours of stomping around the garden, his feet and hands blue with cold despite thick socks and gloves, Peter went indoors to get warm. By this time, Teddy and his sister were sprawled out on the central-heating boiler, and Peter got the sense they were thinking: 'Why were you outside so long in this weather?'

Boots, jacket, hat and gloves were pulled off and Peter stuck his feet into his cosy slippers, then held his frozen hands over a radiator. His hands warmed up quickly, but it took longer for the circulation to return to his feet; in fact Peter's left foot was decidedly numb. Whilst eating lunch and reading the newspaper, Peter noted that both cats sat unusually close to his feet. An hour later, Peter's left foot was still bothering him, the lack of circulation now of some concern, especially as he is on heart medication. So Peter ripped off the slipper to give his foot a rub.

Teddy sprang forward in obvious delight: 'At last!' was probably the message being communicated, as he sniffed the slipper. Peering inside, Peter found a young rat curled in the toe, but dead – the reason for the numb foot, rather than a circulatory problem. Uttering an expletive, Peter tapped the slipper so that the creature fell to the floor, then removed it to outside. Throwing his socks into the washing machine and running a bath, Peter soaked his feet, scrubbing the left one until it glowed pink. Teddy slunk into the bathroom to watch, a supercilious look about his narrowed blue eyes that said: 'I am highly amused. What fun we are having.'

A week later, on my return, it was not difficult to tune into Teddy and get the story from his viewpoint. He had come upon a teenage country rat lurking near the woodpile around which Peter had conveniently cleared the snow. Downwind of it, Teddy had crouched by the summerhouse and studiously watched the rat's movements ... until it ran forward and straight into Teddy's mouth. I could imagine the awkward stroll through the snow, the rat dangling between Teddy's legs as he dragged his hapless victim back to the house. Popping into the utility room through the cat flap, Teddy had dropped the depleted rat,

which had then escaped into a nearby dark hole that happened to be one of Peter's slippers. How incredulous Teddy would have been that my husband was not tuned in enough to be aware that a creature was residing in his slipper when he stuck his foot into it. I was, of course, very sorry about the rat's fate, but there was little sympathy for my husband.

A pony's joke

The pretty young pony made eye contact with me, as she basked in the sun. I had gone out for a stroll amongst a feral herd, wanting to breathe air as a wild living animal, without sight and sound of the stultifying encroachment of technology to dull my senses. The herd had no particular interest in me; I was not a threat, just hanging around, hungrily observing every detail of their relationships, one with the other. In the midst of the herd, the handsome proud stallion grazed, surrounded by his mares. Colts and fillies would every now and again approach the stallion to sniff him. Some he shooed away, others were allowed to remain in his space. I sat down on a grassy hummock and almost drifted off into a slumber as I listened to messages from the herd. No, far more than that, I was – through their graciousness – experiencing a level of awareness far beyond my own. There is a particular date in May when I always sense the energy of new growth at its zenith, and it was that very day, a hum of life unfurling and renewing. Overhead, lapwings sang their lyrical and soulful song – *pee wit, pee wit* – heralding high summer days to come.

Someone broke the spell by lifting my hat off my head. The young pony with whom I had sensed the earlier connection was waving my hat up and down in her mouth. Unceremoniously, she dropped it onto the top of a gorse bush, as the herd in unison turned to watch, heads high, ears forward. A vignette of action formed, with me in the centre. The stallion was the first to look away in disinterest, then his mares too went back to their grazing. The culprit pony continued to stand next to me, idly flicking her flaxen tail from side to side while she watched me. I had a broad grin on my face as I retrieved my hat, telling the pony it was a good joke and something cheerful to remember the day by. The pony then wandered off to join the others, her job as mood enhancer done.

A dog's laughter

For a few glorious days, I took a break to stay with special dog friends and tuned into their simple ways, sharing walks and happy games as well as just hanging out and being. I poked around in rock crevices, ran after balls on beaches, sniffed the breeze, shared fistfuls of blackberries with inquisitive wet noses, lay on the floor against warm furry bodies, talked about dog life to my heart's content and even strolled around the garden in the moonlight with a dog in my arms. During every waking second, I let myself be doglike in order to extract the most happiness from each moment: an intense state of being, yet one with which it was easy to flow, as my soul got busy with the business of spiritual renewal.

On the fourth morning, I rose early to pack before going down to breakfast. As I opened the kitchen door, I was greeted by a dog missile; it was Blue leaping up to grab my body with his front paws whilst making soft groaning noises. I kissed the top of his head and, on doing so, sensed the expectation of fun tinged with sadness. Blue knew I was leaving soon, even though I had not consciously told him this. As Blue nuzzled my ear, I heard him asking me, very firmly in fact: 'Can't you stay a while longer? Maybe .... even ... forever?'

The other four dogs joined in the jubilant melee, and I slid to the floor in the middle of an encouraging embrace. Noses rubbed my hands and my face, tails wagged on cupboards, making a soft drumming sound, and various dog barks added to the whirling energy. Blue pointed his head upwards and gave a whine – a gesture of lament that it was my last day of this particular visit. The youngest dog, Connie, leapt backwards, looking shocked. 'On no!' I heard her say. Wise middle-aged Patsy grinned her signature smile, her laughter twinkling in my senses. 'You will be back again, though, I am sure of it,' she communicated, at which the doggies became even more exuberant and teeth softly pulled at my sleeves in a bid to hold me back. Patsy was right, of course: I have returned many times, drawn like a magnet to my place of healing.

Spending time with any animal is a heavenly place to be, and I can't get enough of it. Through their communication, animals invite us to share not only in their fun, but a healing hug, a divine look, a loving touch – and just watching them can be heart-warming.

Keep talking and listening to animals, hearing their stories, telling them yours. Laugh, play and love together, for animals bring high notes of colour to brighten our days.

Animals are masters of simple but effective communication. The words on the facing page are the most common messages that animals communicate, and they will have a unique resonance for each of us. Look at each word and consider what it means to you; how it triggers memories as well as hopes and aspirations. Then think of animals that you know or have known, and, using your intuition, sense what inspiration they are sending especially to you through these words. Finally, look at the whole page and absorb the composite meaning. As the message from the animals washes over you, feel the healing power.

Touch me with your **LOVE** each moment as if it were your last

I hear **YOU**

Healing thoughts make a difference to all beings

LISTEN with your **HEART**

WE ARE ALL IN THIS TOGETHER

LIFE LASTS **FOREVER**

What you do to me you do to yourself

because the **SOUL** is eternal

FEEL and **SENSE** who I am

TALK to me because I am listening

INTUITION is a bridge to unseen worlds

Special Thanks

An important aspect of writing a book is the support received from other people. I am indebted to Judith Kendra, publishing director of Rider Books, for inviting me to write another book. Special thanks go to commissioning editor Sue Lascelles, who has again been a valuable advisor and mentor, and done a brilliant empathic edit of my manuscript. My appreciation also goes to copy editor Helen Pisano. It is wonderful to continue working with the excellent Rider marketing team, including PR manager Caroline Newbury. Designer Bob Vickers has taken my ideas and words, and turned them into a beautiful book.

Ali Brett has ably and cheerfully supported me with secretarial assistance and an ability to read my messy handwritten notes. Huge thanks to specialist vets Sue Devereux and Nick Thompson for their valuable time in checking areas of text and supplying information, and also to vet Cheryl Sears for her input. I am indebted to Dr Anne McBride, from the Department of Psychology at Southampton University, UK, for advice about animal behaviour. Appreciation goes to my colleagues chartered veterinary physiotherapists Amanda Sutton and Marjoleine Riezebos, as well as animal osteopath Tony Nevin for everything I have learnt from you and the awesome experiences.

Thank you to family members for your patience whilst I threw my social life of the window to complete the book. To my animal soul mates – where would I be without your encouragement and teachings? Huge thanks to my friend Valery Johnson for the time I spent with Sheltie friends Lillie, Patsy, Blue, Gina and Connie and whose enthusiasm for life is truly inspirational. Cat companions Teddy and Lilly have made an art form of radiating peaceful healing energy and thus helped me through the pressurised writing process. The horses who continually enter my life remind me why I do, what I do through imparting their wisdom. To these, and all the animals that I meet or which surround me in their wild state, thank you from the bottom of my heart.

Hugs and special thanks to the animals who posed for the book cover photos. Julie Walls' sixteen-year-old stallion, Radian, a Pura Raza Espanola (PRE) champion breeding, riding and dressage stallion is on the front cover. On the back cover is beautiful Viszla Ellie, a show dog, and my devoted cat Teddy, who knows everything about me and no doubt could write a tome about that.

This book contains many photos of animals, most of whom I am privileged to have met, and I am honoured to have them grace these pages. There are numerous animal-loving people that my work brings me into contact with, and who share their stories with me, and for this I am humbly grateful.

Thank you to artist Emily Mayman for the use of her horse illustrations (www.theequineartist.co.uk), and to artist Cate Hamilton for her dog illustration (www.catehamilton.com). (The cat illustration is a drawing by myself.) Included in the book are two amazing images – of a dog with a deer and dog with a horse – kindly donated by professional photographer Isobel Springett (www.isobelspringett.com). Professional photographer Sabine Stuewer donated the wonderful image of the dog cuddling a kitten (www.sabinestuewer.com). Singer/composer Maria Daines and muscician Paul Killington have turned my poem 'Awakening to Animals' into a wonderful song (www.mysonginamillion.com).

I send my love, healing and heartfelt thanks to animals everywhere for without you I would not be fulfilled. Thank you for being generous, patient, loving and awesome teachers, and for your soul blessings.

Picture credits: Line illustrations by Rodney Paull. Photographs on page(s) 2, 75 by Marianne Barcellona; 12, 25, 45, 78, 132, 156, 172, 185, 216, 245, 246, 248 by Margrit Coates; 19 by Shari Gittleman; 36 by Oephebia; 54, 215 by Isobel Springett; 65 by Katherina Dohlen; 83 by Anna Pell; 99 by Yvonne Allen; 190 by Peter Coates; 106, 117, 121 by Birgit Volesky; 136 by Mia Sampietro; 146 by Festina Lente; 152 by Sabine Stuewer; 163 by Liz Mitten Ryan; 208 by Sarah Archer; 229 by Beverley Pasque; 242 by Adele Hasley Wells; 250 by Francine Labossiere.

Index

Abraham, Marc 7
ACPAT 234, 235
Acupuncture 221, 230, 231–3
Afterlife 183
Altruism 29
American Association for the
    Advancement of Science 212
Animal insight 15, 18, 26, 39, 56,
    70, 95, 105, 140, 143, 149, 169,
    179, 189, 213
Animal nation 30
Animal Roadshow 1, 205
Animal Zen moment 10–11, 23, 41,
    63, 102, 148, 158, 176, 187, 194,
    203
Anxiety 220, 223
Apes 212
Awareness 18, 41–2, 103, 129, 191

Banff National Park, Canada 195
Behavioural problems 218-19, 222–8
Behaviour, animal 37, 38–9
Bears 66, 195, 196, 199
    black 196
    grizzly 195–8
Bees 70
Bird, Christopher 193
Birds 66, 67, 192, 207–9, 213
    eagles 66–7
    hummingbirds 67
    Jimmy 98
Books, recommended 239–41
Born Free Foundation 2
Breathing 24, 42, 83
Butterflies 64, 71–2

Carey, Jill 130
Cats 40, 65, 90, 161, 191

behavioural problems 225–6, 229
    books 239
    diet 236
    Friday 139–42
    Ginger 74–5
    Lance 149–50
    Lily 62
    Louis 47
    Luzie 167–71
    Simba 181
    Teddy 243–5
    Thomas 155
    Tiger 166
Chakras 136
Channeling healing 134, 135, 136,
    137, 138
Chase, Lorraine 7
Chiropractic 233–5
Chopra, Deepak 134, 241
Churchill, Winston 201
Clunes, Martin 7
Colles, Chris 113
Communication 17–19, 20, 29, 56,
    80, 82, 168, 214
    animals' abilities and 17–19, 27
    developing skills in 20, 23–24,
        27–8, 34, 41, 50, 80
    distant 147, 153–71, 210
    human–animal connection 14,
        17–19, 27–8, 50, 61–2, 81–2,
        84–6, 138, 140, 151, 217
    levels 80
    multiple participants 93–4, 146,
        164
    non-domesticated animals 48–9,
        192, 195, 199, 203, 214
    photographs 155, 179
Communicators, animal 223, 237–8

Companion animals, grief and 220, 221
Company, animals' need for
Confidence, animal 102
Confusion 92–3, 227
Consciousness 29, 31, 60, 103
Cosmic material 21
Counselling, animal 223–4, 226–8
Coyotes 67
Culture clash, humans and animals 217

Daily Mail 1
Death 134, 163, 171, 173–89
Deer 48–9, 64
Definitions 29–30
Diet 135, 227, 236–7
Dodds, Jean 230–1
Dogs 38, 65, 191, 222, 247
  Batschi 178–9
  Beethoven 61
  behavioural problems 222-3, 224–5
  Billy 159–60
  Bobby 95–6
  books 239
  diet 236–7
  Duffy 51–2
  Finn 104–5
  Flops 72–4
  Frostie 61–2
  Gemma 96–7
  Gus 165–6
  Jodi 145
  Michiko and Miki 45–6
  Millie 13–17
  Red Bearen 138–9
  Riley 183–4
  Ryley 147–9
  Sasha 25–6
  Tanya 62–3
  Tasha 94–5
Dolphins 70, 212
Dreams 160–1, 184
Dragonflies 68

Eagles 66–7
Egan, Peter 7
Electromagnetic fields 100, 153
Elephants 69, 209–12
  Anne 209–12
Emotional release 210–11
Emotional surrogacy 33
Emotions, animal 31–4
Energy 20–1, 80, 82, 85, 98–100, 131, 133–6, 137, 173, 188, 232
  depletors 100
  enhancers 100
  exchange 60, 76, 138
  healing 1, 129, 133–7, 138, 139, 140, 141, 149, 150–1, 221
  quantum 20
  universal system 18, 21, 134, 142
Environment, pet health and 157, 203, 226
Exercise 135, 221
Eyes, communication and 81, 91, 131, 139, 206
Explanations, importance of 100–2

Fear 163
Festina Lente 129, 130
Free will 60

Gandhi 201
Ghosts 179–81
Grasshoppers 71
Grief 182, 220, 221, 228
Gurney, Carol 2, 84, 239

Hands-on healing 140, 146, 147, 149, 150–1, 170, 174, 182
Harrison, Justine 111–12
Healers 134, 150
  animal 142–5
Healing energy 1, 129, 133–7, 138, 139, 140, 141, 149, 150–1, 235
Heart 30, 175
Herbs 221, 231
Hitchcock, Mary 204

Homeopathy 221, 228–31, 233
Horse insight 129
Horses 62, 65–6, 90, 103, 107–31,
      245
   Basil 126–7
   behaviour 110–12, 120,
   Boo 11
   books 240
   Chico 187–8
   communicating with 108, 114,
      121, 131
   Ed and Wilfie 127
   emotional disturbance 123
   George 161–2
   Ginger Ann 128–30
   handling 120
   health and wellbeing 120–1, 125
   living conditions 121
   Maddie and Sabine 115–19
   mirroring humans 109–10
   Mistral 114
   natural horsemanship 112
   Narfee 166–7
   observers, as 115
   pain, physical 122–3, 229–30
   Portia 127–8
   Radian 9–10
   Rocky 113
   trainer/handler empathy 112,
      124–5
   Victor 125–6
   Zeb 115
Horse Zen moment 11, 110, 125
Human mismanagement, animals
      and 112, 124–5, 221, 227
Hummingbirds 67
Hutto, Joe 192
Hydrotherapy 234

Interspecies communication 8, 79,
      85, 103, 189
Intuition 8, 10, 18–19, 20, 22–7, 34,
      38, 73, 79, 83, 84–5, 112, 124,
      131, 135, 137, 154, 178, 192,
      193, 195, 201, 217, 221, 228

and telepathy 24–6, 73
and sixth sense 8, 23, 24, 27, 73,
      124

Kangaroos 204–5
Kindness, animal acts of 33–4

Language, body 38–40, 217
Language, verbal 18, 23,
LeGrand, Mara 160
Lines, Julie 238, 239
Longleat Safari Park 209, 212
Lost animals see missing animals
Love 48, 81, 133

May, Brian 7
McElroy, Susan Chernak 2
McKenna, Virginia 2
Meditation 24, 42, 83
Memory 43
Mental powers, animals 31–3
Messages 11, 82, 89, 249
   interpreting 14–15, 92
   receiving 82, 90–2
   sending 81, 82, 86, 109
Mind, human–animal connection 81
Missing animals 162–71
Misunderstandings, animal–human
      217, 227
Moffett, Heather 121
Morgan, Huey 7
Music 135, 240

Natural therapies 228
Nature 63, 135, 183, 191, 192,
      193–5, 197, 200–1, 203
Negativity 81
Neutral state, the 82, 83–4
Nevin, Tony 234, 235

Oneness, The 55, 56
Open Center, New York 1
Organic food 228
Osteopathy 233–5
Overlap mode 168

Pain, emotional 123, 173, 221
Pain, physical 122–3, 219
Personal frequency 21
Personality 61–2, 79
Pet Nation 1, 7
Pet's Corner 1
Physiotherapy 233–5
Pictures, communicating in 16, 80,
    82, 89–90, 157–9
Pigs 157–9
    Freddie 157–9
Predictions 188–9
Problems, small animals 218–19

Questions, how to ask 86–9

Rabbits 186, 205–6
    behavioural problems 226
    books 239
    diet 237
    Hazel 205–6
Ranquet, Joan 165
Reiki 235
Reincarnation 189
Relaxation 24, 42, 83
Ryan, Liz Mitten 103

Sampietro, Mia 166
Sears, Cheryl 232
Secret Life of Plants, The 193
Secrets 10, 96
Self-awareness 29, 41, 44–7
Senior, Niki 157–9
Sensory input 23
Simmons, Emma 130
Simonds, Mary Ann 110
Sixth sense 8, 23, 24, 27, 38, 124,
    162, 183, 217
Small talk 33
Soul 30, 160, 173–4
    voice of 30, 57–8, 59, 85, 137,
        140, 192, 209
Squirrels 69
Spirit forms 174–7
Spirituality 29, 56, 103, 192

Stress 210, 222
Subconscious 17, 62, 160, 192

Tarbuck, Liza 7
Tarrant, Ingrid 7
Telepathy 14, 15, 19, 27–8, 38, 80,
    82, 86, 159, 164, 167, 169, 178,
    203, 207, 208
Thompson, Nick 228–30, 237
Time, perception of 197
Tolle, Eckhart 201
Tompkins, Peter 193

Universe, the 10, 26, 30, 55, 188,
    195, 209
University of Bristol 32
University of Southampton, the 1,
    217

Vets 217, 220, 227, 230, 236
    Abraham, Marc 7
    acupuncturists 233
    Colles, Chris 113
    Dodds, Jean 230–1
    herbal treatment 231
    holistic 217, 220, 228, 230, 231,
        232, 236, 237
    homeopathic 228–31
    Sears, Cheryl 232
    specialists 237
    Thompson, Nick 228–30
Visitations 184–6
Vocalisation, animal 57–8

Websites, recommended 228, 230,
    231, 233, 235, 237, 239
Webster, John 32
Wetnose Awards 7
Whale 212
Wild animals 49, 191–213
Wild Horses in Winds of Change
    160

Zen 11